GAMING SEXISM

Gaming Sexism

Gender and Identity in the Era
of Casual Video Games

Amanda C. Cote

NEW YORK UNIVERSITY PRESS
New York

NEW YORK UNIVERSITY PRESS
New York
www.nyupress.org

References to Internet websites (URLs) were accurate at the time of writing. Neither the author nor New York University Press is responsible for URLs that may have expired or changed since the manuscript was prepared.

Portions of chapter 5 were previously published as A. C. Cote, "I can defend myself": Women's strategies for coping with harassment while gaming online, *Games and Culture* 12(2) (2017), 136–55; and A. C. Cote, Curate your culture: A call for social justice-oriented game development and community management, in K. L. Gray and D. J. Leonard, eds., *Woke Gaming: Digital Challenges to Oppression and Social Injustice* (2018) 193–212, University of Washington Press, reprinted by permission of the copyright holders.

Library of Congress Cataloging-in-Publication Data
Names: Cote, Amanda C., author.
Title: Gaming sexism : gender and identity in the era of casual video games / Amanda C. Cote.
Description: New York : New York University Press, 2020. | Includes bibliographical references and index.
Identifiers: LCCN 2019041466 | ISBN 9781479838523 (cloth) | ISBN 9781479802203 (paperback) | ISBN 9781479802210 (ebook) | ISBN 9781479802197 (ebook)
Subjects: LCSH: Gender identity. | Identity (Psychology) | games—Social aspects.
Classification: LCC HQ1075 .C678 2020 | DDC 305.3—dc23
LC record available at https://lccn.loc.gov/2019041466

New York University Press books are printed on acid-free paper, and their binding materials are chosen for strength and durability. We strive to use environmentally responsible suppliers and materials to the greatest extent possible in publishing our books.

Manufactured in the United States of America

10 9 8 7 6 5 4 3 2 1

Also available as an ebook

MIX
Paper | Supporting
responsible forestry
FSC® C013604

To my parents, for more reasons than I could ever list

CONTENTS

Introduction

Diversification and Resistance in Gaming's Casualized Era

When my older brother bought a Nintendo Wii in 2006 or 2007, he brought it on our annual family vacation. My grandmother, who had never shown interest in any video game except a pre-programmed, handheld *Yahtzee*, proceeded to spend the rest of the week absolutely destroying anyone who challenged her to a game of *Wii Bowling*. This small event, of my grandmother playing video games, enjoying them, and doing well at them, was emblematic of Nintendo's "Blue Ocean Strategy," which it had introduced with the Nintendo DS handheld gaming system and fully pioneered with Nintendo Wii.

As described by Perrin Kaplin, Nintendo of America's vice president of marketing and corporate affairs, "Blue Ocean is the notion of creating a market where there initially was none—going out where nobody has yet gone. Red Ocean is what our competitors do—heated competition where sales are finite and the product is fairly predictable" (Rosmarin, 2006). Nintendo was avoiding direct competition with other video game producers by deliberately reaching out to unexpected gaming audiences, such as moms and the elderly. In doing so, they not only got my grandmother to game, but they also helped usher in a new era in video game history, which I term the "casualized era."[1] In this era, from the mid-2000s onward, so-called casual games, or easy-to-learn games targeted at broad audiences, have become a major player in the overall games industry. Although casual video games existed for many years prior to the Nintendo Wii, in games like *Solitaire* and *Minesweeper*, they were often considered tangential to the main industry, included on home computers for free, and rarely thought of as "real games."

The Wii brought these games to the forefront of the industry and made them a major part of the console market, which was traditionally a bastion for more involved, time-intensive core games.[2] Because

1

Nintendo had been struggling to compete with its rivals in terms of technical superiority, core game creation, and audience numbers, they made the DS and the Wii under completely different assumptions, and it proved to be a successful approach. In the year it was introduced, the Wii outsold both its competitors, the Xbox 360 and the PlayStation 3 (Kuchera, 2007), and by 2008 it had surpassed the Xbox 360 in overall sales to become the top-selling console worldwide, even though the 360 was released a year earlier (Kim, 2008).

Along with the DS, the Wii provided widespread evidence that diverse groups of people were interested in video games and undermined the idea that games were a technology for men. Its marketing campaign and easy-to-learn games directly targeted families, older individuals, and women as well as more traditional "gamers,"[3] and its success was rapidly followed by other industrial changes that also diversified imagined game audiences. For example, the growth of Internet-enabled smartphones increased the reach of mobile games, while social media platforms like Facebook helped promote social games like *Farmville* or *Words with Friends*, which leverage players' existing relationships as a game mechanic.[4] All these offerings focus on large audiences and entertaining mechanics rather than top-tier graphics and technical superiority, potentially creating new expectations for game producers and players. After all, no one could argue that *Candy Crush Saga* or *Clash of Clans* offers cutting-edge visuals. However, their entertaining, pick-up-and-play nature and their convenience have netted their developers billions in sales (Shontell, 2014; Takahashi, 2016).

At the same time, game culture has also seen a backlash against nontraditional players, including female gamers, LGBT gamers, and/or gamers of color. In terms of gender specifically, a variety of major sexist incidents have targeted female gamers, game developers, journalists, and cultural critics throughout the 2010s. Thus, games appeared to be simultaneously opening up and becoming more exclusionary. How is such a paradox possible?

In this book, I argue that these two positions are, in fact, not a contradiction but rather the expected result of a change to the status quo. For decades, games have targeted a narrow young, male audience. And that audience has, in turn, defined itself through its engagement with games and other "geek" areas of culture. As games have started to diversify, some members of this narrow audience have come to fear the loss of their privileged position. As a result, they have reacted forcefully to maintain games as a small, exclusionary area with limited audience members and have worked to build a barrier between traditional core games/gamers and newer casual areas. Sexism and misogyny are, unfortunately, some of the mechanisms through which this occurs.[5]

To understand the conflicts of the casualized era, their impacts, and how exclusionary forces in gaming can be overcome, this book provides a multifaceted analysis of how sexism currently shapes game communities and practices. It argues that the identity of a gamer is still defined in masculine terms, complicating female players' interactions with other gamers, setting hurdles for their entry into game culture, and encouraging them to take on subject positions that are fragmented and messy. At the same time, women's continued engagement with games, especially core games, outlines potential ways in which players, developers, and researchers could capitalize on the conflicts of the casualized era to build new pathways towards more inclusive gaming cultures. So, let's get started!

Games and Masculinities

Video games have a long history as a masculinized technology.[6] This is not to say that only men play games; women have always been present in gaming. Rather, it means that a variety of forces have constructed video games as something meant more for men than for women. For instance, cultural historian Carly A. Kocurek (2015) argues that attempts to legitimate arcade gaming, the rise of video game competitions, cultural anxieties around games' moral influence, boys' longstanding associations with technology, and more all worked to make male gamer identity more culturally salient than female gamer identity during games' early decades, the 1970s and 1980s. Some of the women I spoke to for this book agreed. As longtime gamers, they had started their playing careers in video game arcades. Despite nostalgia about the early years of gaming, their anecdotes showed that men dominated this environment. One participant, Harley, stated, "There were very few girls. Some of them were good though. The ones that did play were good. But there were a lot of men, college kids, and you just barely saw one [woman playing]. [. . .]

The rest of them were cheering their boyfriends on or they were on the side." Women were primarily spectators to arcade culture, with only a few becoming active participants.

Early home consoles and computer-based games provided an exception to arcade games' overall masculinization, advertising primarily to families in the recognition that parents would need to allow video games in the home and purchase them (Williams, 2006; Kirkpatrick, 2015). However, even early video game advertisements that showed families gaming together often defaulted to presenting the boy as the authority, teaching other family members how to play (Newman, 2017). The content of games also drew on masculinized hobbies like sports or war games, complicating ostensibly broad advertising (Newman, 2017).

These masculine associations grew even stronger in the mid-1980s, following the game industry's devastating crash. In the early 1980s, console game companies were producing large numbers of low-quality products and failing to innovate effectively, driving away consumers (Kent, 2001). This, combined with an overall economic recession, effectively destroyed the US video game market between 1983 and 1985. When producers tentatively returned to making games, they redefined their audiences more narrowly to manage future risk (Graner Ray, 2004; Williams, 2006; Shaw, 2014b). Because young men had been visible game players during the arcade era, and because of masculine discourses present in gaming magazines (Kirkpatrick, 2015) and other areas of the industry, developers focused on this group as a proven consumer base. With these forces and many others at work, video games were firmly masculinized by the mid-1990s (Kirkpatrick, 2012), naturalized as a hobby for men and boys. In turn, this affected and was reflected in audience demographics. "As late as the mid-1990s, 80 percent of players were boys and men" (Dyer-Witheford and dePeuter, 2009, p. 20). Industry members constructed games as a product for young men, and "gamers" became narrowly defined along similar terms. Although we did not realize it at the time, my female neighbors and I, who grew up playing video games together, were exceptions rather than the rule.

The only real attempt to change games' masculinized construction occurred in the 1990s. At this time, several developers and feminist activists tried to address gaming's gender gap and draw in more women and girls (Cassell and Jenkins, 1998; Laurel, 1998). They sought to create games that appealed to girls by drawing on their preexisting interests, such as social relationships and cooperative exploration (Laurel, 1998; Graner Ray, 2004). By separating "girl games" from "games," unfortunately, the movement maintained gaming itself as a masculinized space, while offering girls only a limited spot on the industry's margins (Shaw, 2014b). Furthermore, many of the companies that targeted girls went out of business within a few years. This business collapse, combined with the fact that game audiences did not actually diversify, marked the girls' games movement as a general failure, and developers made few other attempts to alter games' gender construction. The industry continued to think of its "gamers" as young men, and cultural texts largely represented them as white, cisgender, and straight. This led to the development of broad cultural stereotypes that also defined gamers in this way, marking individuals who were not straight, white, and male, but who did play games, as abnormal or "other." Game culture has been more accessible for certain kinds of men than for anyone else.

At the same time, games are in an interesting position because the masculinity of games and gamers does not always necessarily coincide with hegemonic masculinity, society's most accepted way of enacting manhood. The specific components of hegemonic masculinity can and do change over time and context, but in Western society, they often include physical strength, athleticism, sexual prowess or power over women, and mastery of technology, including weaponry, vehicles, or even musical instruments (Brod, 1987; Hanke, 1992; Connell, 2000). Hegemonic masculinity is an ideal more than it is a position most people embody; as sociologists Raewyn Connell and James Messerschmidt (2005) write, "Hegemonic masculinity was not assumed to be normal in the statistical sense; only a minority of men might enact it. But it was certainly normative" (p. 832). Consider the idealized jock who is a fixture in teen movies and TV shows—handsome, smart, good at sports, etc. Most of us do not know anyone who perfectly embodies all those characteristics in real life (and especially not in high school!). But that *type* of representation matters, because it promotes an ideal version of masculinity against which real people are expected to measure up. When they do, they attain social privilege; when they do not, they can face social censure.

Gamers often possess a "geek masculinity" (Taylor, 2012) that embodies some of the characteristics of and privileges associated with hegemonic masculinity, such as competition and technological mastery. At the same time, geek masculinity is frequently positioned as adolescent or lacking. Digital media scholar Derek A. Burrill (2008) describes gamers as embodying a "digital boyhood," while others like Anastasia Salter and Bridget Blodgett (2017) trace how gamers and geeks are generally associated with an "inability to engage in or understand sports and [a] general lack of attractiveness to women" (p. 3). Compared to hegemonic masculinity, geek men can feel marginalized (Massanari, 2015; Braithwaite, 2016; Salter and Blodgett, 2017). Many have reacted by celebrating their difference from the norm, prioritizing intellect over athleticism and other markers of hegemonic masculinity and pinning their identity on *being* outside the mainstream. When geek spaces start to become more mainstream, existing community members may feel as if new entrants cannot be real geeks, because they did not join the community while it was marginal and experience that marginalization (Salter and Blodgett, 2017). Geeks' feelings of marginalization also mean that "critiques of the immense amount of capital (particularly cultural and intellectual capital) that geeks possess may be met with skepticism or outright hostility" (Massanari, 2015). Therefore, geek masculinity can be resistant to change in geek communities and often employs toxic measures to bar new entrants (Salter and Blodgett, 2017).

Theorizing the Casualized Era

I bring this up in relation to the casualized era because this masculinized-but-marginalized position is key to understanding how the current era of gaming is progressing. As mentioned previously, the mid-2000s started a series of industrial changes, the first of which was Nintendo focusing its attention on families and nontraditional players, such as moms and the elderly, with the DS and the Wii. They were wildly successful in this approach, and many producers followed their lead. Other console manufacturers introduced motion-enabled controls to compete with the Wii, while growing mobile and social media technologies brought games to everyone's pocket and browser. With the introduction of more casual play to core consoles, and the subsequent rise of casual gaming on mobile and social platforms, casual games became a major player in the overall industry. Furthermore, they started redefining who was or could be a gamer. As video game theorist Jesper Juul (2010) writes, "The rise of casual games has industry-wide implications and changes the conditions for game developers, pushing developers to make games for a broader audience" (p. 7). Rather than expecting all gamers to be young, white, cisgender men, developers, players, and researchers like Juul believe that gamers now embody many different identities.

At the same time, the casualized era has seen a backlash against diverse players, including women. For instance, 2012 saw professional gamer Miranda Pakozdi quit her competitive team due to sexual harassment from her coach, who focused the team's webstream camera on Pakozdi's body while making lewd comments (O'Leary, 2012). In the same year, media critic Anita Sarkeesian proposed a project examining tropes surrounding women in video games; in response, swaths of the gaming community published her personal information online, threatened her, and even created a video game in which users could beat up her virtual representation (Sarkeesian, 2012). As Sarkeesian released her video game analyses, threats continued, to the extent that she has at times been driven from her home for her own safety (Campbell, 2014).

Although these events received outraged protests and a high level of publicity, these responses were not enough to prevent further issues. Perhaps the most significant incident of ongoing sexism was Gamer-Gate, a 2014 Twitter movement that began when game designer Zoë Quinn's ex-boyfriend accused her of having sex with a games journalist in exchange for positive coverage of her game *Depression Quest*. The claims were later disproven, but they outraged many "gamers" who took to Twitter trying, ostensibly, to decrease political correctness in gaming and improve ethics in game journalism. In actuality, they developed a sustained harassment campaign against Quinn that also caused her to leave her home, fearing for her safety (Auerbach, 2014; Wingfield, 2014). GamerGate involved virulent misogyny and the online harassment of female game developers, cultural critics like Sarkeesian, and anyone who supported them, including popular male developers. For example, Phil Fish, creator of the critically acclaimed independent (indie) game *Fez*, had his personal information hacked and publicly posted online after he defended Quinn, leading him to sell his game company and leave the industry (Maiberg, 2014).

Individuals face further problems if they possess multiple characteristics that make them a gaming minority. The impact of this intersectionality can be seen in the treatment of comedian/actress/gamer Aisha Tyler, who was widely criticized when she hosted game company Ubisoft's press conference at the 2012 Electronic Entertainment Expo (E3), gaming's largest industry event. Tyler has been deeply involved in the gaming community for years and responded to the harassment with an open letter detailing her experience and love of the medium. Despite this, many community members still felt that her position as a black woman meant that she could not possibly be "a real gamer," that she had to be an outsider Ubisoft brought in as part of a publicity stunt (Tyler, 2012; Jackson, 2012; Narcisse, 2012; Stuart, 2012). Tyler defended her "gamer cred" extremely well, but the fact that she had to do so in the first place demonstrates the strength of community stereotypes and expectations, as well as their exclusionary nature. Furthermore, it indicates how gaming culture can bleed into other areas. In Tyler's case, harassment by gamers played off broader racial issues, in that they assumed she was a "diversity hire" for Ubisoft, rather than a skilled equal. Discriminatory trends both draw on and feed into wider cultural issues.

Harassment is not limited to public or industrial figures; female players speak eloquently about the day-to-day issues they face, particularly when they choose to play video games online. Some interviewees I spoke to for this book state that male players treat them as a "nuisance," while others describe more offensive experiences, such as frequent rape comments or threats of assault. Due to their gender, players often target female entrants into the gaming community as outsiders, and women face many serious barriers to the gamer identity they want to embody.

These instances demonstrate that, although some industry members and players support diversification, others seek to preserve the gendered, racialized, and overall exclusionary nature of gaming. They see games as a homosocial space in which men can be men, without having to be "politically correct" or sensitive to the feelings of others. Games also allow geek men to band together against their perceived marginalization from the mainstream, and changes to the industry seem to threaten this preserve. To protect it, some "gamers" deploy harassment to drive away anyone who may change what gaming is or what it means. Thus, while gaming has long possessed sexist structures, these have become more salient in the face of potential change.

I refer to this conflict as a "crisis of authority," borrowing the term from Marxist cultural theorist Antonio Gramsci.[7] Gramsci is perhaps best known for his theories about cultural hegemony, or the process by which social, political, and cultural power is maintained through normalization (Gramsci and Hoare, 1971). That is, hegemony occurs when a particular way of viewing the world (generally one that supports the ruling class) comes to be taken for granted; once this view becomes "common sense," it is very difficult to question or change, which helps maintain the existing system. In gaming, industrial decisions, such as the focus on limited audiences and genres, have normalized games and gamers as masculine. But hegemonies are *not* actually natural; they are built through social, cultural, and political systems. Because of this, alternative ways of viewing the world—counterhegemonic forces—also exist.

Hegemony thus requires constant attention, as members of both the ruling and the subordinate classes at times realize the constructed nature of their positions and how power might be enacted differently. When they make this realization, subjected groups push for more power. At times, the dominant group will engage in what Gramsci calls "passive revolution," making small concessions to the oppressed to limit the scope of changes and maintain overall control. At other times, which Gramsci referred to as "crises of authority," real power shifts can occur. In these moments, extensive pushes for change can redefine the dominant order, although the previously hegemonic group will deploy all the forces at its disposal trying to prevent this.

Gramsci argued that the "crisis of authority" was the time when the veneer of common sense would slip away, and the established order would no longer be taken for granted. At this moment, the ruling group would resort to pure force to maintain power. In the case of gaming, we can see the casualized era as a "crisis of authority," in that the success of casual games and audiences has undermined the commonsense notion that gaming is a masculine hobby and gamers are men. "The ruling class has lost its consensus, i.e. is no longer 'leading' but only 'dominant,' exercising coercive force alone" (Gramsci and Hoare, 1971,

p. 556). We have seen such dramatic instances of sexism, racism, and other forms of discrimination in gaming in recent years because of this; these acts are forms of "coercive force," trying to resist change to the hegemonic order.

A crisis of authority has one of two outcomes—change, or the successful use of force to prevent change. The casualized era has the potential to redefine gaming more broadly, but it also has the potential to fail, if exclusionary tactics are successful. Therefore, the era needs more attention before we can understand what specific exclusionary measures are being employed, how they affect targeted gamers, and how they can be overcome to redefine games more inclusively.

The Goals of *Gaming Sexism*

The sexism of the casualized era has not gone entirely unaddressed. Researchers, developers, and players have responded to gaming's misogyny with deliberate efforts to call out inequality and promote inclusive gaming spaces. For instance, in 2012, a game developer asked why there were so few women in the industry. In response, industry members employed the hashtag #1ReasonWhy to illustrate the extensive sexism they faced within the field, affecting everything from hiring processes to day-to-day working conditions to game play (Blodgett and Salter, 2014). The spinoff hashtag #1ReasonToBe was then used to highlight positive experiences and remind women (and other marginalized creators) why they were developers in the first place. This worked to "provide support and mentorship for others seeking to gain a foothold in this context of production" (Harvey and Fisher, 2015). Numerous incredible organizations were also created for the purpose of solving inequalities in game production spaces; Dames Make Games, the Pixelles, Code Liberation, and Girls Who Code are some of the many groups founded in the early 2010s to support underrepresented game developers, as a means for diversifying the production of games. Similarly, game critic and diversity activist Tanya DePass originated the Twitter hashtag #INeedDiverseGames, then developed it into a nonprofit organization that works to "provide a safe online space for gamers of color and gamers of any other marginalized identities," "promote the work of creators in the gaming industry, including journalists, developers, artists that are marginalized and would otherwise go unheard," and "encourage and defend diversity in all forms of gaming," among other goals ("About," n.d.).

These efforts are necessary to address gaming's inequality in all its forms and to promote real change. But not all players have development aspirations, and many marginalized gamers do not know other players like them (Taylor, 2008; Eklund, 2011). Existing collectives may thus be limited in terms of who they reach, necessitating further attention to the issues of where individual players already are and how they manage their engagement in games. This book therefore addresses the experiences of women who see themselves as standard, everyday gamers, who chose to enter gaming spaces before they were normalized as "for everyone," and who often still fight to find space in masculinized areas of gaming. Through their experiences, we can better understand the different forces at play in the crisis of authority, what they mean in terms of power and gender, and how sexism persists or is combated at the individual level. This is necessary to address continuing issues and formulate appropriate responses to sexism and discrimination.

Female gamers also need more attention as past gender and media research has often studied feminized media more than masculinized media. American studies scholar Janice Radway's *Reading the Romance*, for instance, studied the paradox of women's engagement with romance novels. Although romance novels are a deeply sexist medium on the surface, Radway's participants constructed the act of reading as a "declaration of independence" (1991, p. 7) and found extensive pleasure in reading them. How they discussed their romance reading, and the specific guidelines according to which they selected novels, demonstrated that women were complex media consumers who used novels as a form of psychological self-care. Because the women Radway studied were generally housewives in low- to middle-income families, most with children under eighteen, the home was their primary sphere of labor, raising challenges when they wanted to take a break from work. The act of reading allowed them to mentally escape from their homes, while the physical book acted as a momentary shield against other demands on their time.

At the same time, participants often experienced guilt because reading took time and resources they felt they should spend on their families. In this way, they both combated and reaffirmed hegemonic notions of the patriarchal family, taking time for themselves but recognizing that this was contrary to expectations about what they should be doing. By prioritizing women's lived experiences, Radway explained how they managed their media environments in active ways and used romance novels, despite their culturally trivialized nature, as important tools for navigating gender roles, patriarchy, and power.

Following Radway's project, many other researchers have done similarly useful, nuanced studies on media, gender, and their mutually constituted nature. Cultural studies scholar Ann Gray (1992), for instance, conducted in-depth interviews with British women whose families owned or rented a video cassette recorder (VCR) in the late 1980s. This was a relatively new domestic technology, and Gray sought to determine how women engaged with the VCR as a part of the home and as a technology. She found that women's relationship with technology and media was conflicted. For example, when asking women to color-code the gender of home technologies like the VCR or the washing machine (blue for masculine and pink for feminine), Gray found the VCR was a strange, detailed mix of both. "The 'record,' 'rewind' and 'play' modes are generally lilac, but the timer switch is nearly always blue, with women having to depend on their male partners or their children to set the timer for them. The blueness of the timer is exceeded only by the deep indigo of the remote control which in all cases was held by the male partner or male child" (p. 248). Analyzing this further led to more complication; many women had not had time to learn how to use the VCR fully, but others *deliberately avoided* learning to forgo having more responsibilities in the home, such as being expected to record shows for the family. Women's interactions with the VCR revealed both their continued burdens of housework and the nuanced strategies they employed to manage these.

Further research has addressed soap operas, Pinterest and fashion websites, gossip magazines, and more.[8] These critical studies have focused extensively on women's relationship with feminized forms of entertainment and how their actions both support and resist existing gender ideologies. Where further work is needed, and where this book offers an intercession, is in the area of women's engagement with media forms that are not feminized but masculinized and structured to exclude women. It is likely that women face many similar conflicts within these areas, and the way they navigate those conflicts is significant.

My questions for this book are broad. First, how has the casualized era changed the face of gaming? Second, what effect does this have on marginalized game audiences, specifically women, as they try to enter game culture and spaces? And finally, what can be learned from women's strategies for managing their presence in a masculinized, often exclusionary space? To answer these questions, I employed a multivalent methodological approach, analyzing industry practices, texts, and themes and conducting thirty-seven in-depth interviews with self-identified female gamers.[9] Although some interviewees were recruited through my personal social network, the majority were recruited through online video game forums, using a general post that explained that I was conducting a research project on women's experiences as gamers and asked interested parties to contact me for more details. When women responded, I gave them more information about the study, the ability to ask questions, and a consent form to sign electronically, before scheduling an online interview via services such as Skype or Gchat. Online recruitment allowed me to speak with women from all over the United States and even from around the world. Because the goal of this study is to address female gamers' diverse encounters with gaming in the casualized era, even a small number of differences between participants was helpful in expanding the experiences they had to relate. For instance, although the sample tended to be young, the inclusion of a few older participants helped provide a perspective on how gaming has changed over time, as well as whether age influences access to power or control.

It quickly became apparent that, despite the positive narratives about games opening up, many exclusionary barriers are still in place and a few new ones have even arisen. Core gaming, in opposition to casual gaming, remains a space defined in masculine terms, where the assumed identity of a gamer is male. This leads to the harassment and exclusion of women as outsiders and frames their negative treatment as acceptable. Nontraditional players also frequently find themselves in a conflicted position where they struggle to embody different parts of their identity simultaneously, as gaming encourages them towards masculinized subject positions even though they identify as female. At the same time, the interventions women make into core games and core gaming, where they are not expected or welcome, provide a means for analyzing and potentially undermining the reproduction of sexism in gaming. They also provide a potential model for addressing sexism in other areas, particularly when women are engaging with a traditionally masculine medium.

A Note on Gender and Identity

I have been referring to "gender" throughout this introduction without necessarily explaining what I mean. Given that this is a key concept, some form of definition may be needed. This book draws on cultural theories that posit gender, and identity more broadly, as what philosopher Michel Foucault calls "discursive practices." This is a complicated way of saying that identities do not necessarily have inherent meaning (Foucault, 1970; Hall, 1996c). Rather, their significance is constructed through discourse—interactions with others, with society and culture, and with language. Take, for instance, the identity of a "gamer." What we think of when we hear this term (e.g., young, straight, white men who are perhaps a bit socially awkward) has no natural connection to the word itself; rather, that meaning has been built up through the ways we discuss, write about, or describe gamers and gamer identity. It then gets reaffirmed as these forms of discussion circulate through culture and as people accept and embody their characteristics. Identities come to have meaning through language.

Because identities are constructed, rather than natural, they can be flexible. For instance, I can emphasize my gender identity by performing femininity, through dress or behavior, or I could emphasize my gamer identity through play and a knowledge of games. I could even do both simultaneously, depending on how I wanted others to see me. As cultural theorist Stuart Hall (1996b) points out, "Identities are never unified and, in late modern times, increasingly fragmented and fractured; never singular but multiply constructed across different, often intersecting and antagonistic discourses, practices and positions" (Hall, 1996b, p. 17). In other words, people are made up of a wide variety of identity components rather than a single unified self, they can draw on these aspects separately to convey different meanings, and these meanings develop through interaction with society, culture, and language. Identity in this way becomes *performative*, something we act out or do rather than something we are.

As a form of identity, this is also true of gender. Gender theorist Judith Butler (1990, 1999) first proposed the idea of gender as performative, arguing that we construct gender as a meaningful category and ourselves as gendered subjects by acting in ways that we have culturally defined as feminine or masculine. For instance, wearing dresses and heels, having long hair, or demonstrating an interest in babies are all characteristics we view as feminine; when we enact and embody these characteristics, we perform femininity. What this theory argues, however, is that one does not need to be biologically sexed female in order perform femininity. As Butler states, "There is no gender identity behind the expressions of gender; that identity is performatively constituted by the very 'expressions' that are said to be its results" (1999, p. 34).

This reimagining of gender as constructed and performed explains how gender norms change over time and context, as they are socially built rather than natural. It also breaks down the idea that gender is or should be a binary, allowing for different forms of expression. Finally, Butler argues that viewing gender as performative opens new possibilities for movements such as feminism, by negating the requirement that everyone working towards feminist change *be* female or feminine. It may, in fact, be easier for people to connect and work towards a common goal when they do not need to share an identity to do so (Butler, 1990, 1999).

At the same time, identity performances have constraints. Individuals who violate existing norms by performing gender in unexpected ways can incur social penalties for doing so; these can range from insults to hate crimes and beyond. For instance, the harassment many women face when they play core games is a form of gender management, as will be explored in chapter 2. Many individuals still consider the categories of "male" and "female" to be fundamentally different and live according to this binary, which has real impacts on their interactions with the world and each other (Taylor, 2012). There are also limits on how we develop and present our identifications, as we often rely on existing representations to show us potential identities we could embody. Scholars like Hall (1996a) argue that the world is continually understood and defined not simply through reality, which is too large for an individual to process in its entirety, but through the interplay of representation and lived reality. Hall describes these two factors as "mutually constitutive"; what exists in reality influences the representations that we see in media, but the trends that appear in media in turn affect how people perceive reality. More simply, the way in which we envision and define ourselves is at least partially related to the way people like us, or unlike us, are represented to us. Media representation is not deterministic—it does not force people to identify in particular ways—but it can make "certain identities possible, plausible, and livable" (Shaw, 2014b, p. 67).

This is significant because representations and identifications are not constructed in a vacuum. Rather, they reflect existing systems of power and control, which can make representations exclusionary. In terms of video games, the consistent representation of gamers as male in news, marketing, and other media presents for men a simple point of identification where they can see themselves taking on the identity of a gamer. This same representational trend can exclude women by making their connection to that identity harder to envision. For instance, a woman who plays games frequently and has a long history with gaming may self-identify as a gamer, as many of my participants did. However, continually seeing largely male representations of players can work to separate her from that identity, complicating her attempts to embody it. In other words, the discourses around gaming and gamers allow limited "subject positions," or places where individuals can see themselves fitting into an identity (Foucault, 1982; Hall, 1997). Masculinized subject positions make more sense than feminized ones when one is interpreting the meanings, power, and management of gaming, and thus they are easier to embody.

Therefore, when I discuss women and female gamers throughout this book, I do not mean to imply that "female" is an essentialized identity that can only be understood in one way. Rather, I use these terms as more concise ways to describe the gendered identity position my participants have taken on and choose to perform, as well as the ways in which sociocultural norms constrain that performance. Similarly, my descriptions of gender identity and gamer identity should not be taken as normative prescriptions about what gender and gamer identity should be. Rather, they are recognitions of how those positions have been constructed already and how they could change.

Viewing identity as nonessential provides an entryway through which games' historical construction as masculine can be questioned and subverted. Female gamers' simultaneous desire for a gamer identity and rejection of many aspects of that identity reveal identity itself to be partial and contested. Through identifying both as women and as gamers, and inhabiting these identities in diverse, negotiated ways, my participants and other "geek girls" (Taylor, 2012) help break down narrow conceptions of femininity and instead outline new ways of being female. Although players rarely refer to their actions as feminist, many of their strategies for choosing games and managing their engagement with game spaces make, as Helen Kennedy argues in her study of female *Quake* gamers, "precisely this kind of intervention" (2006, p. 198). Furthermore, by revealing the constructed nature of this hierarchy, they undermine the existing hegemony in gaming that prioritizes men over women.

These strategies are not without their challenges. Women's interventions into gaming culture and gender identity involve many levels of acceptance and resistance. Their interventions are constrained—by a desire to protect themselves from harassment, a desire to enjoy individual pleasures in game play rather than fight for acceptance, and more. However, their intervention strategies demonstrate how individuals can take feminist action even in an environment that is structured as exclusionary and where they often feel isolated and alone, knowing few other female players (Eklund, 2011). While traditional feminist politics are about banding women together, my participants show how women can embody feminism on their own, as well as how or when they cannot. In doing so, they lay out strategies for managing misogyny not only in games but also in other masculinized or exclusionary areas. Female sports fans, for instance, often struggle to belong, and sports-oriented environments such as bars and stadiums are primarily homosocial spaces for men. Women also face exclusion and misogyny on many online platforms like Twitter. Therefore, insight into women's possible interventions in gaming may serve as a model according to which resistance on other platforms could be explored. This is particularly significant given the cultural contexts of the casualized era, especially with regard to gender and feminism.

Feminism, Postfeminism, and the Cultural Contexts of the Casualized Era

Since the 1980s, the United States has been facing a strong push-back against the feminist movement. This can be seen in media portrayals of women as miserable, stressed by the demands of their careers, and lacking love and family due to their ambition (Faludi, 2006). It appears in increasing regulations on abortion access, women's health care, and reproductive rights (Rohlinger, 2016), as well as in the argument, advanced by writers like Hanna Rosin, that women have not only achieved equality but have actually begun to supersede men in terms of economic, social, and even political power (Rosin, 2010, 2012; Sommers, 2013). These elements are part of an overall sociopolitical milieu known as postfeminism, in which feminism has been "taken into account," treated as something that has achieved its goals and is therefore outdated (McRobbie, 2009). Postfeminism argues that structural barriers to female achievement have been removed, and individuals and movements who push for continued political change are trying to become superior to men rather than simply equal.

Feminist scholars have, of course, emphasized how feminism has not achieved all its goals, pointing out that many structural barriers to full gender equality have merely shifted form while ensuring that the glass ceiling remains intact (e.g., McRobbie, 2009). Furthermore, the challenges that women now face are often invisible or easy to dismiss. This is due to the forces of embedded feminism, a concept described by gender and media scholar Susan Douglas, who argues that women's accomplishments have become a visible part of the cultural landscape (Douglas, 2010, p. 9). Many women have achieved high-powered positions; Hillary Clinton, Madeleine Albright, and Condoleezza Rice have been secretaries of state, and Fortune 500 companies hit a record high of thirty-two female CEOs in 2017, although that number is now down to twenty-four (Mejia, 2018). Fictional media is also rife with powerful female cops, top medical professionals, attorneys, and high-ranking politicians.

Both real-life and fictional examples of female power normalize women's success and highlight their achievements, but they also mask continued problems. Many women are still underpaid in comparison to their male counterparts, men head 476 Fortune 500 companies, and research into household labor shows that women still complete more at-home chores than men (Mejia, 2018; Schulte, 2014). Representations of feminine power, however, make it easy to focus solely on the successes of feminism and to feel as though it is overreaching. This is especially true as privilege is often invisible to its bearers, and awarding the same privileges to others can appear to be giving them undue advantages. Sociologist Michael Kimmel (2013) compared this to a race: "It may be hard for white men to realize that, irrespective of other factors, we have been running with the wind at our backs all these years and that what we think of as 'fairness' to us has been built on the backs of others. [...] Efforts to level the playing field may feel like water is rushing uphill, like it's reverse discrimination against us" (p. xiii). This is further affected by the fact that, while men, and white men specifically, are privileged as a group, there are distinct disparities in the power they obtain individually. Many believe that if they were truly privileged, they would feel more powerful or more successful. In short, they feel entitled to more than they possess.

For some men, this has led to a push-back against further changes to the sociopolitical environment and even a desire to reverse feminism's gains. The past decade or so has seen a rise in websites and online communities devoted to topics of men's rights and how feminism infringes on them. For example, writers like Jared White detail how men and their children are turned away from domestic abuse shelters due to their gender, how women primarily receive custody of children in a divorce while men are forced to pay child support, how men who suffer domestic abuse are not given the same level of help as women, and how men are more likely to be accused of rape than women are, at times even falsely (White, 2011). In these ways, White argues, the feminist movement's attempts to protect women have detrimentally affected men. While organizations such as the Southern Poverty Law Center have combated these claims (Potok and Schlatter, 2012), many men gravitate to these allegations as evidence of reverse discrimination, and their anger and frustration over these points "is 'real'—that is, it is experienced deeply and sincerely" (Kimmel, 2013, p. 9). Despite the arguments that can be made to the effect that men are still privileged, large subsections truly feel that their position in the world is being overtaken and that they are not free to be the kind of men they want to be.

This connects strongly to gaming's crisis of authority, in which changing expectations around gaming are perceived as evidence that other groups are achieving power at the cost of men. Because of games' masculinized history, gaming has frequently served as a homosocial space for men to bond with other men. Men's homosociality, or intragender socialization, often takes place in specifically gendered spaces, such as sports bars and locker rooms, or through masculinized media such as male-hosted talk radio or sports talk radio (Lipman-Blumen, 1976; Wenner, 1998; Nylund, 2004). Interactions in these areas serve to reaffirm traditional masculinity, through interpersonal behavior policing, but can also provide a space in which to talk about gender and sexuality in meaningful ways without surveillance by women. The loss of these spaces, through the entry of women, could therefore seem threatening, especially given geek masculinity's already precarious position between power and marginalization.

Because of this, players lash out against change. Harley, one of my longest-playing participants, argued that the elevated levels of misogyny currently present in gaming were a new development; although gaming had always been a male-dominated space, specific efforts to keep it that way only started recently, according to her account. That is, until the masculine orientation of gaming was questioned, it did not need to be firmly protected through overtly exclusionary measures like sexist harassment. Greater misogyny in gaming may also reflect overall antifeminist, and often antiwomen, trends in modern politics and culture. Regardless of the specific nature of the relationship among games, gender, and overall sociopolitical movements, it is clear that gaming's current struggles relate to broader cultural trends and can serve as a small microcosm through which to examine these trends.

Book Structure

To begin this intervention into gaming sexism, and sexism more generally, chapter 1 opens with an exploration of the video game industry in the casualized era. First, it lays out a theoretical framework for the book in its entirety by engaging with the concepts of "core" and "casual" and how they embody games' hegemonic and counterhegemonic forces. Although both terms are generally deployed as industrial, generic adjectives for particular types of games or players, I use them instead to show how discourses in gaming spaces separate new type of players from traditional ones and position both in a hierarchy that prioritizes core and dismisses casual. In determining what is allowed in the core and what is relegated to the margins, as well as in analyzing how this changes contextually, I work to show how the core of gaming is a nonessential space. Rather, it is changeable and can be challenged and reimagined. This chapter then uses a critical analysis of gaming news to demonstrate that this reimagining is an already existent process that has provoked a crisis of authority, where previously powerful members of the community fear losing control and are exerting extra force to maintain their privileged position.

Chapters 2 and 3 then assess the forces women encounter that attempt to maintain core as a definable, masculine sphere, such as direct harassment, gendered stereotypes, and being treated with surprise, among others. They show how these behaviors and themes separate women from gamer identity and relegate them to the margins of gaming rather than allowing them to enter the core—a maneuver accomplished through overt sexism, where the sexist nature of a behavior or trend is obvious, and inferential sexism, which rests on commonsense assumptions about gender and gender relations. These two forces serve to preserve core gaming's existing hegemony and power for male gamers over female gamers. However, these chapters also weigh the significance of different types of exclusion, comparing the impact of overt sexism's more obvious nature to inferential sexism's subtler but perhaps more damaging influence. In this way, they both address new aspects of women's experiences in masculinized spaces and provide insight into the continuing challenges of the casualized era.

Chapters 1–3 having established the many challenges women face when entering core gaming, chapter 4 asks why they would bother to do so. It summarizes the many pleasures women find in gaming, and then lays out how they can and already often do embody a gamer identity. It addresses the many subject positions women embody as they game and how these are encouraged by or resistant to the overall culture of gaming. Through this analysis, it demonstrates how women are a diverse, rather than essentialized, group and how both gender and gamer identity can be embodied in multiple ways. Women's preferences for gaming are personal, contextual, and rarely specifically gendered. However, this chapter also continues to show that female gamers' interactions with games are conflicted, with interviewees struggling to embody both their gender identity and their gamer identity without being singled out for this seemingly contradictory combination.

Chapter 5 demonstrates that women are capable managers of their media environment, outlining the specific strategies they employ to cope with the conflict between core and margins. From choosing an appropriate game to responding to harassment, women are willing and able to fight for equality in an unequal space. Unfortunately, their experiences also show that managing a conflicted identity involves a significant amount of work, and thus may not be sustainable. From their existing strategies, however, it is possible to see where developers or activists could make useful intercessions. Amid gaming's crisis of authority, these intercessions could be particularly critical for increasing gender equality in gaming.

Recognizing that the original interviews for this project were conducted in 2012, and that major events in gaming history have occurred since then, chapter 6 reconnects with interviewees five years later. It asks participants to address events like GamerGate and explores how their gaming habits have changed over time. In doing so, this chapter reveals that large-scale events, like GamerGate, do not meaningfully affect female gamers' day-to-day experiences, but the garden-variety sexism they face regularly continues to structure their decisions around play. This chapter provides a relevant update to the information and conclusions put forth in the preceding sections and situates GamerGate and play within broader contexts.

Collectively, *Gaming Sexism* works to demonstrate how, despite gaming's perceived diversification, many barriers to true equality between different types of gamers persist, and it invites you to consider what is lost when sexism and misogyny are allowed within a significant subsection of popular culture. Given the existing cultural climate around feminism and postfeminism, there is a strong likelihood that inequality in gaming will not stay limited to the screen or to game-oriented spaces. Indeed, many events have already shown this to be the case.

1

Core and the Video Game Industry

Changing Perceptions of Power

When I saw the first trailer for *Assassin's Creed* in 2007, I was immediately mesmerized by the game's stealth mechanics, parkour-like free running, and beautifully crafted environments. These elements, combined with the games' story about a centuries-long struggle between the Assassins and the Knights Templar, continue to draw me back to the series again and again. At the same time, many *Assassin's Creed* games have moments that signal that I am not part of their intended audience. In an early *Assassin's Creed II* segment, for instance, my character, Ezio, needed to sneak into his girlfriend's bedroom for an illicit tryst. At other times, succeeding in a mission required me to hide among scantily clad courtesans. These moments do not ruin my enjoyment of the series, but they do tend to draw me out of the action; given that I am a straight woman, my character's attitude towards women often diverged strongly from my own.

This anecdote helps illustrate how masculinity defines and structures many aspects of games and game culture. Within games themselves, these range from character design, which overrepresents men and underrepresents women (e.g., Waddell et al., 2014) to the structures of game mechanics and play (Burrill, 2008) to storylines and genres that tend to focus on traditionally masculine interests (Newman, 2016), although some of these factors are changing as casual games become more prominent. Outside of game texts, masculinity can be found everywhere from marketing (e.g., Behm-Morawitz, 2017) to how game press addresses its audiences (e.g. Cote, 2018b; Kirkpatrick, 2012, 2015) to the many industrial structures that make it easier for men to develop games than for women to do so (e.g., Blodgett and Salter, 2014; Johnson, 2011).

Collectively, game scholars Janine Fron, Tracy Fullerton, Jacquelyn Ford Morie, and Celia Pearce (2007) have referred to these forces as "the

hegemony of play" (p. 1). This term draws on Marxist philosopher Antonio Gramsci's theories about cultural hegemony, in which he argued
that powerful classes maintain their power over the oppressed not by
force but by naturalization. The ruling class draws from the aspirations
of nonelites and/or manipulates the values and beliefs of society in order
to create a "commonsense," self-justifying worldview that supports their
continued power (Gramsci and Hoare, 1971). This process has occurred
in gaming through the promotion and maintenance of narrow views
around what qualifies as a game and who qualifies as a gamer, such as
those listed above. Fron and colleagues point to three specific "areas of
crisis" in which this status quo (or hegemony) develops: the production
process of games, the technologies of play, and the cultural positioning
of games and "gamers." Each of these, the authors argue, plays a role in
narrowing the types of games that get produced and the audience for
these, in the end limiting the commercial success of the gaming industry
as well as marginalizing many potential players. They also normalize the
idea that gaming is a hobby for men and boys.

This masculinized hegemony has persisted for decades, and Fron and
colleagues rightly point out that researchers have not paid enough attention to it in the past, often ourselves buying into and using industry-
defined categories for games and gamers rather than questioning their
assumptions. At the same time, the end of the "Hegemony of Play" article
recognizes that the authors were writing on the edge of "subtle but tec-
tonic shifts" (p. 8) in video game culture. Specifically, they recognized
that the rising forces of casual, social, and mobile games and their associated platforms and players had the chance to fundamentally redefine
who could be a gamer or what games meant. Rather than focusing on
traditional young, male audiences, casual games engage many different
types of players and encourage different play styles. In other words, casual, social, and mobile games serve as a counterhegemonic force, bringing into question the taken-for-granted nature of the existing order and
its legitimacy. Counterhegemonic forces can promote real shifts in power
and in determinations of who has access to different areas of culture.

Because of this, the traditional "hegemony of play" is no longer the
only force present within game culture and industry. Rather, it is one of
two competing forces, which I will refer to using the terms "core" and "casual." Respectively, these terms are apt descriptors for gaming's existing

hegemony and the counterhegemonic casual, social, and mobile games that are challenging that hegemony's normalization. "Core" and "casual" describe different play styles, games, or players, but both also mean more than this. "Core" is often used as a marker of centrality, to guard the significance of the games, platforms, and players the gaming industry has traditionally prioritized. In contrast to this, "casual" is associated with nontraditional players, such as women or older gamers, and is often dismissed and treated as less serious than core. Accordingly, these terms already embody the divide between hegemony and counterhegemony,[1] and they are already commonly used in game culture.

By integrating an overall examination of industry trends with specific conclusions drawn from an in-depth, critical discourse analysis of video game magazines from the start of the casualized era (2005–2008),[2] this chapter shows how core and casual have been constructed as different, as well as how this binary breaks down under closer inspection; for every example of what core is, there is an example of a game or player that undermines that definition. Because of this, I argue that the divide between core and casual is a socially and culturally constructed attempt to maintain games' existing hegemony. Finally, I explain how narratives around the start of the casualized era frame casual as a "threat" to core, provoking the crisis of authority I described earlier. Discourses around gaming often frame it as zero-sum, whereby success in one area necessarily means the decline of another. This belief drives core players to exert all the forces at their disposal, including sexism, to protect core from the incursion of casual games, players, and platforms. In this way, this struggle over what games mean needs to be addressed before we can solve some of gaming's existing toxicity.

Defining Core

When I use the term "core" throughout this book, it means two things. First, "core" is a reference to the video game industry's historic attention to male audiences, console games, and masculinized genres. I argue that all of these, including a focus on consoles, have normalized men's participation with games over women's. Second, "core" comes from "hardcore," an adjective describing a level of commitment and a particular kind of content. Through connotations developed in other areas where "hardcore" is used, as well as through the way it is applied to games, this connection both masculinizes core games further and sets them up as the "natural" center for the gaming industry. Collectively, these forces have worked to build an intrinsic relationship between gaming and masculinity and to prioritize games and players that fit this relationship. They are key contributors to games' existing hegemony.

Take the game industry's traditional focus on console games. Although gaming first arose on university and research laboratory computers and then spread to arcades throughout the 1960s–1980s, over time, home consoles and personal computer (PC) games became the dominant force in the market. Not only were home games more convenient for players, who could play in their living rooms, but they were likely to be less expensive for serious gamers. Home consoles were pricey up front, but continued play did not cost a quarter per life. These characteristics also made home console games a favorite of parents, as "younger children would be safe from the perceived threats of the world outside, and parents would be relieved of worrying about kids squandering pocketsful of quarters in coin-operated machines" (Newman, 2017, p. 99). Additionally, as game consoles developed swappable game cartridges or discs, their attraction for developers increased. While arcade owners and game providers had to replace arcade games regularly to maintain player interest, the infinitely changeable nature of home consoles and their cartridges meant that a single system had a much longer shelf life and that individual games were cheaper to make and to buy (Kent, 2001).

For these reasons, the gaming industry has traditionally focused its attention on home consoles. This is evidenced by industry sales statistics, which, until the late 2000s, concentrated almost entirely on console and PC games. For instance, sales figures collected by the Entertainment Software Association (ESA), the trade organization funded by gaming's largest publishing companies, did not even measure digital sales until 2009 (see figure 1.1). Instead, it measured only physical sales of games from retail locations. This prioritizes console games, which were primarily available in cartridges and CDs prior to the mid-2000s, and PC games, which also came on physical discs (although they have been available for digital download for longer than console games, as Internet connectivity spread faster via PC). Even as this shifted, and the ESA added in measures of

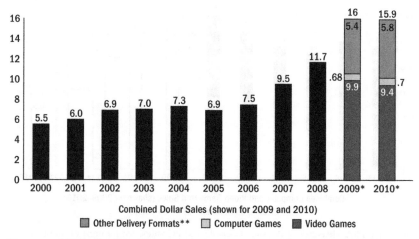

Figure 1.1. ESA Dollar Sales Figures, 2011. Entertainment Software Association (2011). Essential facts about the computer and video game industry [Press release]. Retrieved from www.theesa.com/.

* Figures include total consumer spend.

** Other delivery formats include subscriptions, digital full games, digital add-on content, mobile apps, social network gaming, and other physical delivery, 2000–2008 figures are sales of new physical content at retail exclusively.

digital sales, it still printed a head-to-head comparison of physical computer and console unit sales up until 2014 (figure 1.2).

As industry scholar Aphra Kerr (2017) points out, most measures of video games sales and profits come from within the industry itself, rather than external forces like governments or nonprofits. Therefore, these stats can be read as a measure of the game industry's priorities, which have long been console games and, to a lesser extent, PC games. Because of concerns about piracy, developers often consider PC games riskier investments than console games. Gaming websites like Polygon, for instance, have reported piracy rates as high as 90 percent for PC games (Polygon Staff, 2012a), indicating that consoles may offer game producers a higher return on investment. Therefore, although PC games are significant, it is possible to argue that console games have been *the* focus of the gaming industry.

There is nothing inherently masculine about a game console, and many women, myself included, own and game on consoles. But consoles have often been developed and marketed with men in mind. When the original Xbox was released, for instance, the controller size was too large for most

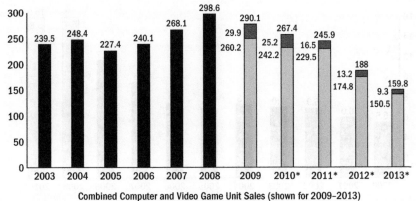

Figure 1.2. ESA Measures of Physical Console and PC Sales, 2014. Entertainment Software Association (2014). Essential facts about the computer and video game industry [Press release]. Retrieved from www.theesa.com/.
* Figures are sales of new physical content at retail exclusively.

women or children to play comfortably (Fron et al., 2007). Furthermore, because computing technology in general is culturally constructed as masculine rather than feminine, many parents will buy consoles and computers for boys but not for girls (Gilmour, 1999; Schott and Horrell, 2000; Bryce and Rutter, 2003; Jenson, de Castell, and Fisher, 2007; Jenson and de Castell, 2011). Finally, measuring only physical console and PC game sales ignores any software that comes preinstalled on a computer, like *Solitaire* or *Minesweeper*, as well as web browser–based games and other casual offerings. Therefore, core's prioritization of consoles narrows the types of games and players that are visible to the industry and to one another.

In addition, the games industry has tended to produce specific genres. In the earliest years of gaming, many games focused on sports, war, adventures in the wild West, or science fiction (Newman, 2017). All of these are collectively elements of Western "boy culture," or what we expect men and boys to enjoy, e.g., that they will be brave and adventurous or that they will fight for a cause. This trend of prioritizing traditionally masculine interests in gaming has continued. Measures of the top-selling games from 2004–2019, the years in which the ESA has released overall industry reports, show a strong focus on action, sports, racing, shooting, and fighting games. Other genres are underrepresented and in many of the reports are classified into the single category "family entertainment." Again, this could be a remnant of the way the ESA measures game sales, often leaving out digital downloads, mobile games, or web-based games in favor of console and PC games. It could also be read as an indication that these masculinized genres are what players really want; after all, these are lists of best-sellers. However, given the aforementioned measurement limitations and the game industry's risk-averse nature, with producers basing their game design on previous successes, it is more likely that these limited genres reflect preconceived notions about who games and what they like rather than real audience desires. The success of games that break the masculinized mold, such as *The Sims*, *Just Dance*, and more, also indicates that the industry's continued use of masculinized subject matter is more their choice than the audience's.

Thus, core comes to be defined by an interaction of game type, platform, audience, and anticipated play style. As American culture scholar Erica Kubik (2009) argues, core games have become heavily associated with "trappings of masculinity" (pp. 62–63). This can be seen in a particular subgenre of gaming that uses the term "core" within its title, the area known as "masocore." "Masocore," a portmanteau of "masochism" and "hardcore," refers to games developers specifically make to be almost impossible to complete. In these games, titles like *Super Meat Boy* and *The End Is Nigh*, players must take pleasure not in beating the game but in proving their skill by making infinitesimal progress through intense time commitment. Masocore games are generally platformers[3] that provide players with unlimited lives, but then set them against difficult game mechanics that require extremely fast reflexes and precise movements. The smallest misstep will lead to the player's death and send them backwards in their challenge. These are games one uses to show mastery, not games one plays for relaxation or enjoyment. Because of this, masocore games possess many masculinized characteristics, such as a desire to dominate game environments and other players through one's skill, and an extreme focus on competitiveness. These elements, combined with their deliberate difficulty and appeal to only a small contingent of obsessive players, further link masculinity to core, tying together hegemonic gender expectations and the idea of commitment to gaming.

The second meaning of core, where it develops out of the term "hardcore," then deepens these masculine connotations. As Merriam-Webster defines it, "hardcore" means "a central or fundamental and usually enduring group or part: as a: a relatively small enduring core of society marked by apparent resistance to change or inability to escape a persistent wretched condition (as poverty or chronic unemployment), b: a militant or fiercely loyal faction" (Hardcore, 2018). Hardcore gamers, therefore, are the most committed, experienced, skillful, and obsessive players; hardcore games are the ones that require this level of obsession to complete. Describing them as "hardcore" also implies that these players and games are central to the development and existence of the gaming industry and game culture more broadly, given the term's association with "enduring" and "fundamental."

Assuming that "hardcore" and core are *only* based on this definition of commitment and loyalty, however, ignores the terms' background and application in other areas, where "hardcore" has come to be associated with varying performances of masculinity. Through these subtler connotations, and often only apparent to those within the described sphere, "hardcore" and core can serve as a political tool that prioritizes a version of hegemonic masculinity based on an ideal of toughness, aggression, and dominance over women and other, nonhegemonic men. Hegemonic masculinity also often involves sexual prowess or power over women as well as mastery of technology, including weaponry, vehicles, or, in the case of music, instruments like drums and guitars. Finally, it can include an emphasis on the male body, its musculature, strength, and ability to withstand injury and pain (Brod, 1987; Hanke, 1992; Connell, 2000). Put simply, hegemonic masculinity prioritizes men's power and control over their environments, selves, and others. In tapping into, reproducing, and inflecting these elements of masculinity, core equates "power" with "men."

Take the use of "hardcore" in punk music. Hardcore was a movement to return punk, which had been affected by corporate interests, to its original anti-establishment rhetoric and political beliefs (James, 1988). The music was faster, louder, and more abrasive than much of the original punk movement, making it more extreme and less mainstream (Blush, 2010). Hardcore punk culture also tried to be deliberately fringe, setting itself up against mainstream society and popular culture. Because of this, it ostensibly rejected social constructions of gender, race, sexuality, and more, fighting against the "isms" associated with these constructions—sexism, racism, etc. However, the ways in which the scene expressed hardcore identity ended up excluding many people its open-minded and anti-establishment definition should have welcomed.

In her study of "straight-edge hardcore" fans, who rejected drugs, alcohol, and sex as a means to avoid consumer culture, sociologist Jamie Mullaney (2007) wrote, "Even as they express commitment to the idea that gender does not play a role in the scene, [third-wave] sXers simultaneously offer a plethora of anecdotes detailing the ways the scene marginalizes women" (p. 386). For example, many straight-edge men, who were avoiding casual sexual encounters or abstaining from sex altogether, were suspicious of women's intentions. They felt women were only "hardcore" as a ploy to get a boyfriend, and this made them a potential threat to men's ability to remain straight-edge (Mullaney, 2007).[4] Furthermore, while many hardcore bands did include women, they were frequently limited to the role of bassist, rather than taking on more prestigious positions as lead singer or guitarist. This ghettoization of women to roles that men did not want helped ensure that they remained marginal to hardcore, despite its ostensibly open-minded nature.

Limitations like this were not only part of straight-edge hardcore. Rather, they echoed throughout the genre and its scene. The physical style of hardcore dancing, also known as slam dancing or moshing, for instance, restricted the extent to which women participated as audience members at shows. Involving a lot of flailing, punching, and kicking, slam dancing often resulted in dancers accidentally or intentionally hitting those around them. Crowd surfing, pushing others out of the way to get closer to the stage, and jumping up and down in time with the music also made being in the crowd at a hardcore show a physical and potentially dangerous option. This relegated many hardcore fans to the margins of concert venues. While some women no doubt became well-practiced slam dancers, anecdotal evidence seems to show that most avoided "the pit," the area in front of the stage where hardcore audience members tended to be most violent (Fenster, 1993; Willis, 1993; Blush, 2010).

It was only in the area of style, a consumption-based practice that hardcore was supposedly against, where women and men achieved parity. Women could look hardcore and were definitionally invited to be part of the hardcore scene. In practice, however, they remained on the margins, limited to only a few carefully delineated forms of participation. Hardcore music was (and is) overall a masculinized sphere, enacted in ways that exclude others.

Another area where "hardcore" has been masculinized is in pornography, where it describes material in which there is "explicit sexual expression" (Escoffier, 2009, p. 1). Within the industry, this generally means the display of erect male genitalia (Hirdman, 2007). Because of this, the material naturally requires male actors and a male presence. While hegemonically masculine elements like the direct domination of women are not specifically necessary for pornography to count as "hardcore," hardcore pornography is still inescapably gendered male, due to its requirement of male body parts to qualify.

Thus, the use of hardcore in other areas shows a clear link with masculinity; these connotations carry over into gaming, and the industry's narrow focus on male audiences, masculinized content, and consoles exacerbates this connection. In other words, core is ostensibly an ungendered term that refers to gaming's most committed players. The way it has been employed and understood, however, defines those committed gamers as male. To tie this back to the identity theory discussed in the introduction, these structures make masculine subject positions more accessible than female ones within core gaming.

Further considering core through "hardcore's" implications of centrality shows how gaming exists in a hierarchy. Rather than core and casual just being different, core developers, games, and players are marked as *better*. This deeply connects to relations of power, in that members of an area's margins generally lack access to sociocultural power in the center and can effect little change on gaming overall. As Gramsci argues, the power of a hegemony comes from its naturalization; the idea that men and boys are more likely to game than other groups, and that they prefer specific types of content, has been in place for so long that it has become common sense.

Defining Casual

Like "core," "casual" describes a set of games, playstyles, players, and gendered positions. The term "casual" also constructs this sphere of gaming as frivolous and less serious than the central, committed sphere that is "core." This is one of the ways through which core gaming maintains power and resists change. Before I explore that claim, however, a deeper discussion of casual may be useful.

Considering first the games themselves, game scholars like Jussi Kuittinen and colleagues (2007) argue that defining a casual game is easier said than done. Definitions range from a game "that is easy to learn, simple to play and offers quick rewards with forgiving gameplay" (p. 106) to one with nonviolent content to specific genres such as puzzles games to particular business models such as advergames, which promote branded products as part of the play experience. Annakaisa Kultima (2009) defines casual games as ones with broadly acceptable content and themes, accessibility for players of different skill levels, and simple, flexible game design. To this, Jesper Juul (2010) adds that casual games are interruptible (players can easily put the game down if needed), have lenient punishments for failure, and provide excessive positive feedback for player actions, which he refers to as "juiciness" (p. 50). Collectively, these definitions all speak to casual games as positively valanced, easy to fit into small gaps of time, and accessible for diverse players to pick up and play.

Because of this, casual games target new audiences, instead of core players. As Juul (2010) said, "Video games are becoming normal; during the history of all games, everybody, young and old, has played games of one kind or another. The rise of casual games is the end of that small historical anomaly of the 1980s and 1990s when video games were played by only a small part of the population" (2010, p. 20). This fits in with Nintendo's Blue Ocean strategy and its marketing for the DS and the Wii; Nintendo was targeting families, the elderly, moms, and as many other nontraditional gaming audiences as it could think of.

However, these casual players soon developed stereotypes of their own; developers expect that a casual gamer "has a preference for positive and pleasant fictions, has played few video games, is willing to commit little time and few resources toward playing video games, and dislikes difficult games" (Juul, 2010, p. 29). The success of games such as *Farmville*, in which friends help you care for your farm, or *Words with Friends*, a social media version of Scrabble, has also led to the stereotype that casual gamers prefer social games that require interaction between players. Finally, developers do not expect casual players to have or desire in-depth knowledge of games. This implies that casual gamers play games in short bursts, have little knowledge of mechanics or game history, and look primarily for entertainment rather than deep storylines, quality graphics or game play, and intense challenges. Regardless of their real play habits, these discourses construct casual gamers, as their name itself suggests, as nonserious players who are only tangentially involved in gaming culture. This starts to build casual as less significant than core by arguing that casual gamers do not contribute as much to the game industry and game culture. These discourses also dismiss the games themselves; as Juul states, many developers and players think "'casual' connotes bland or shallow games" (2010, p. 26).

Casual games are further culturally dismissed due to their gendered status as a feminine sphere. As game studies scholar John Vanderhoef (2013) states, "There has been a long history of linking mainstream or popular culture with the feminine for the purpose of denigrating both" (p. 1). And developers and discourses around casual gaming have emphasized the presence of female players. In looking at press releases from casual game developers, for instance, Kuittinen and colleagues (2007) found that "one notion which is highlighted in these press releases is that the majority of casual gamers are women and that the majority of these women are middle-aged and older" (p. 106). Similarly, gender and games researcher Shira Chess (2017) found that casual game designers tend to picture their audience as middle-aged, middle-class, female, maternal, white, and often from somewhere in the midwestern United States. She refers to this construction as the "designed identity" of a casual gamer and sees it resonate through game design, industry conventions, and marketing decisions. Although all the aforementioned authors are careful to point out that expectations for casual games do not necessarily reflect the real habits of players, these discourses have constructed casual as both feminine and trivial.

Although casual games are economically significant, the discourses around core and casual set them up as peripheral to gaming culture. As new media researcher Christopher Paul (2018) points out, "A key rhetorical construction in video games is that some games and 'gamers' are more 'real' than others" (p. 66). Game discourses also often treat women and other nontraditional gamers as "new" additions to gaming communities, ignoring the many individuals who have always played games despite the medium's masculinized history. This limits them to the margins of gaming culture, as they are not expected to have significant experience with games, and can prevent women's future access to gaming communities and the identity of a gamer. Because of this, core and casual need to be seen as strategic rather than natural.

Breaking Down the Binary

The association of casual and core games with different audiences serves as a discursive attempt to maintain an unequal hierarchy of power in gaming, by separating the traditional straight, white, male market from newer, broader audiences. Furthermore, it attempts to define core games as the more serious and important segment of the gaming community, taking on core's connotations of "central," while framing casual games as nonserious entertainment or "stupid games" (Anderson, 2012). This politicizes seemingly simple descriptors, endowing one with importance and the other with frivolity (Kubik, 2009; Vanderhoef, 2013). Further, it reserves cultural power and significance for traditionally male audiences and games, maintaining a hierarchy that excludes women and other "new" audiences from control over gaming culture.

These expectations affect many areas of gaming, such as when non-casual development teams push for greater gender equity. For instance, *The Last of Us* developer Naughty Dog had to request that its popular postapocalyptic survival game be focus group tested with women prior to its release; the research group conducting the tests considered women to be outside the game's target audience and excluded them from testing (Agnello, 2013). This assumption reveals to some extent the degree to which men and video games are still intimately linked in cultural imagination despite the rise of casual games and their supposed diversifying influence.

At the same time, the stereotypical definitions of casual and core do not necessarily play out in the lived experiences of players. Chess (2017), for instance, was careful to argue that the designed identity of "Player Two" was an industry construct, and therefore not entirely reflective of actual casual players. Juul and other scholars have also shown strong evidence that casual games can be played in core ways and vice versa (Chess, 2014; Consalvo, 2009; Consalvo and Begy, 2015; Juul, 2010; Shaw, 2014a), arguing that a game's design and its actual impact may differ dramatically when players engage with the game.[5] Game studies scholar Mia Consalvo (2009) has even titled a piece on this practice "hardcore casual," indicating how these two terms do not meaningfully represent real player practices. However, popular understandings of the terms have not changed greatly as a result of this research. Media and audience discourses continue to treat casual and core as polar opposites, ignoring the heavy overlap between these areas (Shaw, 2014a).

The fact that core and casual are not as simple as they appear offers a challenge to gaming's existing power divide. As Gramsci (1971) points out, hegemony is not immutable. Rather, it is a continual struggle between the ruling class, which works to make its culture appear to be commonsense, and subordinate classes, who sometimes consent to and sometimes resist this construction. Core and casual embody this struggle. Specifically, hegemonic gamers and developers use notions of core to bound and police a hierarchy that prioritizes them, expanding or retracting the perimeters of core as needed to delineate what matters to game culture—their game culture—and what does not.

However, core is a flexible and paradoxical concept. For each possible indicator of what core is, there is an example of a game or player that undermines that definition. If core is marked out by time investment, the many players who spend hundreds of hours on social media games like *Farmville* would seem to indicate that this game should count as core, and they should count as core players. If core is decided by platform, with PC games and console games as the locus of core, then *Solitaire* and *Wii Sports* would both be included, while detailed, complex mobile games like *Injustice: Gods Among Us Mobile*[6] or *Horn*[7] would not. If core is determined by player gender, the many experienced, skillful women interviewed for this study would be ignored or left out, while any male player would be included regardless of play style, game preferences, or skill level. Core and casual are extremely complicated terms that encompass many different elements at once.

The flexibility of these boundaries allows subordinated gamers to take on some core characteristics while ignoring or deliberately avoiding others. This is a necessary step in breaking down and altering gaming's current gender hierarchy by denaturalizing it and showing how it can be constructed in different, more inclusive ways. Drawing out fractures in what core means, and the ways in which players who are not generally seen as core can embody its characteristics, is one path towards undermining the importance of these characteristics. This has also been happening through the rise of casual games. As casual games grow increasingly significant to the overall industry, they challenge core's taken-for-granted status. This has resulted in conflicting perspectives on the new game environment.

Concerns about Core: Anxious Discourses in Gaming Magazines

To see how journalists and other members of the gaming community framed the rise of casual games, I conducted a discourse analysis of video gaming magazines from the start of the casualized era (2005–2008).[8] I chose this time frame because it is when many industrial shifts originated; Nintendo introduced and released the Wii, mobile gaming grew in market share and scope, and audiences expanded. The way these changes were discussed as they began set the stage for later concerns about core and its casual competition, making this a key moment to focus on. And by analyzing discourse, or the language patterns surrounding core and casual in these publications, I was able to see what, if any, consistent themes and patterns were circulating and how they might affect readers' perceptions of the changing industry.

I found that the rise of casual as a counterhegemonic force was discussed in two distinct ways. On the one hand, many innovative elements of the casualized era are lauded for their creativity, their focus on quality game play over pretty graphics, or their popularization of gaming. For instance, some articles celebrated the Wii's introduction of intuitive, motion-based controllers as a new way to make games immersive. Others pointed to mobile, social, or web-based casual games as a chance for developers to break away from the constraints of big budgets, large teams, or restrictive relationships with publishers.

On the other hand, and perhaps more importantly for the questions of this book, the magazines also expressed many anxieties about the future of core gaming. Writers recognized that casual games were extremely popular; because of this, they feared that industry resources would move towards this area and away from the games they preferred. In fact, "Some players are explicit in their complaints that growth in some areas—such as casual and social games, which are often targeted to women—means that fewer budgets and development teams will be focused on traditional titles and genres such as First-Person Shooters and Action games" (Consalvo, 2012). This comes through clearly in press coverage from the start of the casualized era, as magazines emphasized the differences between core and casual audiences, focused on developer flight to the casual sector, and compared core's expensive and uncertain future to casual's success. These anxieties frame casual as a threat to core, which is probably one of the factors provoking the casualized era's crisis of authority.

Fundamental Differences

As I and other researchers have demonstrated (Cote, 2018b; Kirkpatrick, 2012, 2015), the language of video gaming magazines frames gamers in specific ways, predominantly as male and young. This is not a monolithic presentation; both *Edge* and *Game Informer* (*GI*), for instance, had issues in which male gamers wrote to the magazine complaining about how their girlfriends, and women in general, just could not play games as well as men. The magazines not only completely dismissed this assertion, claiming that it was one of the stupidest things they had ever heard, but they also prioritized response letters from female gamers in ensuing issues. At other moments, the magazines spotlighted articles written by female gamers, addressing problems they faced in gaming spheres, or recognized claims that gaming audiences were already more diverse than stereotypes would expect, such as when *Game Developer* (*GDM*) cited ESA statistics showing how women make up significant parts of game audiences (February 2005).

However, these few moments were somewhat minimized by the many times the magazines portrayed nontraditional gaming audiences, and especially casual audiences, as old, female, and disinterested in challenging games. In short, the magazines drew on many of the previously mentioned stereotypes associated with casual games and gamers, while implying that their audience of core gamers was not any of these things. For instance, when *Game Informer* asked readers for their opinion of the Wii, PS3, and Xbox 360, one reader lauded the Wii for its multiplayer capabilities. However, he did so using his sisters as an example of the quintessential nongamer, stating, "My sisters have never been into games. I hate to be stereotypical, but they're sisters. They'd rather do their hair than save the world. They've actually started playing with me [on the Nintendo Wii] and they've had fun" (February 2007, p. 39). It might be hard to believe that anyone would opt to style their hair over saving the world, but this player's use of stereotypical alternatives clearly expresses the idea that women are fundamentally less interested in games than men and therefore are not gamers. In *Edge*, one of the magazine writers stated that he recommended the Xbox 360 as the best system for a gamer but changed this recommendation to "the Wii if they're an old person or a girl" (January 2008, p. 124). Elsewhere, nontraditional gamers are named as grandmas, "soccer moms and retirees," "baby boomers," "housewives, schoolkids, people like that," "moms, kids, and anybody who can move a mouse," and, of course, as "mum" (*Electronic Gaming Monthly* [*EGM*], Holiday 2007, p. 14; *EGM*, November 2008, p. 16; *GDM*, November 2005, p. 11; *Edge*, March 2005, p. 14; *GI*, March 2008, p. 42; *Edge*, Christmas 2007, May 2008).

In contrast to this, "gamers" are described as "young, white, and male," "the high school and college age crowd who will buy violent games like *Gears of War* by the millions," and "the young man who is 18 to 34" (*GDM*, February 2005, p. 18; *GI*, July 2006, p. 17; *GDM*, March 2007, p. 16). Furthermore, magazine discourses argued that casual gamers need easier games than hardcore gamers do, including statements like "Games for 'gamers' can be too difficult for casual players, but games targeted towards the mass-market are often viewed by the hardcore bunch as being too dumbed-down and not worth playing" (*GDM*, April 2006, p. 30).

This deep divide between the way traditional "gamers" and new gamers are described sets them up as completely disparate groups. One is old, female, and uncompetitive, looking for something to just pass the time, while the other is competitive, tech savvy, young, and male. This dismisses the possibility of any common ground between the two groups, even though casual players might play extensively or hardcore players might occasionally prefer a less challenging game. It also, despite the moments when female gamers or older gamers were recognized in the magazines, largely minimizes their presence in gaming, leaving them out of mainstream discourses about who is or can be a gamer.

With this strong separation as a foundation, it is easy to see why other aspects of casual games, such as their growing attractiveness to developers, might seem threatening. Because casual games are positioned as so popular, core gamers could see many of the industry's resources moving towards this area and away from core games. Because new games are also positioned as unappealing to core gamers, this perspective comes with a real sense of loss.

Developer Flight

The magazines of the casualized era are rife with press releases from big companies and interviews with developers that indicate a desire to reach a broader market. Nintendo led this charge with the DS, the Wii, and its deliberate targeting of nontraditional gamers, but other companies quickly got on board. Between 2005 and 2008, big publishers like Electronic Arts (EA) and Ubisoft opened branches specifically focused on the casual market, with EA forming a mobile games branch and Ubisoft announcing a series of educational games for the Wii. Although both are traditionally core companies, creating some of the industry's most well-known console franchises, they saw the potential of casual to bring in fresh players and revenues. They were not alone in this. Id Software, the company that created *Doom*, started a mobile branch in 2008, while well-known developers like Yuji Naka, the creator of *Sonic the Hedgehog*, also moved towards casual, creating "simple, easy-to-play games for the Wii" (*GDM*, December 2008, p. 1).

Many developers framed this decision as one made for the good of gaming audiences overall. Shigeru Miyamoto, the legendary Nintendo game designer responsible for the *Super Mario*, *Legend of Zelda*, and *Donkey Kong* franchises, among others, explained, "We're going to continue to create new and unique experiences for people that are currently playing games and hardcore gamers. But, at the same time, we need to continue to invite new people into gaming, because those are the people who are going to become the next generation of hardcore gamers" (*GI*, December 2005, p. 48). He argued that modern games and controllers had become too complicated for most people to pick them up and play easily, and this excluded many potential gamers. To prevent losing these people entirely, and to help them start building facility with and interest in games, the Wii revolved around easy-to-use, motion-based controls and simple, fun games. This, Miyamoto felt, was essential to the future of gaming.

Other developers, such as *Doom* creator John Carmack, explained their company's entry into mobile or casual games as a way to be more innovative and test new gameplay ideas that would excite gamers. Carmack stated, "The short cycle time [of mobile] allows us to try out more experimental ideas and actually evolve the gameplay concepts a whole lot faster" (*GI*, October 2005, p. 34). He felt designers could use less expensive, more casual outlets to develop material that would then be used in more traditional formats, without risking failure on a big-budget project. In this way, mobile and casual would be contributors to core rather than detractors.

However, these positive narratives were not the only explanations for developers' interest in casual markets; some were more mercenary, explaining how broader markets made financial sense. While Miyamoto described how the DS and Wii would benefit core gamers, Nintendo's senior vice president of marketing, George Harrison, positioned the Wii as a move away from core gamers, asserting, "Men under 25, that segment has been declining, the general population is going to start to decline. So, we realized that they had to attract some people who maybe hadn't played games before or hadn't played games recently" (*GI*, April 2006, p. 55). This statement located core gamers as part of the desired game market, and a small part at that, rather than prioritizing them as the heart of the industry.

Nolan Bushnell, the founder of Atari, similarly focused on getting large audience numbers rather than just core gamers. Following his departure from Atari, Bushnell was involved in several other entertainment ventures, including founding Chuck E. Cheese. In the mid-2000s, he was working on bringing digital entertainment into adult restaurants with uWink, a company focused on casual party play. Bushnell said, "When people talk about the size of the video game market, they're talking really about the habits and the money of 15 million people in the United States. [. . .] I'm trying to get back to the number of game players that existed basically in the '70s. In 1979, 40 percent of the population—250 million—self-identified as a game player, meaning that they'd played a video game within the last week. When you look at that, you say what happened?" (*GDM*, June–July 2008, p. 4). Bushnell specifically blames the masculinization of games, their overt violence, and their growing complexity for narrowing potential markets significantly. Because of this, he, like Miyamoto, sees casual gaming as the way forward. However, he speaks of this simply in terms of the market and sales, rather than positioning casual games as a path towards becoming core.

With these discourses in mind, readers are likely to have one of two reactions. The first type of explanation for developers' moves in the casual arena could help ameliorate gamers' fears that core would lose out, helping them see casual games as useful and necessary. However, this second, market-focused approach could have the opposite effect. Being told that one's market segment is "declining" could provoke anxiety that this segment will no longer be important to developers or publishers at all. Furthermore, Bushnell's explicit statements about violence and a lack of female players as a problem could lead gamers who like violent games, or who are not female, to fear that developers will stop making the types of games they enjoy. The likelihood of this happening is exacerbated by the many discourses that position casual and core as fundamentally different. Rather than seeing casual games as a separate section of the industry with different audiences and interests, discourses around broadening the market may make it appear that core developers are selling out to the bigger casual audience.

Core Costs and Casual Alternatives

The rising cost of core games, and casual games' lower development budgets and high potential for growth, also contributed to gaming's shifting hegemony and related anxieties. The video game consoles released at the start of the casualized era were, apart from the Wii, extremely technically advanced. This meant that development costs increased exponentially for core games, and the pages of game magazines were rife with concerned journalists and developers attempting to predict how this would affect games.

In 2007, *Edge* listed the cost of developing console games at, on average, $10–15 million (*Edge*, Christmas 2007), while others cited even higher numbers. These budgets, *Game Developer* pointed out, "are huge and scary things" (*GDM*, January 2007, p. 4). *Game Informer* simply stated, "The video game industry is getting more complicated and more expensive. This is no surprise to anyone, but the magnitude of the challenge is stunning" (March 2006, p. 42). For core console producers, most journalists agreed, the rising cost of game development changed the conditions for production. Specifically, they argued that it decreased the possibility for innovation, new intellectual properties, and risk taking.

In order to get the funds needed for a multi-million-dollar project, developers generally must contract with, or be owned by, a larger publishing company like Nintendo, EA, or Ubisoft. However, these companies expect a significant return on their investment. Companies like EA and Ubisoft anticipate yearly earnings in the billions, meaning they need to release either thousands of games that net $1 million in profit or fifty to sixty multi-million-dollar games (*EGM*, August 2008, pp. 14–15). Traditionally, they opt for the second choice, increasing the need for each individual game to succeed. *EGM* continues, "With so much money invested in so few games, publishers are much more wary of failure and this greatly contributes to the industry's current bout of sequelitis" (August 2008, p. 15). Investing in proven series can make game production less risky. However, it also prevents innovation and the rise of new intellectual property. And for developers, continually working on the same projects as part of a large team can be exhausting.

Independent game production, in smaller, employee-owned companies, did not necessarily offer a full escape either, as many also faced ballooning budgets. In 2005, for instance, competitors in the Independent Games Festival had average game budgets around fifty thousand dollars, with some as high as $1.3 million (*Edge*, May 2005, p. 59). A couple of years later, when Robert Walsh, the CEO of independent development studio Krome, was asked if indies could survive in the modern era, he responded, "In a time of skyrocketing budgets, huge development teams, and the ever-increasing technical requirements of next-gen platforms, it's a legitimate question. More challenges than ever are facing developers, and some studios will find them insurmountable. But there are also more avenues available for developers to find a way to succeed" (*GI*, January 2007, p. 48).[9]

For some developers, casual was this way to succeed. Although indie games that strove for core characteristics like cutting-edge graphics were likely to face ballooning budgets, those that did not aim for technological superiority could produce at a more reasonable cost. *Game Developer*, for instance, argued that Nintendo's push towards casual games, and the lower technical specs of the Wii compared to the PS3 and 360, meant that they were opting "to target those developers that cannot afford the huge budget leap that many report will be required for Xbox 360 and PS3 development" (June–July 2005, p. 4). Downloadable games, through services like Steam or the Xbox Live Arcade, also provided developers with opportunities, without demanding intense graphics or high-cost effects. Developers could then price games more reasonably, sell fewer units, and still make a profit (*GDM*, March 2007).

Others leaned towards the promise of mobile games, arguing that they offered "what many complain is missing from the mainstream— cheap games, passionate startups, and in the best cases, back-to-basics gameplay" (*Edge*, June 2006, p. 13). Mobile game budgets at this time averaged three hundred thousand to five hundred thousand dollars (*GDM*, September 2005), which, although high, was nowhere near the millions needed for core development. Furthermore, much smaller teams could produce these games. As *Game Developer* pointed out, "The average development cycle for a console title is about 24 months, and developers work on a team of 30 to 40 members or more. [. . .] But in the same two-year period, a mobile developer might work on a closely-knit team of only three or four people, have ownership of a broader skill set, and fully complete four or five projects" (December 2006, p. 34). Mobile gaming was largely still in its infancy in the mid-2000s, and modern mobile powerhouses like the iPhone had not even been announced.[10] However, it was clear to some developers that mobile had a quality future, particularly in contrast to the expense involved in core console development.

A decade later, we know that core gaming has not gone away, and consoles remain a significant part of the gaming industry. At the time, however, their fate was uncertain, especially as counterhegemonic forces like mobile and casual games were a relatively new phenomenon. These challenged "how we define 'player,' 'gamer,' and even 'game'" (*GDM*, February 2006, p. 2). "Gamers" who were used to being the industry's sole concern saw their own importance threatened as developers targeted other markets, ones they felt they had little in common with. Because of this, many core gamers and producers experienced real, deeply felt anxiety about what their role in gaming would be.

Fear and Loathing in Core Gaming

These anxieties played out across the pages of mid-2000s gaming magazines with regular frequency. For instance, a 2008 *Game Developer* editorial on "The Hardcore Niche" asked,

> Will it be possible to make a game like ASSASSIN'S CREED or BIO-SHOCK in 2015? It's already becoming difficult to justify large budgets for single-player experiences, and it stands to reason that it will get more difficult as time goes on. What does that mean for developers of these games? What happens to the concept of a game auteur? [. . .] Certainly there will always be the hardcore players that will want that deeper experience. There's no doubt about that. But the question is—in an industry where we're getting our asses kicked financially by web developers, of all people—who will pay us to make it? (*GDM*, June–July 2008, p. 2)

In this piece, editor Brandon Sheffield pointed out that if "blockbuster" titles were ones with the highest sales, core games no longer counted; rather, blockbuster titles were casual games like *Club Penguin*, an online hang-out for children. He predicted that this trend would lead gaming money to flow from core into casual, turning core into a niche market. In *Edge*, a letter from a reader expressed a similar sentiment, asking, "Are we, the gamers of old, going to feel out of place in this new world?" (*Edge*, March 2007, p. 126). *Game Informer*'s editor reminisced about the video game crash of 1983 and recommended to readers, "Find games you like and play them. Because if you don't, you could wake up one day like I did and find them gone. It's not cool. Trust me on this one" (*GI*, February 2006, p. 10). He put the burden of responsibility on core gamers to keep their favorite genres and formats alive by investing in them and proving that their audience was still significant. Other articles simply expressed concern that developers would focus too intensely on casual markets, to the detriment of hardcore gamers.

Not all writers or gamers took this doom-and-gloom approach, with many arguing that "gaming isn't an either/or hobby, and one type of game doesn't need to replace the other. Just like movies, you can enjoy the big-budget releases right alongside the smaller, independent titles" (GI, July 2008, p. 12). Others lauded new types of games for their innovation and welcomed new types of players, assuming their hobby could only benefit from further attention and sales. The reason I have focused more intensely on the negative rather than the positive is simply that this anxiety about shifting game culture and priorities, even if it only affected a small number of gamers, matters as one of the root causes behind the intense sexism and other discriminatory trends modern gaming has faced. These discourses present casual as something that will detrimentally affect core. In so doing, they contribute to the crisis of authority and core gamers' felt need to protect "their" space from incursion. And this felt need remains significant as, although core has not gone away, counterhegemonic forces have continued to strengthen over the past decade.

Continued Challenges of the Casualized Era

In addition to the rise of casual, social, and mobile games described in the introduction, the casualized industry has undergone several other changes, such as stagnating console technology and rising mobile technology, and the growth of new distribution and funding mechanisms. These developments have shaken core ideas about who makes games, what "good" games are, and what the gaming audience looks like, allowing for potential diversification and demonstrating clearly how core is a constructed rather than a natural concept. Rather than being permanent, core can change and is even in the process of doing so now.

Changing Technologies

Although video games can be produced for many platforms, the gaming industry's focus has long been console games, and its revenue has generally come from this sector as well. Only recently have other market segments, like mobile and casual PC games, become competitive with console games in terms of profits (Rayna and Striukova, 2014). Consoles and personal computers are also the platforms primarily used for core games like first-person shooters, helping to centralize these systems further. In the casualized era, however, consoles have in many ways lost their privileged position, facing challenges from both lower-end and higher-end technology. *TechCrunch* reporter Natasha Lomas (2014) illustrates this through the following quotation from an anonymous veteran game designer: "The PS4/XB1 is the first generation to have technology that is worse than what is already out there. [. . .] This means whilst the casuals are moving to mobile/web, the high-end enthusiasts are moving to PC where games are better looking. The traditional consoles are caught in a pincer movement."

Although their convenience, smaller size, and technological competitiveness with arcade games allowed home consoles to win the market in the first place, other technologies are rapidly catching up. Mobile gaming, for instance, has made enormous strides in the casualized era due to the spread of smartphones and game distribution channels like the Apple App Store, as well as their continuous improvements (Hachman, 2013). While mobile games cannot offer the graphical quality of console games, their high level of innovation and easy access make them appealing to many players, especially as they demand less investment than more time-intensive and expensive core games.

Personal computers (PCs) also offer a new threat to the living-room console. PCs have long competed with consoles for players' time, especially as the two share many games and genres, but top-of-the-line gaming PCs have generally been far more expensive than consoles, often costing thousands of dollars. Now, however, PCs are not only competitive in terms of graphics quality, genre offerings, and more, but they have become much less expensive. In 2013, *PCMag* branch *ExtremeTech* ran a test to see if it could build a gaming computer competitive with the PlayStation 4 in performance and price. The magazine staff concluded that it was possible, building a computer with comparable technical specifications to a PS4 for barely over four hundred dollars (Anthony, 2013). They did not include the cost of a gaming keyboard or mouse, but this shows that PCs now have price points similar to those of consoles. Thus, although PCs still face piracy concerns, the availability of low-cost

technology may make them more attractive than consoles. This is especially true as companies developing games for game consoles need access to their development kits, while PCs are programmed consistently
and freely.

New Means of Funding and Distribution

As technological changes have potentially undermined the hegemonic
role of consoles, new means of distribution and funding have changed
the stakes for game development costs and pricing, again forcing a
reconsideration of traditional industry structures.

One major change has been the growing role of digital downloads
as a means for distributing games. Although mobile game technology
existed on PDAs and Blackberries as early as the late 1990s, these brands
were marketed primarily towards business purposes. The launch of the
Apple App Store in 2008 changed these expectations, indicating that the
iPhone was an entertainment tool for anyone rather than just working
professionals. The App Store made low-cost casual games widely available as part of this marketing push. When consumers responded enthusiastically, Apple's competitors moved to emulate their success, and
other phone providers rebranded and sought out gaming markets. This
created an entire sphere of gaming that occurred solely through digital
distribution.

Digital distribution has also made major inroads into both PC gaming and console gaming, which were traditionally dominated by physical
game copies. Steam, the largest market for traditional PC downloads,
has been open since 2003, but its addition of a Macintosh platform in
2010 greatly increased its reach and capacity. In the same year, Wolfire
Games introduced the first Humble Bundle. Humble Bundles are small,
privately curated collections of digital content such as video games that
players can purchase for highly discounted rates. Buyers choose what
they want to pay for the bundle, with extra content offered to those who
pay above the average contribution or above a certain cut-off point.
These mechanisms and others like them have offered smaller developers new opportunities to get their games to an interested market, often
at lower cost to themselves.

This opened the potential for studios to take new risks and innovate in their game designs (Spock, 2012). As game designer Chris Swain explains, "Digital distribution cuts out a tremendous pressure: games purchased from a retailer retain only 17% of the price for the publisher, along with the complete lack of profit from used game resale. Digital distribution [. . .] would retain 85% of the retail price, along with removing limits of selling the long tail back-catalogue of previously published titles that a brick-and-mortar store cannot stock" (Lipkin, 2013, p. 12). Game producers save heavily on this distribution method, cutting out the high overhead of CD printing and physical game distribution. Furthermore, they never risk overproducing or underproducing their games; no retailer ends up with empty shelves or unpurchased copies. They also benefit from the lack of a used game market, in that they do not lose customers who share game copies with friends.

The same is true in a console setting. Microsoft introduced the first major network, Xbox Live, on the original Xbox in 2002, then continued this service onto the Xbox 360 and the Xbox One. In order to compete, Sony and Nintendo introduced the PlayStation Network and Nintendo's Virtual Console in 2006. All allowed players to explore new games, download material, and update their physical game copies via the Internet. While big-budget games are often still distributed via CD, console networks allowed new types of games—specifically low-cost games by independent producers—to reach gamers who might not have considered them previously, due to a preference for living-room gaming over other methods.

Funding methods have also changed in this time period, furthering new game forms and a focus on new audiences. "Perhaps the most promising form of opposition is the rise in popularity of crowdsourced funding platforms, such as Kickstarter and Indiegogo. Rather than forcing developers to develop projects on the side or push unfinished goods to market and finish them over time, platforms like Kickstarter enable money to come in up front—a luxury previously reserved for large established developers and those under patronage of major publishers" (Lipkin, 2013, p. 20). Crowdfunding allows new ideas to have a chance to reach the market; rather than having to pass proposals through potentially risk-averse large developers, who also want to avoid competition with their own titles, crowdfunded games need only appeal to potential players.

Furthermore, crowdfunding helps designers interact more closely with their potential markets, to see who supports their project and to market even as they are producing the game itself. This allows for better tailoring of the game to the intended consumer, as well as the potential to change who expected markets are. While core games still tend to focus on the young, white, male market, crowdfunded games can, and often do, move beyond this stereotype. Not all games succeed via crowdfunding options, and those that do may receive disappointing reviews if they veer too far from the proposed design (Hiscott, 2014). They can also struggle with the sheer number of competitors who seek funding via the same sources, splitting the potential investments a single market is likely to make. However, crowdfunding still offers a new approach to game development that reduces the personal investment needed upfront, allows for greater innovation, and provides a means of reaching the gaming market without needing traditionally established publishers.

Rising Competition and Changing Assumptions

These changes in technology and distribution and funding are providing new opportunities for smaller developers and innovative teams who want to reach new audiences. And many of the new games they produce are successful. Independent game *Journey* provides a prime example; it was produced by a team of fourteen people and went on to win the Game of the Year award at the Game Developers Conference in 2012. It was also nominated for a Best Soundtrack Grammy, the first in video game history (Statt, 2013).

This success is breaking down the expectations of core games' historical focus on straight, white, male audiences and genres like first-person shooters by showing that other people play, and that other types of games matter. *Journey* was incredibly successful without following traditional industry expectations for the production and distribution process or for audience targeting. The game, in which players control a robed figure on a quest to reach a distant mountain, has little in common with core games of the past and decidedly did not target a stereotypical straight, white, male audience. In fact, the developers deliberately stepped away from the trappings of boy culture, such as when they re-moved their characters' arms to avoid players even thinking about "pick-ing up some kind of weapon and hitting something" (Smith, 2012).

Journey is not alone in changing how developers and audiences ap-proach games and players. As *The Last of Us* director Neil Druckmann points out, indie games focus on nontraditional audiences far more than core games do, something that he sees as a benefit (Sinclair, 2013). "He specifically called out *Gone Home* and *Papers, Please* as two games with impressive narrative components, saying he was 'blown away' by the kind of stories they told, and the mechanics used to tell them" (Sinclair, 2013). *Gone Home* is an interactive story game in which the playable character returns home from a year-long trip to find her house empty and her fam-ily gone. As she investigates the house, she finds objects and clues that reveal her sister's relationship with a girl from school, exploring deep questions about relationships, family, sexuality, and coming out. *Papers, Please* puts the player in the role of an immigration officer who needs to evaluate applications for entry into their fictional country, trying to screen out terrorists while allowing legitimate applicants through. These games deliberately told new stories, exploring the experiences of immi-grants and gay women. In doing so, they targeted new audiences, extend-ing past "gamers." As video game magazine *Polygon* wrote, "Games allow us to walk a mile in the shoes of another, and thanks to indie games, those shoes no longer belong solely to white beefy men."[11]

The same is true of mobile or social games, such as *Farmville, Angry Birds*, or *Candy Crush Saga*. Taking advantage of the many platforms players can access and the low-cost nature of digital distribution, these games have reached audiences in the hundreds of millions and brought in billions in sales (Anderson, 2012; Shanley, 2013; Dredge, 2015). They cut down on overhead and can be downloaded and played for free, with optional purchases to speed up slow processes, to help beat difficult lev-els, or to get extra experience or items. But most importantly, they de-liberately aim for the widest possible audiences. Their success through this approach necessarily changes the conditions for game production and subverts the idea that "gamers" are the only people who play video games.

New types of games are also challenging traditional expectations about what "good" games look like. For example, the popular indie game

Fez uses blocky, 2D graphics as a key gameplay component. In *Fez*, "You play as Gomez, a 2D creature living in what he believes is a 2D world. Until a strange and powerful artifact reveals to him the existence of a mysterious third dimension!" (*Fez*, 2012). Although the game graphics are 2D, the player can rotate the environment to view 3D space from different sides, using this ability to help the character navigate through and solve puzzles. *Fez* received several awards, such as the Grand Prize at the 2012 Independent Games Festival and the Game of the Year award from *Eurogamer* (Independent Games Festival, 2012; Bramwell, 2012). Games like *Fez* necessarily force a redefinition of gaming's core values, due to their critical and popular success despite their lack of high-caliber graphics or masculine themes.

Industrial changes have undermined the expectation that gaming only exists to target a core audience and that the best games come out of core studios. Many developers and players see this as positive, both for players who are now discovering the fun of gaming and for developers who have new markets to tap. Furthermore, there is little reason to believe that game companies will return to their prior practices; such industrial and technological changes are a natural part of any media industry. Television, for instance, is currently experiencing its own changes due to digital distribution, with streaming services like Netflix, Hulu, and Amazon becoming content producers to rival traditional broadcast and cable channels. In fact, video games' historical insularity is unusual, as every media industry from radio to books to film has previously recognized the benefits of extensive markets. One would expect that producers would be interested in gaining as many potential consumers as possible, which of course includes more than young men.

What is most interesting about these changes in terms of video games and gender is not the fact that they are happening, but rather the types of discourses about gaming's future that they have provoked. As Aphra Kerr points out in *Global Gaming*, her excellent overview of the modern video game industry, console games, PC games, mobile games, and social games can best be thought of as different segments of the video game industry. Each possesses its own funding and distribution methods, and its own desired audiences and content patterns. In short, these different sections may overlap, but they often focus on unique audiences and consumers (Kerr, 2017). Within discourses about gaming, however, they are generally conflated into an overall gaming industry. This is not inherently a problematic way to discuss games. However, it appears to have increased concerns about the future of core, positing gaming as a zero-sum industry in which success in one area necessarily means the decline of another.

Conclusions

Although it may seem obvious to conclude this section by stating that changes in the video gaming industry have resulted in a medium in flux, such a realization is a necessary foundation for the rest of this project. As game studies scholar Adrienne Shaw (2010) reminds us, the masculinized nature of gaming culture often goes unquestioned. Other than small, relatively unsuccessful attempts like the girls' games movement of the 1990s, little has been done in the past to change or undermine the idea that gaming is a hobby for boys and men, not for women and girls. The rise of counterhegemonic forces in the casualized era, however, has provided a foundation upon which a real attempt to undermine games' masculinized history can take place, a basis from which core can be questioned and redefined.

At the same time, this does not happen without resistance, and the rise of alternatives to core has seen many challenges. Although new games are critical hits and economically successful, players and critics often treat them as less serious, less significant, and less important than older styles of games. For example, although *Gone Home* is one of the games Druckmann specifically praised for its inventive storyline, and although it won game site Polygon's 2013 Game of the Year award (Grant, 2014), critics, particularly core gamers, often claim that it does not actually qualify as a game (Kohler, 2013; Gaynor, 2014; Sheffield, 2014). Many are quite negative about *Gone Home* because of this, arguing that it is overrated, too expensive, or simply distracting players, developers, and journalists from "real" games. Even when players speak positively about their experience playing *Gone Home*, insisting that it is not a game is an attempt to maintain gaming's status quo, as a medium for a specific audience and specific games, in the face of industrial changes that broaden or redefine that core. It is an attempt to maintain exclusivity and to continue to define gaming boundaries in the way they have always already been defined. And although it is a more positive way of defining boundaries than the sexism and misogyny "gamers" also employ, it is still a mechanism for maintaining gendered hierarchies.

More interestingly, players seem to deploy the "not a game" argument selectively; for example, although popular sandbox game *Minecraft*, like *Gone Home*, does not necessarily have a way for the player to fail, or combat or puzzles for a player to face, its gameness is rarely or never questioned the way *Gone Home*'s has been. This could simply be the case because *Minecraft* does offer options for elements like combat if players seek them out, but evidence suggests that the negative reaction to *Gone Home* (and *Journey*, *Flower*, *Her Story*, or other recent offerings that face the not-a-game argument) is at least partially due to its focus on new audiences and storylines (Gray, 2015). In the face of changing industry standards, some players, especially players who are part of gaming's longstanding straight, white, male audience, are deploying ideas of quality and what constitutes a game as a way to valorize games that target them, and that have always targeted them, as more important than newer offerings.

This is probably further connected to the discourses that frame the gaming industry as zero-sum, in which casual games' normalization of gaming (Juul, 2010) and the ensuing increase in non-"gamer" players become a potential threat to the kinds of games core players enjoy or prefer. That is, industrial changes and the broadening of gaming audiences have motivated a Gramscian crisis of authority, where previously hegemonic male gamers fear losing their privileged position in this space. As a protective measure, they are deploying many forces to maintain core as exclusive and exclusionary in terms of both content and broader culture. Defining the quality of games in specific ways is one attempt at this. The rise of greater misogyny in gaming is probably another, especially as participants for this study, particularly those with long histories as gamers, argue that gaming's blatant sexism is a relatively new development.

Because of this, the interventions female gamers make into gaming's gender exclusivity potentially matter now more than ever, while the future of gaming power is being decided. A crisis of authority has two outcomes—the exertion of enough force for the subjected class to resume its position of powerlessness or the success of the counterhegemony. As the editor of *Game Informer* wrote regarding the Wii in 2005, when it was still codenamed "Revolution," "Like any revolution, it can either upend society as we know it, or be squashed under the power of the ruling class" (*GI*, May 2006, p. 10). The rest of this book, therefore, analyzes how women who play games encounter the boundaries of core—forces that work to uphold gaming's existing masculinized nature—as well as how their entry into gaming as skilled, experienced players subverts those same boundaries. Understanding *how* and *when* essentializing forces are deployed, undermined, or changed in gaming offers a means for analyzing relations of power and understanding masculinized or exclusionary spaces in greater detail.

2

Tits, Tokenism, and Trash-Talk

Overt Sexism in Game Culture

Although the gaming industry has started to diversify its target audience, as recounted in chapter 1, this effort has not yet fully redefined expectations about who games and how. Interviewees for this book related significant forces that still work to bar them from gaming. Specifically, they encountered both overtly sexist problems, such as character representations and harassment, and subtler, inferentially sexist forces, like being treated with surprise by others while they are gaming. Each of these serves as a barrier between women and gaming's core, in that they mark female gamers as "other."

Now, given that games researchers have looked extensively into the history of sexism in gaming and have explored many factors that are off-putting to female-identified players,[1] it is possible to ask, Why return to tread this old ground? I would respond with three points. First, although we have recognized many sexist elements of gaming in the past, the fact that games are diversifying and game audiences are changing necessitates a return to these earlier topics. As Mia Consalvo and Jason Begy (2015) point out, the contexts in which play occurs deeply matter. In their study of *Faunasphere*, a short-lived casual MMO, they found significant differences in how players interpreted and played the game when it was in beta, when it opened to a broader public, when it was integrated with Facebook, and when it was announced that it would be closing down. The contexts of the casualized era are very different from those of prior eras in game history. Therefore, it is likely that player experiences are similarly changed.

Second, some past research has tended to essentialize female gamers and present their preferences unilaterally. Although this is understandable, given that much of this work has been activist in intent, deliberately working to draw more women and girls into gaming by focusing on what *most* might want or prefer, it is important to recognize the fractures and divides between members of ostensibly the same group as we move into a more nuanced era of gaming. This is significant as female gamers vary in how they see their gaming, with some viewing it specifically through an activist lens while others heavily buy into identity positions or beliefs that have exclusionary roots. They also differ in what they find off-putting and the extent to which it affects them; sexist forces that drive some women out of gaming entirely are easily laughed off by others. Understanding their different perspectives can provide insight into how hegemony is challenged or changed.

Finally, it is true that we have long recognized many elements of sexism in gaming; however, a number of these persist. Therefore, although I might be repeating previous findings here, they *bear repeating*, as only continued attention to inequality and calls for change can actually result in change. With this in mind, the next two chapters work to understand what factors in gaming provoke the most struggle for female-identified players, and why. They do this not to replace the excellent existent research on games and gender but to build on it by prioritizing the diverse experiences of women who play core games and updating their concerns for the casualized era.

Overt and Inferential Sexism in Gaming

During our interviews, female gamers mentioned numerous challenges they encounter while playing games. In the past, researchers have often divided these according to the traditional media studies lines of text/content, audience, and industry. While this was originally my intention, it did not resonate with the experiences of the gamers I spoke with. To them, these areas were inextricably linked. For example, if they were concerned about the hypersexualization of female characters in games, they first worried about how this was off-putting to women who would seek other content. But they also feared that hypersexualization would affect their interactions with male players, who would be more likely to objectify or harass female players if the texts they were consuming continually indicated that women were there for their pleasure. And they were frustrated with the fact that rampant hypersexualization revealed deeply seated industry practices that prioritize male players over female. This one area of concern spread across text, audience, and industry.

Rather than dividing by production, content, and reception, therefore, I draw on Stuart Hall's (1995) concepts of overt and inferential racism to categorize exclusionary forces in gaming according to their overt or inferential sexism. I apply Hall's framework to sexism not to argue that racism and sexism are the same, as they each have very different backgrounds, impacts, and modes of enactment, but because the concepts of overt and inferential are deeply reflective of my participants' experiences. They also serve an activist purpose; much past work on games has focused heavily on the obvious forms of sexism that pervade gaming, but less has been done on inferential issues, which my participants found to be as off-putting as, or at times even worse than, overt ones.

In discussing race and media, Hall divided racism into two categories. Overt racism occurs when the racist nature of a policy, argument, or narrative is clearly evident. Inferential racism, on the other hand, takes place when the racist nature of a policy, argument, or narrative functions due to unquestioned, naturalized assumptions that have a racist basis. Although both forms of racism are potentially damaging to cultural relations between groups, Hall and others have argued that inferential racism can be a more insidious problem, because it "is the kind of racism that doesn't explicitly declare itself as such, yet still forwards damaging racial stereotypes—stereotypes that are made all the more damaging by the casualness with which they are forwarded, and by the speaker's unquestioned assumption that their statements couldn't possibly be racist because they are, at least according to the speaker, *true*" (Phillips, 2015, p. 95). Inferential racism can be so ingrained and subtle that it can even be employed in antiracist contexts; popular culture scholar John Fiske (1996) points out that the use of the term "minority," a generally politically correct way to describe nonwhite ethnic groups in the United States, carries connotations "of being a minor, not yet fully adult, and thus one who can properly be spoken for and looked after by members of the majority" (p. 37). This framing minimizes minority groups in inferential ways. Both overt and implicit forms of discrimination matter for the maintenance of inequality.

Similarly, the cultural environment of video gaming is rife with obviously sexist themes, such as the lack of female characters, the hypersexualization of the female characters that do exist, and the direct harassment of female players in gaming's social spaces. But gaming also contains many inferentially sexist elements that female gamers describe as equally frustrating. In these cases, they face content themes, audience members, or industry trends that are not meant to be negative or sexist. However, these elements rest in deeply naturalized assumptions that "gamers" are and should be men.

Collectively, overt sexism and inferential sexism reaffirm the masculinized core of gaming, requiring female players to assume multiple and contradictory subject positions in order to navigate these spaces. Female gamers deeply identify as just that: gamers, or individuals who are invested in playing and enjoying video games and who have extensive knowledge about these texts. In this way, they embody many existing characteristics of core. However, their self-identification as gamers runs contrary to the overall cultural definition of "gamer," which means that they find their ability to take on this identity complicated. As described in the introduction, the process of building and communicating who we are—which we call identification—is at least partially influenced by forces outside of ourselves, including how we see our desired identities represented in media and culture. As "gamer" often means "male," identifying as female at times precludes identifying as a gamer, and vice versa. Women work to combine these identities, but they face extensive struggles in trying to do so.

Because gaming's overtly sexist forces have received extensive coverage in the past, it makes sense to start by updating these topics, detailing why they remain of concern to female gamers. The remainder of this chapter will therefore address the overtly sexist elements of gaming culture that interviewees marked as problematic. It will also analyze how and why these elements affect gaming's power structures more broadly. Following this, chapter 3 will explore the inferentially sexist aspects of gaming culture that made it difficult for participants to conceive of themselves as a core part of the gaming community, as well as how the subtle nature of these factors makes them potentially more damaging to gender relations.

Game Tokens: Missing or Underdeveloped
Women in Games

When researchers have studied games in the past, especially when they have been working to get more girls and women to play games, one of the biggest areas they have focused on is character representation. Various content analyses have found that video games systematically underrepresent women, particularly as primary characters. For instance, media researchers Berrin Beasley and Tracy Standley (2002) had players complete the first twenty minutes of a random selection of PlayStation and Nintendo 64 games, the most popular systems at the time, then coded the material for character gender and appearance. They found that 71.5 percent of characters were male. Later studies looked at a wide variety of game texts and paratexts, including advertisements, reviews, magazines, and video game packaging, and affirmed these results (Behm-Morawitz, 2017; Burgess, Stermer, and Burgess, 2007; Dill and Thill, 2007; Downs and Smith, 2010; Ivory, 2006; Jansz and Martis, 2007; Miller and Summers, 2007; Scharrer, 2004; Waddell et al., 2014). Each tallied how frequently women appeared in these materials in comparison to men and found the gender ratio to be between 60 percent and 86 percent male. It is, of course, important to note that these studies were conducted on traditionally core games; similar studies of casual games (Wohn, 2011) have found that they overrepresent women in comparison to real-life population statistics.

As my participants played many core games and often saw themselves as core gamers, many noted that games offer few female characters, especially as playable options. As interviewee Emily said, "I definitely have noticed that a lot of times I'm forced to be a boy in a game. And then it's ok, but there's definitely not as much of a feeling like this is a real story action-adventure about me." Female players find that games, even ones that seem gender equitable on the surface, often presume a male subject and interpellate the player as if they identify as male.[2] The *Assassin's Creed* series, for example, was popular with participants, but its main installments have only recently started to include female protagonists.[3]

To complicate matters further, even when women were included in games, they were often not well developed. Rather, participants saw them as afterthoughts—"token" characters that designers would include to try to draw in a small female audience without having to try too hard. "Token" characters were flat, lacking personality, backstory, or character development. As Helix argued, "I think the industry is starting to realize they need to cater more to female players but are currently stuck at 'If we stick a girl in it, it's good!' Hopefully things will continue to get better. (I'd like to commend a few games, like *Dungeons of Dredmor* and *Portal*, for being a little ahead of the curve there.)" Because of this, participants frequently preferred a game that completely lacked female characters to one in which they were included just for the sake of having a female character.

Players do not need characters to be like them in order to identify with them. As games scholar Adrienne Shaw (2014b) found, "Interviewees did not always see identification [with game characters] as an important goal. In part, not needing to identify with characters occurred because individuals fulfilled different needs through their media use" (p. 87), such as relaxation or competition. Shaw also found that characters were often too shallow or underdeveloped for participants to identify with, that players liked to use characters to try out different ways of acting or being, and that game context mattered deeply to how players looked at game characters, among other things. She then used this finding to argue that developers should diversify representations in games specifically because they do not matter to participants as much as previously thought; because of this, more diverse representations can improve cultural perspectives on differing groups and identities without ruining the game experience.

My participants, however, felt the lack of female characters did matter, because it indicated that they were not a significant market for developers, especially core ones. Like Shaw's participants, my interviewees' desire to identify with or as a game character was not fixed, but rather contextual and fluid. They would often happily sacrifice gender identification for other forms of identification (e.g., personality or backstory) or for other enjoyable aspects of games, such as when the rich storyline and environments of *Assassin's Creed II* made up for playing as a womanizing young Italian man. Being offered primarily or only male characters, however, made them feel as if they were afterthoughts to core game creators, who had not bothered to represent women in meaningful ways.

Interviewees were also concerned about the messages both male and female players would take from core games as, when female characters were included, they were often highly constrained, overly sexualized, and tangential to the game. As Helix stated, female characters were "a vast indistinguishable pile of boobs and ribbon," built to unrealistic proportions, hypersexualized, and overly girly. To participants, these trends were not necessarily exclusionary, as they obviously chose to play games anyway, but they were frustrating, often affecting players' choice of games and their enjoyment of them.

Existing content analyses show that core games predominantly represent women as oversexualized, dressed in clothing inappropriate for the storyline, and with unrealistic body shapes. In Beasley and Standley's study, "The majority of female characters [were] dressed in such a way as to bring attention to their bodies, particularly their breasts" (2002, p. 289). Again, later research mirrored these results across various texts and paratexts. Studies analyzing total game content, introductory videos to games, magazine articles, and online reviews all found that women were less commonly shown but still more likely to be sexualized than their male counterparts (Beasley and Standley, 2002; Behm-Morawitz, 2017; Burgess, Stermer, and Burgess, 2007; Dill and Thill, 2007; Downs and Smith, 2010; Ivory, 2006; Jansz and Martis, 2007; Lynch et al., 2016; Miller and Summers, 2007; Scharrer, 2004).[4]

My participants expanded and built on these concerns with specific references to dress, body type, and character role. For example, Angela related an anecdote about playing a female character who, even though she embodied the same role as similar male characters, had a very different appearance. She said, "I remember playing *Persona 3* and getting an awesome armor piece that worked for the female character on my team which, when equipped, basically looked like a bikini. Which was irritating, because it's cool to have that option, but to have the equipment with the better stats pretty much default to bikini is very . . . limiting, I guess." The same armor, when equipped on a male character, was not revealing. Rather, it was a normal suit of armor, covering essential body parts to protect the wearer in battle. Many other participants discussed experiences like this, where the same equipment was portrayed differently on male and female characters despite similar abilities. For instance, Helix referenced how characters in *Diablo III* have an extensive array of clothing and gear, but "all the female wizard gear shows the 'panties' portion and all the demon hunter gear has high heels." Given these clothing options, she preferred to play male characters.

Body type was also a concern, in that most female characters in core games were similarly built. As one interviewee said, female characters were almost always "the big-breasted, scantily-clad, tall, tiny-waisted woman" (Spinach, interview 1). This meant that participants, if they wanted to play as a female character, were required to play as a specific type of character, one with which they often did not identify. Participant Feather expressed this clearly, and with evident frustration, when she said, "I would like it if there were more variation in characters especially for female characters. [. . .] I'm a curvy, sort of short girl, and there are very few video game characters that look like me that aren't hobbits and trolls and squat, gangly things. [. . .] Why can't we have more than the set 5'10", 200 pounds, non-realistic, big-boobed anime girl?" In her opinion, women were limited to playing overly sexualized, model-pretty characters or deliberately ugly characters, with few options in between.

Finally, participants recognized that women's roles in games were often limited, with many being damsels in distress. One of my favorite illustrations for this trend is games' classic damsel in distress, Princess Peach, who has been kidnapped or held prisoner at least fifteen times since she was first introduced as Princess Toadstool in the 1980s (see table 2.1). Other female characters were represented as "hot side objects" (Emily) for male players to admire or sleep with. When Caddie played *Star Wars: Knights of the Old Republic 2* (*KOTOR 2*) as a male character, for instance, she found that "as soon as you meet every single female character, they're throwing themselves at your feet. Which, I suppose I could see why, if you were a male playing that, it would be nice, but as a female playing as a main character, you're just like, 'This is weird. Women would never do this.'" Although she argued that other games allow women to take on empowering roles as the main character, games like *KOTOR 2* objectify them by presenting them as prizes.

TABLE 2.1. Princess Peach's Fate in Primary Mario Bros Games

Game	Release Year	Princess Peach's Fate
1. Super Mario Bros.	1985	Kidnapped
2. Super Mario Bros.: The Lost Levels	1986 (Japan), 1993 (US)	Kidnapped
3. Super Mario Bros. 2	1988	Playable Character
4. Super Mario Bros. 3	1988 (Japan), 1990 (US)	Kidnapped
5. Super Mario Land	1989	Kidnapped
6. Super Mario World	1990	Kidnapped
7. Super Mario Land 2	1992	N/A
8. Super Mario World 2: Yoshi's Island	1995	N/A
9. Super Mario 64	1996	Imprisoned in her own castle
10. Super Mario Sunshine	2002	Kidnapped
11. New Super Mario Bros.	2006	Kidnapped
12. Super Mario Galaxy	2007	Kidnapped
13. New Super Mario Bros (Wii)	2009	Kidnapped
14. Super Mario Galaxy 2	2010	Kidnapped
15. Super Mario 3D Land	2011	Kidnapped
16. New Super Mario Bros. 2	2012	Kidnapped
17. New Super Mario Bros. U	2012	Imprisoned in her own castle
18. Super Mario 3D World	2013	Playable Character
19. Super Mario Maker	2015	N/A
20. Super Mario Run	2016	Playable Character
21. Super Mario Odyssey	2017	Kidnapped

Italicized entries indicate games where Peach was kidnapped or otherwise incapacitated (15 of 21 total games).

In doing so, the game interpellates the player as if they are a heterosexual male. Game designers are assuming first that players identify as male and second that men would appreciate having female characters pay them attention and appear sexually available, drawing on patriarchal masculinity's notions of men as sexually voracious (Lotz, 2014). Ensuing development choices then encourage players to embody a masculine subject position, as game narratives and content make the most sense from this perspective. Although players could avoid this, doing so puts them in conflict with the game they are engaging with.

Feather described a similar situation she encountered when playing *Dynasty Warriors*, a game series in which the player controls different individuals in China's dynastic history and engages in nationalistic wars to advance the goals of the empire. As the series has progressed, each game has added new characters, with the most recent installment, *Dynasty Warriors 9*, featuring ninety separate offerings. Most of these are male, at a ratio of approximately five to one. In addition, Feather argued that the characters' motivations differed systematically by gender. She said, "I hate that there are seven girls to choose from and all of their ending stories involved them being in love with their husbands, because that's what all of them are." While the male characters were leaders who took control of the country at the end of the game, Feather felt that the female characters were relegated to side roles after the fighting was done. They served as support for the male characters rather than taking action on their own. Furthermore, any action they did take seemed to be externally motivated by the male characters around them, rather than intrinsically motivated by their personalities, morals, or beliefs. This frustrated Feather, who wanted her female characters to be as interesting and complex as their male counterparts but found they often fell short of this.

These content trends limit the types of stories told by games and the identities made possible through this medium. Identity is a flexible, contextual entity; individuals can and do inhabit different subject positions depending on their circumstances. However, identity and identifications are partially shaped by media representations. Because core games frequently rely on a male hero/female reward dichotomy, defining masculinity as active and femininity as passive, they offer only limited, retrograde gender identities to players. This is not to argue that games inherently make people identify in these ways; such a point would oversimplify the process of identification and would also be untrue for most players. But it does mean that in circumstances where players *want* to identify with their characters, where it would add to their experience of playing games, they have few options for diversity.

Overall, women found core games offered them only three options for identification. They could embody the masculine subject position, engaging with games on the terms that they offer while minimizing their identification with their chosen gender identity. They could inhabit a female subject position that is passive and deferential to men, where men act while women wait to be rescued. Or they could take on a powerful, active female persona, but must expect that at least some of this power is due to hypersexuality and the character's ability to control men through their objectification of her. Drawing on Douglas's (2010) concept of enlightened sexism, this third subject position posits that "it is precisely through women's calculated deployment of their faces, bodies, attire, and sexuality that they gain and enjoy true power" (p. 10). Although female characters often have the same strength or skill with weapons that male characters have, the emphasis core games place on their bodies implies that sexuality is an inextricable part of female strength.

Participants struggled with these limited positions, desiring greater diversity and the ability to take on less traditional gender roles, ones that allowed them to have power both as male and as female characters and that did not necessarily rely on sexuality to achieve their goals. Because such a position was a rarity, they frequently found identifying simultaneously as both female and gamer to be inherently contradictory.

Obviously, given interviewees' self-defined status as gamers, these issues were not enough to stop them from playing games entirely, and some felt as though there were plenty of alternative options available. Taylor Ryan, for instance, stated, "I think a whole lot of fuss is made over the supposed over-sexualization and powerlessness of females in video games, and, sure, there are some definite examples of this within the game world—LOTS of examples. But for each negative example, I can always think of several incredibly strong, powerful, dynamic female heroines as well. They're not always the protagonist, but I would absolutely say that there are many, many positive female role models in the video game world." For her, these positive character examples were more than enough to make up for the negative choices. Other players were also able to find games that they would enjoy, either by carefully seeking out positive representations of women or by focusing on other aspects they liked within a game.

Despite this, some participants still found the overall industry trend towards objectified women to be disheartening, simply because of its prominence. This was true even for the few who really enjoyed playing as sexualized characters. Bear said in her interview that she played games for the gratuitous violence and sex. However, she argued that the ubiquity of sex was a problem. "I think games are entertainment and porn is entertainment and it's fine for them to overlap. The thing is, there's very few exceptions. I'm tired of playing a conventionally attractive character ALL THE TIME if I choose to be a lady. I want to talk [strategies] without talking boobs."

The preponderance of sexualized and potentially exclusionary female characters helps maintain core gaming as a masculine space, as women require a more extensive knowledge base than men do to navigate games. Because female players are more likely to encounter demeaning or sexist representations of characters that share their gender identity, they need to know extensive details about a game before deciding whether it is likely to be enjoyable or offensive. As male characters are rarely objectified or tokenized in the same way as female characters,[5] male players do not need these details in order to start. Laine, for instance, said, "I hate the overly sexualized nature of females in video games. Will that make me stop playing them? No. Will the way a particular character is portrayed make me choose another game (such as the case of *Lollipop Chainsaw*)? Yes." Making this decision, however, requires her to understand a lot about a game before selecting it. This acts as a barrier to entry into core gaming culture, in that women have to develop repertoires for reading games and choosing what they might want to play well before they even start to play. Without this skill, they risk encountering distasteful material. And even if they develop this skill, narrow character roles could still be a problem; as Emily said, the hypersexualization of female characters "would probably turn some women off of playing those games," excluding women who find navigating game options too tiresome.[6]

Furthermore, women often have to seek the knowledge they need to navigate games from men, who are socially encouraged towards games more than women are (Gilmour, 1999; Schott and Horrell, 2000; Bryce and Rutter, 2003; Jenson, de Castell, and Fisher, 2007; Jenson and de Castell, 2011). This gives men a privileged position from which to develop a strong knowledge base about gaming and from which they can invite others into gaming spaces. As researchers like Aphra Kerr (2003), Nicolas Yee (2008), and Lina Eklund (2011) have shown, most women who game are introduced to video games by male friends and relatives. This was also true among my participants. Although all were now committed gamers, most had been introduced to games by a male relative or friend, who helped them find games they would enjoy while avoiding ones that would be offensive, demeaning, or just not fun. This need for greater knowledge, and tendency to get that knowledge from men, helps bar women from equal power in gaming by requiring them to work harder to enter game spaces. It also encourages a mentor/mentee relationship, where male players are presumed to be more knowledgeable and experienced.

Games' character representations also encourage women to develop a mentality of avoidance, where they do not play sexist games. This can exclude them from large parts of gaming culture and communities and, in turn, perpetuate a cycle in which women's avoidance of certain games marks them as casual or not "real" gamers, because they lack direct knowledge of a cultural touchstone. The *Grand Theft Auto* (*GTA*) series, for instance, was one interviewees referenced as disagreeable, due to its frequent inclusion of violence against women; Emily referred to *GTA* gameplay as "beat up women with a shovel." However, *GTA* is an enormously successful and popular game series. It has been critically acclaimed for its use of satire and humor as well as its open-world nature. Players can complete objectives and missions assigned to them by the game, or they can simply drive around in fun cars listening to the radio. The game makes multiple playstyles possible. Due to its positive critical feedback, its sizeable audience, and its economic success, the *GTA* series is a large part of video game history, and committed core gamers, who often compare their knowledge of games and their experience playing with others, may feel pressured to play at least part of the series. Female gamers who choose to avoid the series given its violence against female characters develop gaps in their skill and experience that other gamers can exploit to dismiss their commitment to gaming. As later chapters will discuss, some female gamers use high levels of skill and experience with games to defend themselves against harassment from other players. Avoiding sexist but popular games can weaken their ability to employ this tactic or can mark women as not "real" gamers in the eyes of the community, again complicating women's involvement in gaming's core and helping it remain masculinized.

Because the lack of diversity among game characters is overt and has been addressed in the past, it may at first appear less problematic. This is especially true as casual games do not tend to include hypersexual-ized female characters (Wohn, 2011) and as many recent core games have worked to move beyond limiting tropes of femininity. Players cited offerings like *Portal*, an innovative 2007 game that combined shoot-ing and puzzle mechanics, as positive examples. In *Portal*, players take on the role of Chell, a human female who is working to escape from a laboratory controlled by an amusing but homicidal female artificial intelligence named GLaDOS (for Genetic Lifeform and Disk Operating System). Players use physics and a gun that places portals, or rings that connect space together, to move through walls, over pits, and around other obstacles. The player can only see that they are a female character if they angle the portals in a specific way; without doing this, they see only a first-person perspective of the portal gun they are carrying. *Portal* makes gender a nonissue through its gameplay but used this to increase the representation of women in gaming. As both Chell and GLaDOS are female, and the only real characters in the game, *Portal* is an unusual example of a female-dominated video game. Other popular examples participants cited, like the *Mass Effect* series, allow players to choose a male or female character, and even more, like the *Tomb Raider* series, have updated their female characters to be less objectified in new re-leases than they were in previous installments.

Until this becomes the norm, however, much core game content works to maintain the status quo of core by providing primarily male subject positions for players. Many core games still only make complete sense if the player is male identified, and male players subsequently pos-sess more control over gaming knowledge and power. Female gamers who try to attain this same knowledge or power often do so at the cost of their own comfort or gender identity; they are continually inhabiting a fragmented position, negotiating between gamer and female rather than comfortably embodying both.

Revealing Industry Assumptions

The overt sexualization and objectification of female characters was also frustrating and potentially off-putting to participants because it revealed deep-seated industry assumptions that prioritized male gamers over female gamers. Interviewees consistently felt that, even if game content itself was not exclusionary because they were able to find alternatives, the motivation behind negative content *was* exclusionary; it showed that industry members were willing to alienate women if they felt that sex and violence would help draw in more men.

Furthermore, although female gamers objected to this trend both through their presence and through explicit statements, they often still bought into the idea that men were justifiably central to gaming—that they were the core, while female players were part of the margins. For example, interviewee Katie Tyler said, "I think that because most guys play video games and most guys design video games, the women are always going to be more sexually objectified. And the men are going to be bulky and strong because that's how in their mind they see themselves. And they kind of want all the girls to be the damsel in distress that gets rescued and falls in love with them." Comments like this show that even though female gamers' presence undermines the idea that games are for men and boys, they still buy into the idea that men are and should be central to gaming, at least in some ways. Katie Tyler is arguing that men's majority presence in gaming justifies the type of sexist depictions that many games put forth, because these games are made *for* them. Another interviewee, Eva, argued the same thing when she stated, "Mostly guys play video games, so I think the way [developers] deal with that is they advertise, they try to appeal to the male gender more than the female gender—I know there's some companies out there that are trying to attract girls more, but this is a business, [. . .] they don't want to, you know, lose their main target, which is guys." Eva, like Katie Tyler, is presenting the idea that sexist themes in games, although not good, are understandable as they bring in male players.

These statements demonstrate the degree to which longstanding ideologies about games normalize their masculinization. Ideology works to explain away sexism, rather than to deal with it directly. Like the industry itself, female gamers have internalized discourses around gaming as masculine and core as made up of men. Attempts to target this core are then seen simply as the standard, rather than being fully assessed for their impacts on power and on gender norms. While other factors probably contribute to the perception of games as masculinized, such as the fact that female gamers' participation in gaming culture tends to be less public than that of men and that female gamers often do not know one another (Bryce and Rutter, 2002, 2003; Eklund, 2011; Jansz and Martens, 2005; Taylor, Jenson, and de Castell, 2009), the role of ideologies around core and gender should not be overlooked. Even dedicated female gamers still see gaming as at least partially male dominated, allowing sexism and misogyny to propagate.

The industry's approach to targeting male audiences also perpetuates sexism by reaffirming hegemonic stereotypes *about men*. Participants frequently argued that male players deserved more credit from developers and that men did not just play games to objectify female characters. They felt that men, like women, enjoyed a well-crafted storyline, the ability to take on another persona, and quality game play, among other elements. Heavily sexualized characters, they contended, were not necessary. At the same time, participants took for granted and accepted industry marketing strategies that relied on the objectification of women. This reaffirms troubling stereotypes about masculinity rather than allowing for more diverse expressions of who men are. Assuming that men need an attractive damsel to save, for instance, implies that they only want to protect someone if that person can offer sex in return, not because of empathy. The persistence of this representation makes men appear inherently sexist, using women rather than treating them as equals. Such an essentializing perspective is, of course, as unfair to men as the assumption that all women are overly emotional or frivolous is to women. However, it contributes to participants' concerns that men will be negatively affected by game representations and that they will harass or objectify female players the same way they are encouraged to objectify female characters in games.

Impact on Men

Finally, participants were deeply concerned about how sexualized content could impact men's expectations regarding women's appearances and anticipated roles in the gaming community and in society. For instance, Anna said that hypersexualized female representations were not really a concern for her personally. However, she elaborated, "The community's treatment of women bothers me more than how women are represented in games, but both are issues that feed into each other." Jessica supported this by describing men's treatment of female characters as attractive objects added to games specifically for their enjoyment. She said, "I know a lot of guys who are like, 'I always play as a girl, so I can stare at her ass as I run!'" In this case, the benefit of playing as a female avatar over playing as a male avatar was the ability to objectify and sexualize one's character.

Another participant, Kay, used *League of Legends* to illustrate specifically how she felt games and character design could negatively impact players, especially male players. She said, "*League* has come out with a stream of female characters right now and they all look really similar. This Zyra character, this Elise character that looks like a spider, they're all just really awkward angles on female bodies and they just look like femme fatales, 'cause that's what they are. Those I'm not a big fan of, because it's creepy to see the community on *League* like, drool over these drawings. [. . .] All these guys are commenting about how they wanna have, like, spider sex with the ladies, and it's kinda creepy." Because female character representations were highly sexualized, participants were concerned that they would make female players, who did not match the characters' unrealistic body proportions, feel self-conscious. They also saw evidence that male players objectified female characters, which created an environment focused on male sexual pleasure at the expense of women's comfort.

Harley had similar concerns, and she took it upon herself to combat them when she could. Because games and gaming magazines hypersexualized female characters and players, Harley feared they would negatively affect her nephew, a young, burgeoning gamer. Specifically, she worried that he would have unrealistic expectations for women's body types and social roles, seeing them as sexual objects rather than as peers. To address this, Harley felt the need to prove herself as a gamer and show her opponents that she was a better player than they were. By presenting herself as a skilled gamer and an equal to her male colleagues, Harley felt she helped combat the objectification of women and diversified the game environment.

This appears at first to demonstrate that female players can combat the stereotypical and limiting representations of women in gaming culture and media. Because games present women in limited ways, female players like Harley see their own presence in gaming as key to providing more diverse gender perspectives. Without their intervention, they are concerned that male players will develop sexist perceptions about women. Demonstrating women's strength and capability is one way to combat this.

However, it is unlikely, given the breadth of women's concerns about games, that simply being present in gaming spaces can completely undermine the systems of power that prioritize men and marginalize women. Furthermore, this perspective puts the onus of equality on the marginalized group, rather than on the developers, journalists, and other cultural contributors who are creating and affirming sexist depictions. Expecting the individuals who are most affected by gaming's sexism to undermine that same system is largely unrealistic. Such an approach also incorrectly situates equality as something to be earned by *being good enough* rather than as an inherent human right to be treated well by others (Nakamura, 2017). Consequently, women's skill may combat an individual instance of sexism, but it fails to change the actual foundation of sexist behavior in gaming, allowing misogyny to continue. It can also help perpetuate the notion that games are a meritocracy, in which skill alone determines success. This hides the existing structural inequalities different types of players face (Paul, 2018).

It is important to note that concerns about the impact of sexist depictions were not consistent across the board, even among people who brought them up. While some participants were concerned about the overall representation of women in games, others only felt it was a problem in specific circumstances. For instance, the sexualization of characters only bothered Nina when they were young. For her, encouraging players to see younger girls as sexual objects was crossing a line, because of real-life power imbalances based on age and gender. Other players considered the context of the game and how players were likely to interpret it. Emily argued, "Games that are fantastical, like *Mario* . . . Princess Peach is obviously a weak character and they don't have a lot of females in that one. [. . .] But it doesn't bother me as much in that, I guess. But the games that are really realistic in terms of graphics and all the women are just side objects or you sleep with them and that's like a big perk of the game, that you can actually do that, or they're ridiculously out of proportion and good looking, I think it's degrading to women." In her opinion, the realistic nature of some characters and the explicitness of their role as rewards or sex objects changed the impact they were likely to have.

Despite the sometimes limited nature of participants' worries, they expressed a deep desire for industry members and game companies to take responsibility for the ways their games could affect audiences. For example, Bear, who was one of the most sex-positive participants in the study and who took pleasure in hypersexualized games, still argued that game makers needed to pay more attention to what their creations meant in a wider societal context. "I think the developers have to be more intelligent about it. I think they have to realize that they're building communities and that those communities are their responsibility. The games are fine but denying responsibility for the culture and community they create isn't. I feel like claiming you're not sexualizing women in society by sexualizing your characters is stupid—it's like a porn company saying they totally don't portray a skewed version of women." Bear felt that the overall gaming community was likely to see women differently after intense exposure to hypersexualized female characters and that, while this was not necessarily a bad thing in all cases, it was at least something that companies should recognize and consider while creating new content.

Furthermore, women wanted this change not only to improve their own situation as players but also for the benefit of male players, who they felt were being unfairly limited. Although participants did at times buy into the industry's construction of men as hypersexual, they temper this acceptance by simultaneously arguing that such a construction is prejudiced and essentialist. Kay said, "Someone wrote this great article about like, 'You know when we just subscribe to loving these female characters for their boobs or butts, that just makes us a pair of balls,' and I thought that was this great line, because . . . it's not just, negatively affecting women, but it's portraying men as who they should be." By catering solely to their sex drive through attractive but flat characters, video game content limited men's ability to interact with different ways of being and present themselves as anything more than "a pair of balls."

This is one of the ways in which, although female gamers buy into the idea of gaming's core as still masculine, they push back slightly against this conceptualization. By showing that core is restrictive to both men and women, they encourage men to demand new types of games and narratives alongside women's own requests for these. They also recognize that men, like women, are not an essentialized, unified group, and that many of them can potentially be allies rather than opponents when it comes to changing gaming culture. Participants' call for greater outside help, from developers and cultural creators as well as from core male gamers, can undermine the existing system that encourages marginalized players to face sexism on their own. As matters stand, discourses around changes to core gaming primarily focus on how they could improve matters for marginalized players; recognizing the benefits to *all* players may be a necessary step for altering systems of power in gaming.

"Games are Kinda Hostile": Trash-Talk and Gendered Harassment in Gaming

In addition to their concerns about how games represent women, female players struggled to navigate the social spaces surrounding gaming. As past research has shown, the core gaming community, particularly in online spaces, often demonstrates deeply negative behavioral or linguistic patterns (Consalvo, 2012; Ivory et al., 2017). This is due to both the anonymity of players and core gaming's overall norms about trash-talk. Past research demonstrates that combining anonymity, a lack of immediate consequences, and a competitive game environment where emotions run high often means that players become more aggressive and offensive toward others (Chisholm, 2006; Fox and Tang, 2014), especially if that person does not seem to belong. Interviewees expect this behavior and take it for granted, as when Elayne stated, "The levels of anonymity plus, you know, no consequences, yields what you would expect just as far as obnoxious behavior." She believed that players' ability to hide their offline identities and the challenges of punishing offenders effectively meant that "obnoxious behavior" was almost a guaranteed part of gaming.

At the same time, this level of hostility only occurs when it is supported by community norms (Chui, 2014). These norms exist in core multiplayer gaming, both in person and online, which is dominated by the presence of interpersonal trash-talking. Many core players see trash-talk as a fun but ignorable aspect of competition; they expect targets to respond in kind and argue that those who react poorly to trash-talk are taking it too seriously (Gray, 2014; Nakamura, 2012). At the same time, core players actively defend their right to behave this way. In researching online harassment, digital media scholar Lisa Nakamura (2012) found "a key paradox of race, gender, and game studies rose to the top: while profanity and abuse are 'trash talk,' a form of discursive waste, lacking meaningful content that contributes to the game, many identified it as a distinctive and inevitable aspect of videogame multi-player culture, and thus to be defended" (p. 4). The content of trash-talk is viewed as nonserious, but the act of trash-talking itself is considered an inalienable right.

However, trash-talk often includes racism, sexism, and homophobia, making it more difficult for marginalized players to shrug off (Gray, 2014; Nakamura, 2012; Salter and Blodgett, 2012). With respect to gender specifically, trash-talk frequently involves rape or assault-based threats (Nardi, 2010; Salter and Blodgett, 2012). These are casually stated, often phrased as descriptors of in-game action, such as the use of "you just got raped!" to stand in for "your character was just killed," rather than as direct personal attacks. Even careless comments of this nature can be upsetting, however, especially to people who have been assaulted. Sexual assault can result in posttraumatic stress disorder, and rape-related cues, such as language, can serve as trauma triggers for affected individuals, provoking anxiety and painful memories (Holmes and St. Lawrence, 1983). While treatment can mitigate the impacts of sexual assault, "Even in the strongest treatments more than one-third of women retain a PTSD diagnosis at posttreatment or drop out of treatment" (Vickerman and Margolin, 2009, p. 431). Continued fears or anxiety are therefore likely even among women who pursue therapy, and the linguistic norms of trash-talk may be deeply disturbing to recovering individuals.

Women who have not personally experienced sexual assault can also find it concerning. Sociologist Amy L. Chasteen (2001) found that women consider sexual assault to be "extremely common" (p. 117). Men, on the other hand, are not socialized to fear assault to the same extent as women. As participant Feather stated, "[Sexual assault is] not something that [men] have to really worry about. Guys don't get catcalled on the streets, guys don't have to worry about short skirts, guys don't worry about those things." Women are taught to police their appearance and behavior carefully to avoid the threat of sexual assault in a way that is not true for men. Therefore, even if male players also tell each other, "You just got raped," it may be easier for them to treat this language as a joke than for women to do so. The "just get over it" approach to trash-talk falsely limits the impacts of trash-talking to the moment of conversation, failing to recognize that off-hand comments may have impacts well beyond a single gaming session.

Within this context, it is unsurprising that participants felt online harassment was a significant issue. In fact, my original interview guide did not ask players about online negativity or harassment; when they volunteered extensive stories about it, however, I adjusted accordingly. It was obviously a significant part of their gaming experiences. For example, Adrianna brought up a common perception about gamer behavior when she said, "My boyfriend in college was addicted to *Halo* and he really became kind of an asshole when he was playing multiplayer matches. You know the stereotype of the 12-year-old with an Internet connection screeching racial/homophobic slurs in *Halo*? He gave it right back and thinking about it now just turns me off to *Halo* and FPSs [first-person shooters] in general." Her ex-boyfriend encountered very negative players in online spaces and responded in kind, creating a cycle of derogatory profanity. Adrianna still finds it hard to unlink FPS games from verbally abusive behavior, making the whole genre unappealing to her. Other players also avoided FPSs and sometimes even online games in general. As Feather stated, "I don't really like the culture that's involved with multi-player games." She played only single-player games and in-person multiplayer, to circumvent online harassment altogether.

Of course, not all interviewees avoided online games. After all, there are multiple core game styles and genres that require many players, such as massively multiplayer online games (MMOs), multiplayer online battle arenas (MOBAs) like *League of Legends*, and others. Online games also provide a wider competitive outlet for players who want to prove their skills against others. Because of this, many interviewees chose to play online or multiplayer games despite their culture of harassment. As Kay said, "Usually [online] games are kinda hostile. Lots of like, rape metaphor, insults, and things like that, but, I dunno, I like . . . probably just the competition, in those games." This demonstrates that harassment culture is not necessarily exclusionary to everyone. However, even players who opted to join online spaces recognized the potential downsides. Although they could choose to focus on elements they liked about multiplayer, the decision to play online games also required them to ignore as best they could many aspects of gaming culture that were not only offensive, but specifically offensive to women.

Because players still perceive online gaming, and core gaming in general, as a primarily white male space, interviewees argued that players who were not members of this group were treated as interlopers and were more heavily targeted for harassment. Some participants stated that male players treated them as a "nuisance" (DT) or assumed that they were bad at gaming simply because they were female. When Helix first joined *World of Warcraft*, for instance, she found that members of her guild "assumed I was bad or couldn't play, with absolutely no evidence." Although a display of skill was often enough to halt further assumptions or questions, associating gender with skill or a lack of skill was very insulting to interviewees, who tended to be highly experienced gamers.

Participants faced other, more offensive experiences as well. Players who attended in-person gaming events were often touched or photographed without their permission (Elayne, Feather), while those who played online recounted many sexualized insults such as "slut," "whore," and "cocksucker" (Harley, Alissa). A few players even experienced threats of assault; Helix described an incident in which, during a group raid in *World of Warcraft*, she won an item that her guild leader also wanted. In response, he "threatened to tear my breasts into bloody shreds." This occurred even though she was playing in a guild composed of her college boyfriend's high school friends; his offline connection to them was not enough to keep them from harassing her using very violent language. Although interviewees were quick to recognize that many of the players they encountered were perfectly pleasant and were just focused on playing the game, most had experienced varying degrees of negativity.

Gaming spaces were even less welcoming for players with intersectional identities. In a study of female gamers of color, for instance, digital media and identity scholar Kishonna Gray (2012) found that "Latina women within the space experience nativism, racism, sexism, and even heterosexism as many identify as sexual minorities. African American women experience racialized sexism stemming from the duality of their ascribed identities" (p. 411). Her findings were further supported by my participants. For instance, Eva, who is Mexican, found the gaming community very intimidating, due to her perception of it as not only a male space but also a white one. She said, "I think everyone online, seriously most people online, are just white guys that are from twenty to thirtyish, and that's it. [. . .] So I'm like, unless you're a white, straight, middle-class male who's like in their twenties and in college, you don't really fit in [. . .] [T]hat's really weird to me because I'm not white, I'm Mexican, and I'm not a male, I'm a girl. So, I think that's why I've always struggled." Because the gaming community felt so homogeneous, Eva's identification as female and Mexican disconnected her from the other players she encountered and made her subject to greater harassment as a perceived outsider. Put simply, she described in-game spaces as "very not friendly towards girls" and "mean."

Although some other participants did not face the joint challenge of identifying as both female and nonwhite in an environment where these characteristics marked them as "other," they also agree that the core community's expectations for players made it difficult to be included. Dealing with trash-talk and profanity can be a challenge for anyone, male and female. Individuals have to find ways to ignore or cope with the negativity, as well as to decide whether to respond. However, women face an extra challenge, because the harassment they face can be more targeted and because their outsider status can draw extra fire.

Research into workplace harassment, one of the most deeply studied contexts for this type of gender issue, shows that sexual and gender-based harassment of women is more likely in male-dominated environments, particularly those that prize traditionally masculine qualities like toughness, aggression, and competitiveness (McDonald, 2012). Although workplace research may not seem to connect directly to gaming research, the two areas share many motivating factors behind gender harassment. In male-dominated workplaces, some men interpret women's presence as potentially threatening to the masculine status quo. Women are seen as interlopers who will interfere with homosocial male bonding or soften the workplace with political correctness and traditionally feminine characteristics, such as emotionality or sensitivity. Therefore, members of the masculine community try to limit women's input or drive them out entirely. As many of these traditionally masculine characteristics also appear in gaming communities, particularly those around shooting, fighting, or other competitive genres, it is unsurprising that women could be seen as a threat to the community's structure.

Furthermore, although sexual harassment was originally conceptualized as a behavior that men directed toward women they found desirable, in order to win them over, newer research has shown that gender and sexual harassment are actually directed most frequently toward individuals who violate gender norms as a mechanism for "fixing" their behavior (Berdahl, 2007). Given that core video games have a longstanding cultural definition as being "for men," women's interest in playing may be seen as an instance of gender deviance that requires correction.

This is particularly significant given gaming's interactive nature. With past media, such as the romance novels Janice Radway's readers engaged with or the VCR that Ann Gray analyzed, women could have a more individual experience. Their husbands might complain that they were spending too much money on romance novels, or their kids might nag them into recording a show they did not want to watch, but these women were generally only navigating a small, private family sphere. And once they were in their novel or could settle down to watch their own tapes, they had a private media experience available to them. They interacted directly and solely with the text.

In core gaming, this is often not an option. It is true that many women game alone and get extensive pleasure out of individual play, and I do not intend to dismiss players who opt for this type of experience. I myself primarily play single-player games, which fit my busy schedule and my preference for in-depth storylines. The fact of the matter is, however, that core games are increasingly networked, with many developers adding more and more multiplayer options to new releases. This means that, if they choose to play the hottest new games and engage with gaming culture widely, women are necessarily doing so in a social, interactive way. They cannot access all that games have to offer without encountering other players. This puts female gamers in a position where they almost always have to learn to navigate the type of harassment and sexism that interviewees described here; unless they choose only to play alone, they are extremely likely to face a situation in which another player perceives them as an interloper and reacts accordingly.

As forces like character representation maintain gaming's core as masculinized, it is unlikely that the specific harassment of women will decrease. In turn, this harassment frequently drives women to play games more privately, to hide their gender identity, or to leave gaming entirely. Their less obvious presence then naturalizes discourses that construct men as gamers by helping the audience appear to be more male dominated than it actually is. This cycle of exclusion is key to maintenance of the status quo and is one of the many forces that will need to be undermined if power structures in gaming are to be altered.

Impacts of Overt Sexism

Many of the issues outlined above only apply to core games and are not seen in casual. Casual games, if anything, overrepresent female characters, and these characters are generally not sexualized (Wohn, 2011). Furthermore, casual game mechanics often encourage players to work together rather than to compete; this makes it less likely that they will develop the social norms needed for sustained harassment to occur (Chui, 2014). In this way, casual offers, as Shira Chess (2017) indicates, a chance for nontraditional players to "hit the reset button. We are moving beyond the traditional depictions of the popular gamer" (p. 8). At the same time, I would argue that matters are not so simple. Not only is casual, as it currently stands, restrictive in its own way—Chess argues that "Jennifer," the imagined casual player, is often defined as white, heterosexual, middle-class, cisgender, and able-bodied—but if we position casual games as the solution for all players left out of core, we do not put pressure on core to change. And if we want true equality within gaming, core *has* to change. Otherwise non-"gamers" will remain ghettoized to the margins of game culture, as they have been in past efforts like the girls' games movement (Taylor, 2008). This will allow core to continue propagating inequality. Instead, we should use casual games as models for how core could also be made more open and push for specific changes that will make both core and casual more inclusive.

Continuing to recognize and critique core gaming's overt sexism is one way to encourage change, and it is important to recognize that some game companies have started to improve in these areas. In fact, participants remained optimistic about the future of games, and many felt that improvements were coming. They described several positive changes in the area of game content, such as the rebooted *Tomb Raider* series. In

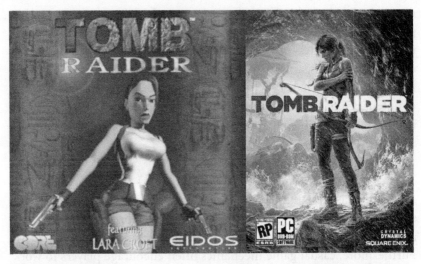

Figure 2.1. A side-by-side comparison of the original and rebooted *Tomb Raider* game covers. Elite Gamer. (2015, November 30). *Tomb Raider* vs. *Tomb Raider* vs. *Tomb Raider*. *Medium*. Retrieved from https://medium.com/.

her original games, Lara Croft, the protagonist of the series and one of the first extremely popular female game characters, had an oversized chest and wore a tight, revealing tank top with short shorts. In the new series reboot in 2013, however, she was redesigned to be less sexualized. Although she still sports a tank top at times, developers altered Croft's body to more realistic proportions and her standard outfit includes cargo pants, rather than shorts (see figure 2.1). The success of the new *Tomb Raider* games gave participants hope that industry members would realize that well-designed female characters are not necessarily off-putting to male players and that they can draw in women, increasing a game's potential audience.

Other positively referenced series included *Fallout* and *Mass Effect*, where players could choose their character gender without affecting the depth of the storyline or the progress of the game. Female characters in these games are just as interesting and developed as male characters. In fact, developers even took some steps to ensure that female and male experiences would be equivalent. In *Fallout 3*, for instance, male and female characters were generally not sexualized, but if they were, it was to similar extents. As Eva described, "In *Fallout 3*, if there was a skimpy dress for the women, there was also one for the men. [. . .] And I was like, 'Oh, that's funny, 'cause usually in most games you just leave it for the girl, not for the guy. So, it was fun to see both of them dressed skimpy and slutty, but most other games don't do that." *Fallout 3* provided realistic armor for both male and female characters, but also provided some joke pieces, such as leopard-print sleepwear, that affected all characters in similar ways, as a reversal of general gaming trends.

In the *Mass Effect* series, developers included the option to play as a female character in each of the three games of the original trilogy and have allowed players to engage in same-sex relationships, to keep each character's storyline options completely open regardless of gender. However, for the third game, developers also made sure to include the female version of the main character, Commander Shepard (colloquially known as "FemShep") in their marketing materials for the game, distinctly promoting her as a feature (Westbrook, 2011). For instance, *Mass Effect 3* included a reversible cover featuring male Shepard on one side and female Shepard on the other (see figure 2.2). The most recent *Mass Effect* game, *Andromeda*, featured only a space-suited silhouette on the cover, masking gender completely, but the game itself included the option to play a male or a female main character. Furthermore, players were required to play a short section of the game as their character's other-gendered twin, meaning that even if a gamer opted to play as a male character, they still got some experience as the female option as well. *Andromeda* did not receive the same level of positive critical feedback that previous games received for several reasons, from storyline to graphics, but it did continue the series' trend of prioritizing female avatars.

Research from outside my interviews shows that games that signal inclusivity by including female, LGBT, and nonwhite characters often outperform their genre competitors (Yee, 2017). Because of this, developers have a profit-based motivation to include diverse character options, and some newer games seem to be moving in this direction. BioWare, for instance, introduced LGBT characters to the popular *Star Wars: The Old Republic* and *Dragon Age II* games, opting to do so in the face of protests from core "gamers" who felt this ruined their immersion (Condis, 2015, 2018). Other series, like *Assassin's Creed*, have started to include more playable female characters alongside their male ones. These changes

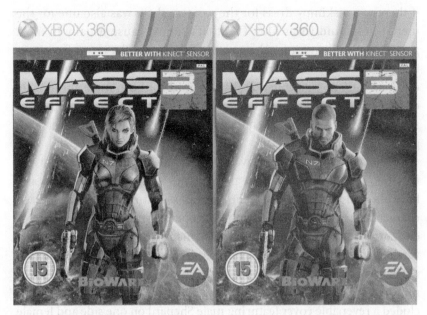

Figure 2.2. *Mass Effect 3* included a reversible cover with male Shep on one side and FemShep on the other. *Mass Effect 3* Covers. (2012). MobyGames. Retrieved August 26, 2019, from www.mobygames.com/.

work to provide more diverse points of identification to players and to tell different stories.

Some developers have also moved to address harassment and trash-talk. Riot, the company behind the popular (but toxic) online multiplayer game *League of Legends*, has, for instance, started to implement community management measures that punish players for insulting or harassing others (Lin, 2013, 2015a, 2015b). These efforts will be discussed further in chapter 5.

At the same time, my participants made it clear that some barriers persist. Although industry members are recognizing the benefits of targeting games more broadly, the optimistic perspective that core gaming is definitely on its way to improvement first underestimates the strength of hegemonic ideologies, especially when they are as longstanding as the idea that video games are for men and boys. Overtly sexist trends, like the lack of representation of women in games and their hypersexualization when they appear, construct gaming as a space for men, rather than for women. Even more so, these trends construct gaming as a space for a specific kind of man, one who revels in power, aggression, and dominance over others. The persistence of this discursive construction then becomes naturalized as "common-sense," and gamers are encouraged to buy into it. This can be seen in how female gamers, although they argued that men deserved more credit, still tolerated marketing tactics that targeted men on the basis of their sex drives. It can also be seen in female gamers' acceptance of limited subject positions in gaming, and the ways in which they avoid games that will offend them but understand why industry members would make those games. Overt sexism is one of the more obvious ways in which gaming's hegemonic and unequal power structure is maintained, and changing or undermining an existing hegemony is far from an easy process.

Second, female gamers' optimism unfortunately ignores the fact that sexism and harassment have been on the rise while change has been happening. Several participants who had long histories in gaming argued that the type of overt harassment they encountered in the casualized era was relatively new; they had only recently started to encounter male gamers who deliberately worked to drive them away from playing. This, combined with incidents like GamerGate and the virulent harassment of public figures, indicates that as the industry has started to welcome in new types of players, some traditional "gamers" have responded with forceful policing of core spaces. Should their attempts to maintain power and exclusivity be successful, female gamers' hopes for the future of games may not be realized.

Finally, participants' optimism ignores the impact of the more subtle, insidious sexism that is implicit in gaming spaces. Representational change, although it intersects in some ways with audience and industry issues, is only one potential area in which women are separated from the gaming community more generally, especially given the ways in which games' interactivity requires female players to deal with others. Core games and gaming spaces contain many inferentially sexist elements that work alongside overt sexism in order to maintain gaming as a masculine space. These aspects of gaming need to be drawn further towards the surface in order to undermine existing notions of gender and core.

3

Girly Games and Girl Gamers

Inferential Sexism and Its Impacts

One year when I was in college, I asked for an Xbox 360 for Christmas. Some of my close friends owned this console, and as we attended schools several states apart, I thought it would be fun to have a system that would allow us to play online multiplayer together. A few days after I requested this from my parents, however, I received a phone call from my older brother. "Hey Amanda," he said. "Mom told me you wanted an Xbox for Christmas, and I wanted to check that she had that right— are you sure you didn't ask her for a Wii?" In this instant, my brother, although armed with the best of intentions (and knowing how little our parents know about game consoles), perpetuated what could be considered an instance of inferential sexism. Again drawing on Stuart Hall's description of inferential racism, I use the term "inferential sexism" to describe an event, policy, or argument that rests on unquestioned, naturalized assumptions that have a sexist basis. These incidents forward sexist stereotypes in a more subtle way than overt sexism does and are all the more problematic because they can easily appear to be simple facts. From my brother's perspective, the Wii was a good choice for me. From my perspective, his assumption that I could only (or would only) want to) play the simpler party games the Wii offered rather than the more complex story or fighting games we both associated with the Xbox was patronizing. Thankfully, once I confirmed that I did, in fact, want the Xbox, the matter was dropped. My brother probably does not even remember this conversation occurring, and he may be rather offended to find out that I am using it as an example of inferential sexism, especially as he is usually the first to nerd out about video games with me.[1] Regardless of intention, however, the conversation appeared to be based on naturalized assumptions linking female players with more casual games, such as those released on the Wii.

In looking to past research and speaking to my interviewees, I found that inferential sexism in gaming is not at all a rarity. A number of studies have indicated that, even at a young age, social forces teach children that technology is a male pursuit. Parents often feel that computing is not an appropriate or useful pursuit for a female child and therefore will not purchase technology or encourage interest in it (Gilmour, 1999; Schott and Horrell, 2000; Bryce and Rutter, 2003; Jenson, de Castell, and Fisher, 2007; Jenson and de Castell, 2011). For instance, early computing research showed that parents were less likely to buy a home computer for a daughter than a son (Gilmour, 1999), limiting the time girls could spend becoming familiar with all the technology's possibilities. Although home computers have become more common overall, gendered differences persist (Jenson and de Castell, 2011).

When girls are introduced to technology, male friends and family members often carefully manage their relationship to it. In terms of games specifically, women are generally introduced to gaming through a male friend or relative, and their continued participation in the gaming community depends heavily on having a social network that also plays (Kerr, 2003; Yee, 2008). Those who lose touch with their gaming friends tend to stop gaming themselves. Other studies indicate that male players frequently take over control of games when women are playing, under the guise of "helping," and that girls who claim to have experience with gaming often admit, when pressed, that their experience is primarily limited to watching male acquaintances play (Bryce and Rutter, 2002, 2003; Jenson, de Castell, and Fisher, 2007; Jenson and de Castell, 2011). This is true even when the technology in question belongs to the female family member, showing how the playing field between men and women is not level with regard to technology and video games.

These patterns also demonstrate the subtle influence of inferential sexism. Parents who do not encourage their female children towards computers and men who "help" their female friends game by taking over their controllers are generally not attempting to bar women and girls from gaming or technology. Most would probably argue that they are trying to help their child develop their existing interests instead, or they are making sure their female friend/child/partner can explore a video game fully. However, the fact remains that these habits are based on naturalized assumptions that equate technology with masculinity and presuppose that men and boys will have a greater facility in this area. And these are not the only inferentially sexist forces that women face when gaming; participants mentioned a wide array of others. For instance, they argued that the specific way in which women are welcomed into gaming from an industrial/content perspective treats them as a minor subgroup—what one participant referred to as a "genre"—rather than a legitimate audience. This ghettoizes them into a small subset of gaming rather than allowing access to all of gaming equally. Furthermore, the ways in which other gamers respond to women's presence, even when they are not being deliberately negative, often marks female gamers as just that—*female* gamers instead of simply *gamers*. Because of this, even positive reactions can increase the gap between a woman's self-identification and how others perceive her.

This indicates how, even as overt misogyny garners attention and is potentially addressed, numerous more subtle forces are still at work to maintain core as exclusionary. Inferential sexism's less obvious nature makes it potentially more difficult to combat as its assumptions appear to be true or at least not damaging. However, it still acts as a barrier to equality in gaming spaces, and potentially in other masculinized areas, by normalizing masculinity while marking women's desire to enter the space as unusual and deviant. Furthermore, participants' experiences show that the casualized era's diversification of game styles, with the introduction of casual, social, and mobile games, does not necessarily solve problems of inferential sexism. In fact, it worsens some of them, as these game styles have become fundamentally linked with femininity (Vanderhoef, 2013). Because of this, they work to "other" female audiences from more general conceptions about gamers. The dismissal of casual as frivolous also encourages players to value core styles of play over alternatives, often making female gamers complicit in their own exclusion by limiting their views on acceptable play styles. In this way, inferential sexism heavily undergirds and perpetuates existing systems of exclusion.

"Dora the Explorer Goes on a Princess Trip": The Restrictive Nature of Games for Girls

Exclusionary outcomes are evident in the first inferentially sexist force interviewees described, the creation and marketing of games for women.

When developers opted to target women, participants felt they did so according to very stereotypical gender norms. Games designed for women relied heavily on traditionally feminine material, such as cooking, dolls, and taking care of families, houses, or pets. The persistent use of essentialized views of gender and femininity, participant Bear then argued, "marginalizes women. It makes women a genre? As opposed to mainstream." She used the term "genre" to refer to how the industry bracketed out women and women's games, treating them as marginal rather than as part of gaming culture as a whole.

Other participants strongly agreed with this perspective. Discussing her experience playing games as a child, Alissa recounted how frustrated she was when, in contrast to adventure games like *Pokémon* or *The Legend of Zelda*, which she felt developers marketed to boys, the games companies marketed towards girls like her were "'Barbie Dream World' and 'raise a horse'" games. The focus was on fashion or caretaking, rather than adventuring through a fantasy world like Hyrule to save it from evil. Alissa described this contrast as "insulting to the point that it was funny" and referenced these early experiences as evidence that the video game industry fundamentally misunderstands women and what they want out of their entertainment.

Alissa felt that newer games were improving their approach to girls and women, but other participants believed that these games were still limited. Specifically, they argued that "girl games" target children rather than adult women, demonstrating the industry's lack of awareness regarding how many adult women play games. Emily said, "I can't think of any game in particular I think is marketed toward adult women. [. . .] When I think of girl games, I think of like that dog game and cooking games and things like that, like Barbie games. I think they are intended for little girls." Participants cited games like *Cooking Mama*, a cooking simulation game, or *Nintendogs*, a pet simulation game, as options developers marketed towards women. They also described games for women using dismissive, made-up titles, such as "Dora the Explorer goes on a princess trip." The sheer frustration and disgust evident in Feather's voice as she named that fictional game as a metaphor for women's video games overall made it an eminently memorable moment in our interview. It also revealed how strongly women felt about their treatment at the hands of the games industry.

Although feminized or domestic games are appealing to many players—including my participants and myself, who often play these alongside core offerings—interviewees found the overwhelming prevalence of these games restrictive or even offensive. It was clear to them that female audiences were an afterthought for most core developers, who showed little understanding of female players' diverse tastes and preferences. The women I spoke with bristled under this lack of recognition and wanted to be taken seriously as significant members of the gaming audience. Taylor Ryan, for instance, said, "Game companies need to stop patronizing us, with games like the 'Imagine: Makeover Studio' sort of DS games. They should just focus on producing more games with strong, appealing female leads, issues that we can relate to, and a plot that is appealing to either gender. That's all it takes. We don't need glitter and pink and stuffed animals." Developers' existing strategies for targeting women dismissed or marked as abnormal women and girls who were not interested in domestic pursuits such as raising children or animals or who did not want to use games to play with fashion and makeup. It also ignored the possibility that women might want to pursue different interests dependent on context—that is, that they would enjoy both beauty games and action-adventure games depending on what they wanted to get out of their media experience at the time.

The targeting of women through traditional gender norms does provide a specific space through which women can enter gaming without having their gender identity questioned or facing some of the overt problems discussed earlier. "Girl games" mark female audiences as desirable for developers and as a part of gaming communities and culture. However, this trend is a form of inferential sexism that helps maintain core as masculinized. First, the separation of "girl games" from all other games constructs a marginal feminine space, rather than undermining or changing video games' overall masculinization. Second, bracketing out female games and players continues to separate gamer identity and gender identity, making a joint female-gamer position difficult to envision and embody. Finally, the stereotypically feminine characteristics used in "girl games" and their marketing reaffirms unequal gender roles that treat men and women as fundamentally different and assign women to more domestic spaces. As media scholar John Vanderhoef (2013) points out, "This discourse promotes notions of difference and distinction that ultimately recreate gender and power hierarchies in games culture and beyond."

Perpetuating outdated, essentialized perspectives on gender also contributes to broader inequalities in socioeconomic power. For instance, as sociologists Arlie Hochschild and Anne Machung (1989) discovered in the late 1980s, although women were entering the workforce in increasing numbers, they were also still primarily responsible for housework and childcare. This illustrates how norms and ideologies around gender roles and responsibilities are slow to change; the feminist movement had encouraged and fought for more equal gender relations in work, home life, and politics, but individuals' lived experiences still reflected numerous pressures from older, unequal gender ideologies that limited both men and women. In a 2014 retrospective on *The Second Shift*, Hochschild pointed out that work culture has still not significantly changed, that there continues to be a large second-shift burden on women, and that overall economic trends such as declining numbers of blue-collar jobs are potentially worsening this situation (Schulte, 2014). Work like this demonstrates how gender inequality persists, highlighting why it continues to matter that games' power structures divide men and women into distinct, unequal groups.

Women did push back against their ghettoization in some ways. While they were still encouraged to accept industry perspectives on gender due to the idea that men make up a larger part of the gaming audience than women do, interviewees once again argued that male players should be given more credit. As discussed earlier, female players frequently have no choice but to play as a male character. However, the reverse was rarely true. Participants struggled to think of more than a handful of games that required players to be female. Obviously, such games exist (e.g., *Portal*, *Tomb Raider*, and *Bayonetta*), but the fact that it took work for thirty-seven committed female gamers to think of examples indicates their rarity. The reason for the excess of male characters and the lack of female characters, interviewees pointed out, was an industry-based assumption that women would play games as male characters if they had to, but that men would be too uncomfortable playing as a woman to choose games that forced them into that role. Therefore, games that only offered female characters would not be successful, at least per traditional purchasing expectations. Players disagreed.

Lee, for instance, referenced the success of the TV show *Legend of Korra* as evidence that men are more open-minded than the industry often gives them credit for being. *Korra* was a spinoff of the popular series *Avatar: The Last Airbender* but featured a female protagonist instead of a male one. Because of this, Lee said, producers were concerned that the show would not do as well, given the traditional logic that boys do not identify with female characters. When the show was put to test audiences, however, "The guys all said that Korra was awesome and they didn't care [that she was a girl]" (Lee, interview 1). Lee admitted that Korra was "a very tomboyish girl" whose creators describe her as "very pugnacious. Kind of in your face" (Farley, 2011). This may have helped her appeal to male audiences by drawing on characteristics traditionally associated with masculinity (e.g., strength, aggressiveness, physicality). But her creators tried to keep her from being a one-sided character, arguing, "She's also funny and has a lot of charm and vulnerability because she's still growing up and trying to figure things out" (Farley, 2011). Therefore, Korra breaks stereotypes, combining traditionally masculine and feminine characteristics into a complex, interesting package. Lee argued that this multidimensionality will draw players, male or female, to a character, regardless of character gender. Flat, one-dimensional characters, on the other hand, will probably avert men and marginalize or irritate women.

Drawing from experiences in other media, women felt that character and gender-role diversity was an area where developers could make progress. They called for greater support in terms of more varied female-targeted games, improved characters, and multidimensional stories, believing that these would have cross-gendered appeal. As games scholar Adrienne Shaw posited, "If [marginalized players] learned to enjoy games that did not represent them, it is likely heterosexual, white, cisgendered men could too" (2014b, p. 144). Although they were often harassed or excluded for being female in the masculinized environments of gaming, participants largely remained positive about their fellow gamers overall, assuming that they would be excited about more diverse representations and more diverse games if these materials were detailed, interesting to play, and innovative.

There is some evidence that this may be true. For instance, in April 2016, the developers of the multiplayer survival game *Rust* introduced

an update that randomly assigned half of their players a female avatar. A previous update had similarly randomized players' race. This was
an unprecedented decision and provoked a backlash from disgruntled
"gamers." The developers, however, have stuck to their decision, arguing
that permanent avatars will make players' decisions more meaningful,
in that a player cannot "attack another then come back later with a different gender or race and befriend the same player" (Newman, 2016).
The developers also argued that "who you are in the game, your race
and gender, makes no difference to the actual gameplay," and therefore
there is no reason not to make avatars diverse. Since this decision, and
in spite of the negative reaction some had to the change, *Rust* has seen
a significant increase in number of players, indicating that gamers may
be more attracted to diversity than researchers, developers, and players
have previously expected.

At other times, gamers and reviewers have recommended that players choose the female over the male option in games where they felt the
quality of the female characters' voice acting and storyline was superior
to the male characters'. In the *Mass Effect* trilogy, for instance, reviewers lauded voice actress Jennifer Hale for bringing dynamic range and
believability to the female version of protagonist Commander Shepard,
colloquially known as "FemShep" (Kauz, 2009; Walker, 2011). In contrast, they argue that Mark Meer's performance of male Shepard is fine
but nothing special (Kauz, 2009). Similarly, reviews of the most recent
Assassin's Creed game, *Odyssey*, have recommended that players choose
the female protagonist, Kassandra, over the male protagonist, Alexios.
They argue that Kassandra is "one of the most complete human characters I've ever played as in a game" (Campbell, 2018), "the most char-
ismatic and interesting of the two protagonists" (King, 2018), or simply
"perfect" (Kain, 2018). This again provides evidence that, if a character
is well crafted, dynamic, and multifaceted, gender becomes less salient
to players, who can enjoy other parts of the character's performance
instead.

Of course, not all recent games that include women have received
positive coverage like the examples above, and some of these reviews still
contained inferential assumptions that the player reading the review was
likely to be male. Game journalist John Walker (2011), for instance, mentioned Hale's voice acting as a reason to play FemShep but also said, "If

I'm honest, my motivations aren't exclusively pure. The other big factor is: whose bum do I want to stare at for 30 hours?" This connects back to the assumption that games should appeal to male players on the basis of sex, and avatar attractiveness is a commonly cited reason why men play female characters (e.g., Stabile, 2014). At other moments, "gamers" have heavily protested games that include female characters. The recently released *Battlefield V*, for example, includes female characters in World War II settings; this provoked many complaints from players who felt the developers were sacrificing historical accuracy for a politically correct, social-justice agenda (Farokhmanesh, 2018a, 2018b). Bracketing out the fact that many women did serve in World War II and that most fighting games are already not historically accurate, the strong negative reaction against this decision shows that the hegemonic definition of core as masculine remains, and challenges to that definition upset many core players. Therefore, there are still barriers to overcome, but participants remained hopeful that negative reactions against diverse characters would come from only a small but vocal minority of gamers, and that developers would stand their ground against these complaints, as the *Battlefield* creators have (Farokhmanesh, 2018b).

"It's So Cool That You're a Woman Who Games!": The Inferential Sexism of Surprise

Other inferentially sexist forces are social in nature. As mentioned earlier, interviewees recount extensive experiences with harassment, especially in online game spaces, and they describe this as an overtly sexist force they must overcome in order to enjoy games effectively. However, their accounts demonstrate that specific gender harassment and negativity online are only some of the many potential barriers they face to being key components of gaming communities. Female gamers also have to combat constant surprise at their presence and strong stereotypes about "girl gamers" in order to continue playing.

Women found that they were seen as a rarity in gaming. As a result, many of them received extra attention when they revealed their gender. In some cases, this attention was positive. Women encountered many gamers who thought it was cool that they played games, and many who asked numerous questions about what games they liked, about how long they had been playing, and about themselves as people. However, even though this attention was positive, the frequency with which it occurred made players feel like anomalies rather than just regular gamers.

For example, one of the first times Eva used voice chat when gaming online, she called for help from her teammates in *Left 4 Dead*, a fast-paced zombie shooter. When she spoke, "He was like 'Whoa, I didn't know girls played this game!' and then his friends were like, 'Yeah dude, sometimes they play.' [. . .] It just suddenly all hit me, 'I don't think girls play that many video games, I don't think this is normal.'" Having her gender become a significant topic of conversation separated Eva from the other players and made her feel out of place. The other players were happy to help her and, according to her account, were extremely nice to her after finding out she was a girl, asking her all about herself and how she got into the game. This behavior only made Eva more uncomfortable, because it was out of the norm. Players in *Left 4 Dead* usually followed the negative behavior characteristic of many online spaces, engaging in trash-talk due to the competitive environment. Rather than treating Eva as just another player and behaving in the same way towards her, other gamers reversed their behavior, marking her as different. Their treatment, although positive, made Eva's gender, rather than her performance or skill, the most salient aspect of her identity and served to "other" her from the general gaming population.

Other gamers also got used to surprised responses to their gender, stating everything from "I grew up as a hardcore gamer, and guys would be totally shocked to hear that" (Taylor Ryan, interview 1) to "Of the hundreds of times I've used [voice chat] with people who didn't already know me well, perhaps two or three I felt like it was not a big deal and/or extremely interesting that I was a woman. Usually it was a conversation-halter" (Helix, interview 1). Some described getting extra attention, similarly to Eva's experience online. Anna, who was part of a gaming group at her university, said, "Posting on the Facebook [page for the gaming group] can be a little creepy though—women get a lot more attention when they post. It used to make me feel special and awesome, but now it's just irritating." Even in a tightly knit social circle based in offline connections, players' behavior differed when they were dealing with a female gamer rather than a male gamer.

Many of these experiences were positive or neutral, but female gamers were frustrated by the fact that they were continually marked as "other" and made to feel as though they were out of place. To borrow an analogy from Helix, being a female gamer is "like wearing a Halloween costume when most people aren't, to work or to class or something. You're not doing anything against the rules and a lot of people will think you're cool for doing it, but other people will judge you and look down on you—and EVERYONE will notice you." Because of this, some players were very uncomfortable revealing their gender, assuming that it would change their experience playing. As Bubble pointed out, when everybody makes "a huge deal out of women playing video games," it gets in the way of enjoying them, because their gender, rather than the game itself, becomes the relevant topic.

The assumption that women are not normal "gamers" also meant that men constantly questioned their presence in gaming spheres. For instance, Elayne attended many in-person gaming events with a competitive team she helped manage. Because she was the only woman or one of very few women present at these events, other players frequently interrogated her as to what her role was. This occurred in part because, as a manager, she was not actively playing, but it also occurred because she stood out due to her gender. These individuals needed to define her position in the event because she did not fit their preconceptions about LAN participants.

Nina has encountered similar responses when she visits friends who stream their games online. Recounting one recent experience, she said, "This weekend I was hanging out with some people who play fighting games, and they play at a pretty high level. [. . .] They were streaming their matches online, and they had one of the cameras pointed to the living room. And some person [. . .] out of nowhere they were typing, like, 'Why is there a girl there? What's a girl doing there?'" Nina's friends tried to save her from being interrogated by lying about her gender, but the players they encountered were relentless and kept questioning her presence. Because fighting games have a majority male audience (Lenhart et al., 2008) and play into gender stereotypes about competition and aggressiveness, Nina's gender was contrary to other players' expectations for the fighting game community. Therefore, spectators called her out as a person who did not belong, despite her close relationship to high-level players and a history of playing fighting games herself.

Being treated as unusual is separate from harassment due to its less aggressive, more positive nature. In instances of harassment, players viewed women as a threatening deviation from the norm that was working to feminize games and ruin their existence as a homosocial space for male bonding. Because of this, players deliberately tried to drive them out through aggression and verbal abuse. But as female gamers like Eva related, other male gamers were often genuinely interested in talking with them and hearing more about how they got into games. They were polite and excited to find a female gamer, and they often offered to help rather than to harass. Male gamers' surprise, however, works to reinforce and perpetuate the masculinization of gamer identity by continually questioning women's attempts to take on that identity and enter gaming spaces.

Male gamers' personal experiences, if they are polite and kind to the women around them or if they witness other male gamers helping female players, can also mask core gaming's overall sexism. In 2012, for instance, popular web comic artist Matthew Inman, of *The Oatmeal*, posted a cartoon comparing gaming as a girl to gaming as a guy (Totilo, 2012; Polo, 2012). In each of the two frames of his comic (see figure 3.1), the pictured player makes a mistake (although the female gamer's is far more serious, resulting in the death of her whole team). The players' teams then respond. While the male gamer is shown suffering a torrent of violent, homophobic abuse, the female player is showered with compliments and friend requests. Inman later stated, "Based on [my experience playing Steam for about a year], and primarily on playing *Left4Dead*, I noticed that anytime a girl was playing everyone acts REALLY nice to her (even if she throws a molly at the team and sets us all on fire)" (Polo, 2012).

To many male gamers, this scenario could look accurate; if they generally game with relatively polite players, or "gamers" who embody the stereotypical "lonely nerd desperate for a girlfriend" geek persona, they may have witnessed female gamers receiving compliments and positive feedback even if they make a mistake. However, as Inman realized when female players responded angrily to his comic, this perspective tells only a small part of the story. Overall, it dismisses the significant sexism, especially in the form of rape threats, that women frequently face online. After being informed that "outside of Steam, [it's] still pretty horrible

Figure 3.1. The Female Gamer Panel from Inman's Comic. Polo, S. (2012, April 19). Props: How to apologize on the Internet for a gender-related mishap. The Mary Sue. Retrieved from www.themarysue.com.

for women to play games," Inman apologized for his comic, removed it from his site, and donated a thousand dollars to Women Against Abuse (Totilo, 2012; Polo, 2012). In this circumstance, the truth of the matter came out, and players recognized female gamers' continued struggles. But in many circumstances, players' personal experiences might not reflect this, allowing them to believe that female gamers are actually treated better online than male gamers are. This helps lay a foundation for continued sexism.

Inferential racism and sexism are potentially more insidious and difficult to combat "because they are, at least according to the speaker, *true*" (Phillips, 2015, p. 95). Given the chance, male gamers who react with surprise to female gamers would probably defend their actions by pointing out that men make up the majority audience in most games, and therefore their actions could not be sexist because they reflect the real lack of female gamers. They could also argue that because they are being polite and honestly interested in helping the women they encounter enjoy games, they cannot be seen as sexist. What such arguments ignore is both the real, felt impact being treated as unusual has on female gamers and the ways in which it works to continue perceptions of male "gamers" as normal and any other type of gamer as aberrant.

Offers of help from male gamers also construct female gamers as *in need of help*, a perspective that most of my participants would not agree with. Given the barriers they faced to entry into gaming, almost all interviewees were determined to make it on their own, to cultivate skill and experience with little to no assistance from others. Being offered help just because they identified as female was, in their opinion, deeply patronizing and dismissive of all they had already achieved on their own.

This behavior also demonstrates the unequal nature of power in gaming; men's offers of help came from a privileged position where their skill was assumed, where they could "naturally" expect that they were better at the game than the person to whom they offered aid. This was often not true—participants were frequently offered help by people who turned out to be much worse players than they were. However, the persistent nature of offers of help and how frequently they occurred clearly shows how longstanding discourses that construct men as naturally better at games than women continue to create unequal power relations in core gaming. Men are seen as able to offer help, and women are thought to need it.

"You're Only Doing This for Attention": Fighting the "Girl Gamer" Stereotype

Finally, female gamers had to deal with deeply embedded stereotypes about their motivations for gaming and how they should behave in gaming environments. Drawing on what I will refer to as the "girl gamer" stereotype, players generally assumed one of two things about female gamers: (1) they were casual players who avoided difficult games or (2) they played "men's games," such as first-person shooters, as a way to get attention from male players. As with most stereotypes, community discourses, media coverage, and diverse other sources have naturalized the idea of the "girl gamer" to the extent that gamers see it as true rather than as a stereotype. Even many female players internalized this stereotype, despite the fact that their own behavior combated it. Because of this, the "girl gamer" stereotype is a form of inferential sexism that divides male and female players, and that makes women struggle with their game choices, interactions with male players, and connections to female players.

For example, participants like Bubble found that their game choices were constantly questioned when they discussed video games with others or when they visited a store to purchase games. She said, "A couple weeks ago, I was talking to a coworker about video games off-the-clock. [. . .] Because I am not a man, he was convinced that everything I play is only because my boyfriend plays it and we only play things together, which is totally untrue. That is just one example. Going to a store to buy a game, they always try to steer me towards some cheesy Wii games or something. Not that there's anything wrong with that, but they don't do that to most people. It almost always happens to me." Because she was female and played games, Bubble was associated against her will with the "girl gamer" stereotype, which dictates that her gaming habits must be either related to the men in her life or strictly casual.

Feather felt similarly judged when she entered a gaming store, saying, "I always worry that I have that look that I'm not here for me, I'm here for someone else, and I'm going to add a game for me on top." Feather played diverse styles of games but was always concerned that video game clerks and other players would see her purchase of shooting games or other core genres as gifts for her boyfriend and her purchase of Nintendo DS games like *Cooking Mama* or other casual titles as games for her. In reality, both varieties of game were for her, but she felt the pressure of stereotypes and assumptions about her gaming habits very deeply.

Others even avoided specific types of games because of "girl gamer" stereotypes. Laine, for instance, avoided playing *The Sims* because of how other players viewed it. In *The Sims* series, players create characters and control them through their daily activities, taking care of their needs, such as housing, food, and social interaction. Although *The Sims* is an extremely popular game series, players viewed it as both casual and feminine, a virtual dollhouse rather than a real game. In Laine's college gaming club, men outnumbered women, a gap that the men jokingly attributed to the fact that "*Sims* is not a competitive game" (Laine, interview 1). Therefore, women who played *The Sims*, and who others assumed *only* played *The Sims*, did not need to join a group where they could find multiplayer opponents. This association of female gamers with series like *The Sims* minimized women's importance to core gaming communities and marked them as "girl gamers" rather than "*real* gamers."

Of course, the very idea that there is one solitary definition of a "real" (read: core) gamer is part of the problem, and by relating my participants' concerns about how others would interpret them, I do not mean to imply that casual forms of play are invalid. Indeed, existing research shows how casual games have their own business models (Nieborg, 2015; Kerr, 2017) and developer expectations (Chess, 2017; Kuittinen et al., 2007; Kultima, 2009), they fulfill a variety of player needs (e.g., Anable, 2018; Consalvo and Begy, 2015; Juul, 2010; Kuittinen et al., 2007), and they even develop their own cultures and communities (Consalvo, 2009). On top of that, casual games are *fun*, and their convenient on-the-go nature makes them easy to fit into small gaps of time when core games would not do. This is why I have played a frankly ridiculous number of levels in *Candy Crush Saga* (over thirty-seven hundred, at the time of this writing); I enjoy fitting *Candy Crush* in between meetings, while on a flight, while waiting for a friend at a coffee shop, and many other times and places when it can provide me a quick break. At the same time, my participants' ambivalent relationship to casual games shows how the casual/female and core/male divide affects female players' participation in gaming spaces.

My participants worked hard to develop a core gamer identity and the corresponding gaming capital needed to defend that position. Gaming capital, as defined by Mia Consalvo (2009), refers to "the form of cultural capital accrued to gamers in part as they gain knowledge about games and game culture, but more importantly, as they share that knowledge with others" (p. 51). My participants, as core gamers, had played extensively, had knowledge of many different types of games, and had solid gaming skills to back this knowledge up. They wanted to be able to use this capital freely to connect with other players and to establish themselves as members of the core community; this was made more difficult when other players assumed they only played casual games. For this reason, women often wanted to distance themselves from associations with casual.

This was also true because, as core gamers, they had internalized many of the value judgments involved in the core/casual debate. As described earlier, core and casual are not just set up as different offerings; rather, industrial and player discourses try to establish a hierarchy whereby core is validated and casual is dismissed. Therefore, female players who were deeply invested in gaming had been exposed to many negative opinions about casual games, which were also then associated with casual female players. Rather than working to change the connotations of casual games towards more positive ones, however, my interviewees instead tended to disassociate themselves from casual games, to protect their gamer identity on an individual level. This involved forefronting their core play and experience, avoiding casual or feminized games like *The Sims*, or feeling guilty when they did opt to play casual games. They often themselves dismissed casual games as "stupid" or "mindless" even as they expressed enjoyment in playing them. Thus, their core gamer identity encouraged them to buy into limited notions of which games were "good," while their attempts to avoid being stereotyped themselves provided only short-term relief and required them to continually manage how others saw them. Increasing the acceptance of casual games more generally would allow diverse players to enter gaming spaces more comfortably, but interviewees did not seem to believe this was possible, demonstrating the difficulty in addressing and undermining inferential sexism.

When female players broke expectations and played core games, they faced a secondary set of challenges—specifically, the expectation that they were playing those games to meet men and that they would therefore flirt with other players. Interviewees described this as a barrier to their full participation in gaming because it continued to mark them as different than other gamers, it meant their skills were constantly questioned, and it made it harder to connect with other women. As Vickie argued, "I feel that I should be represented as just a normal gamer too. [. . .] You'll hear some people talk about like . . . that was their impression of female gamers, that they always got something for free, or they did it to get help . . . I always tried to avoid having that connotation." Being a female gamer changed the terms according to which one participated in the gaming community and required women to work harder to be accepted.

This problem was complicated by the fact that women honestly did feel as if many female players bought into the "girl gamer" stereotype, opting to use their gender to get attention and to succeed in the game. Because this subset of women was happily invested in being "girl gamers," the stereotype persisted in the community and was also applied to women who did not want this identity. Feather illustrated this when she said, "I've had friends who are much better looking than I who play video games much more than I, and they fall into that 'gamer-girl' category very easily where they become very much like, 'I'm a girl and I'm a gamer and get out of my way, I'm gonna use my sexuality to get ahead in games.' I'm not into that but I know that if I get too much like, 'Oh video games, video games, video games . . .' it's going to be sort of like, 'Oh well, she's cute and she's talking about video games; she's just trying to get guys.'" Because men encountered some women who did want attention rather than just the chance to play games, they assumed that Feather wanted the same thing, grouping all women into a single entity rather than recognizing their diverse motivations to play.

This also put women in a position where their in-game successes were questioned. Other gamers were often not sure if a female player was skilled or if she, as the "girl gamer" stereotype suggested, had used her gender to get help and advance that way. Because of this, women had to work extra hard to demonstrate that they were good players. Elizabeth stated, with great frustration, "You also have to show other people you're good, because a lot of girls use their gender as an advantage, and they like, send fake pictures or real pictures to guys to get things in the game, and therefore they're highly geared and stuff like that. It pissed people like me off, cause it's like, I actually work for what I have, I don't just . . . fling myself at a bunch of guys." While players of all types have their skill questioned in regular trash-talk, women also faced a deeply embedded stereotype that linked their success in games to the amount of assistance they received from men, even when this was not actually the case.

Again, participants were demonstrating clear value judgments about other players and about the "right" way to game. Rather than seeing flirtation as a legitimate strategy to get ahead in a male-dominated space, women looked down on players who employed this tactic. This is probably the case because of the work my participants had put into being independent and proving themselves; they had made it and therefore felt other players could do the same. They also disliked how other players' actions reflected on female gamers more generally. At the same time, these attitudes displayed limited, meritocratic ways of looking at games. As game researcher Christopher Paul (2018) explains, "Players are routinely taught, through both the things they do in play and the stories in which they participate, that they earn their success because they started from the bottom and have risen to the top through the quality of their efforts" (p. 61). He and digital media scholar Lisa Nakamura (2017) point out, however, that these narratives are not true; games are *not* a meritocracy, and marginalized players must work much harder than "gamers" do in order to be accepted. As a solution, Paul suggests that developers move away from meritocratic game designs and diversify how players can succeed in games. He also recognizes a need for players, game writers, and more to avoid marginalizing games that do things differently, as this diversification is the only thing that can outline new potential ways to play and to structure game culture. To this, I would add that gamers should avoid marginalizing other players who engage with games in different ways, as doing so forecloses on players' ability to develop diverse play styles. Does this mean that all female players should use flirtation as a means to get ahead in gaming? Obviously not. But it does mean that players should be free to try out different approaches without risk of censure from their fellow gamers, especially those who are already fighting their own marginalization.

Such an approach would also help solve the last "girl gamer" issue my participants grappled with: the fact that it made them more suspicious of other female gamers. While interviewees generally wanted to befriend other female players, they also internalized the community's overall perception of "girl gamers." They were afraid that women they tried to befriend would be among the group that embraced the "girl gamer" stereotype and that they would therefore have very different goals while gaming. When Elayne attended LAN events, for instance, she often wanted to talk with the few other women present. However, she found herself questioning their motives for attending, just as male gamers questioned hers. She said, "You're just not sure if they're going to use their femininity to try and, I guess, manipulate people around them. [. . .] I really do wish it was easier for me to approach another girl at [a LAN event] and for it to just be cool." Rather than being able to openly associate with her fellow female gamers, the "girl gamer" stereotype and the possibility that they were at the event for men, rather than for the games, interfered with Elayne's ability to interact easily with other women.

Participants also mentioned that "girl gamers" were often not happy to see other women playing. If, as the stereotype argues, these women were actually gaming to meet men, the presence of other female players would disrupt this goal, splitting men's attention between multiple women rather than allowing them to focus entirely on one. To quote participant DT, "A small minority of girls who really like attention probably don't like the fact that maybe two girls in a party would sort of take the attention away from them." The presence of other women would also make the "girl gamer" less unique, and therefore less special. Because of this, participants felt, some "girl gamers" were very rude to other women, rather than welcoming them into the community as colleagues.

These negative interactions, or even the possibility of them, made it difficult to form social connections between female gamers, a problem games researcher Lina Eklund (2011) noticed in her study of *World of Warcraft* players. Although Eklund intended to find women to interview via snowball sampling, where players she talked to would introduce her to other female gamers they knew, very few women knew others who played. In reflecting on my recruitment for this project, I realized that I faced the same issue. I recruited a small number of participants through my social network, but each was primarily introduced to me through a male, rather than female, friend. Furthermore, I asked each participant at the end of our interview whether they had any female gamer friends who might also want to participate in the study; most did not have any suggestions. Those who did recommend a friend generally only suggested one. This lack of connection between female gamers is probably due to many factors, such as women's tendency to hide their gender to avoid harassment, but it may also be related to the fractious relationship female gamers have with one another due to the "girl gamer" stereotype.

Like other inferentially sexist elements of gaming culture, the "girl gamer" stereotype persists because players can generally point to one or two instances where it has been true. Many players know or have at least encountered a female player who is happy to take extra help from male players and to play up their gender identity as a means for getting attention. They have also been in situations where other female players were dismissive of or outright hostile to them. Although this may not have been motivated by their gender—the other player may just be an aggressive person—the perceived implication that the female opponent resented losing men's attention to another woman acted as support for the "girl gamer" stereotype. Anecdotes about these incidents perpetuate notions of women as catty, competitive with each other, and in gaming as a means for reaching men. Compounded with extensive discourses that outline the correct way for core gamers to play and succeed, these stereotypes then have extensive impacts on players and their interactions with one another.

Conclusions

Participants clearly self-defined as gamers and possessed many of the characteristics that are associated with core, such as extensive knowledge of games and a long history playing them. Despite this, they encountered and struggled to navigate a wide variety of forces that made their desired gamer identity very difficult to embody. Furthermore, the challenges they describe are those faced by women who have seen the potential downsides of gaming and who have opted to play games regardless. These women had already overcome many of the social and ideological forces separating them from technology and gaming; that they had more to face shows how, despite increased attention to diverse audiences, "gamer" identity and core video games themselves retain many expectations of masculinity. These are policed through both overt and inferential sexism.

Specifically, limited representations of women in games, the direct harassment of women in gaming spaces, developers' use of stereotypical gender roles, players' continuous surprise at encountering female players, and "girl gamer" stereotypes all helped link core gamer identity firmly to masculinity. For instance, "girl gamer" stereotypes spread the idea that women are in the gaming community to get attention from men. Therefore, their investment in games appears fake, barring them from fully taking on the identity of a gamer. Because core characteristics include long histories with games, deep investment in playing and learning about them, and high levels of skill, the idea that women are only gaming to meet men undermines their ability to develop these characteristics and the likelihood of others taking them seriously when they do. While men are always presumed to be gaming because they want to, women's reasons for gaming are questioned or outright dismissed. Their ability to be just a regular gamer like anyone else is limited.

Overt and inferential sexism in games also encourages women to accept core gaming's limitations: to take on masculinized subject positions if they want to receive the full attention of the gaming industry, to accept or ignore sexist depictions, and to mistrust other female players. In many circumstances, interviewees at least partially bought into the very notions that they found so damaging, such as when they justified and explained away sexist character depictions based on the notion that men are a numerically larger part of the gaming audience or when they judged players who were not playing in the "right" way. This also shows in how they struggled to connect with other female gamers, questioning their motives for being in gaming spaces.

Collectively, the divide between gender and gamer identities made female players very defensive about their gaming habits. Although cultural studies scholar Janice Radway was addressing romance reading, a feminized pursuit, her participants and those of this study shared feelings of guilt about their choice of hobby. Radway's readers often had to defend their purchases to spouses or children, as well as to themselves, due to the cultural conception that romances were trashy or a waste of time. Similarly, female gamers struggled with the cultural construction of games as pure entertainment and as masculinized. They felt guilt about their time spent gaming, which was seen as unproductive, and the need to defend their hobby in the face of cultural norms that indicated they should not be playing. For instance, Bubble played games at night to hide them from her parents, who felt they were a waste of time. Others faced social pressure from friends or colleagues to avoid wasting time or to avoid masculine pursuits. The many forces working to maintain core games' masculinization complicated female players' relationship with them and meant that their enjoyment of games was heavily mixed with doubt, insecurity, or a need for concealment.

In addition, the interactive and networked nature of games means that female gamers had to defend themselves not only to family and friends but also to strangers who doubted that they could be "real gamers." This put participants under intense pressure to prove themselves, especially if they were up against specifically gendered roles. For instance, in group raids in *WoW*, where a team works together to beat a high-level opponent, players divide among three overall types of characters—tanks, damage-per-second or DPS, and healing. Tanks are heavily armored characters that attract the attention of the boss opponent and absorb damage while other players attack. DPS characters try to damage the boss as much as possible, decreasing its health. Healers keep the other players on their team alive by casting spells that give them health points back after they have been hurt. Although anyone can play all three types of characters, tanks and healers in particular have associated gender stereotypes, where players expect tanks to be men and healers to be women (Condis, 2018; Eklund, 2011; Nardi, 2010; Ratan et al., 2015). When Vickie played a tanking class in *WoW*, she said, "There were some times that people were surprised that there was a girl being a tank. So, it—I didn't feel like I had to do better to prove that I could do better, but I felt like I had to do better to be like . . . 'F you, girls can be better at this' kinda thing." Vickie felt she had to prove that *women* could be good in a stereotypically male position within the game, rather than just feeling that she had to prove *she* was good. Alissa similarly expressed insecurity about her *WoW* play, stating, "I think as a female there's a lot of pressure to make sure that you don't mess up. Like in *WoW*, I was a class where I was supposed to do a lot of damage, and I was always conscious of trying to outperform the guys in my group because I wanted to make sure that they thought I was an asset that helped out the team." Other players felt they had to defend their knowledge about games, their long history of playing, or even the types of games they played to avoid reflecting badly on women in general, for example, avoiding *The Sims* in order to avoid playing into stereotypes, as Laine did.

Interviewees saw little to no benefit from being female. Rather, they viewed it as a severe detriment, both because other players expect them to fail and because they fear that any failure on their part will continue to play into stereotypes that women only succeed in games due to help from men. Elayne argued that when players know a gamer is female, "You're now labeled and you're 'outed' and everything you do will be scrutinized twice as hard, and every mistake you make, you'll get criticized for it even more, and it's just, there's no benefits to being honest about your gender." The fact that women are still not allowed to just be gamers keeps them from simply being able to play and only worry about their own success or failure. Because "female gamers" are separated from "gamers" in general, their individual preferences and choices end up reflecting on all female players.

Participants' experiences clearly show that core aspects of game culture are still a retrograde preserve for prefeminist constructions of gender, in which the inequality of men and women is largely taken for granted. Female players are consistently expected to be worse at games, to need help from male players, and to be gaming as a means for getting attention, rather than because they truly enjoy the hobby. To combat this, they often have to work harder than their male colleagues, as being among the best players is one of the few options they have for undermining negative stereotypes. This not only makes women's equality into a trophy to be earned rather than an inherent right (Nakamura, 2017), but it also is a somewhat unsustainable strategy, and many female gamers end up changing their gaming habits or leaving gaming entirely when being the best takes too much time or energy.

Overall, interviews showed that concerns that games are a zero-sum industry and that the rise of casual games will undermine men's control over gaming culture are largely unfounded. Although games have been in the casualized era for a decade, the discourses and ideologies that construct core as masculinized are still strongly in force. The masculinization of core, and the way it plays out in players' interactions with each other and with gaming culture, has allowed video games to serve as a bastion of misogyny largely untouched by the gains of feminism. In many elements of gaming, the inequality of men and women is protected and preserved.

Also important to this conversation, however, is how or why marginalized individuals still choose to play games and strive to identify as gamers given the many problems they have outlined above. When they have to struggle to navigate the gap between core gamer and gender identity, why would women still want to be gamers? And, more importantly, how can their choice to do so, to identify with this identity that is clearly marked as not for them, indicate means for undermining and changing the core/margins relationship in a masculinized space? Accepting that games are deeply exclusionary, women's choice to engage with them anyway is a seemingly paradoxical, self-damaging one. But understanding what women get out of gaming, as well as what strategies they use to manage their gaming experiences and protect themselves from the impacts of sexism, can begin to break down the barriers of core and centralize the experiences of women as important to gaming culture. More importantly, it can illuminate pathways along which damaging hegemonic power structures can be undermined and altered in masculinized media spaces.

4

Already Core

Women's Entry into Gaming

Despite all the indications that core gaming was not for them, women were still able to find many pleasures both in games themselves and in the communities surrounding them. This is not surprising, as past research has outlined numerous factors, in both casual and core games, that make them fun for male and female players alike (e.g., Jenkins, 1998; Kennedy, 2006; Kerr, 2003; Taylor, 2003; Nardi, 2010). Thus, this chapter moves beyond the simple, easy-to-prove idea that women can enjoy core gaming and demonstrates how they do so, providing a more nuanced picture of their strategies for prioritizing the elements of games they enjoy while dismissing those that are troublesome. It also indicates that women's enjoyment of gaming spaces can serve as a form of incipient feminism, in that it diversifies conceptions of what women are and how they behave.

Further, women's pleasure in gaming could work to start bridging the gap between core and casual. In their interviews, female gamers demonstrate how women adopt a proactive identity fluidity that allows them to prioritize their positions as women, gamers, and female gamers in varying ways dependent on the demands of the situation they are managing at the time. These flexible repertoires of meaning making help them overcome the dominant discourses marking them as abnormal for their involvement in gaming and also allow them to connect to elements of core. Extensive histories in gaming, skill at playing, and affinity for games are some of the many factors women draw on to read pleasure into video game play.

Many of these are characteristics they also share with male gamers. That is, male and female gamers can be seen as part of a shared interpretive community. Literary theorist Stanley Fish, who pioneered the concept of interpretive communities in 1976, defines them as "made up of those who share interpretive strategies not for reading (in the conventional sense) but for writing texts, for constituting their properties and assigning their intentions. In other words, these strategies exist prior to the act of reading and therefore determine the shape of what is read rather than, as is usually assumed, the other way around" (Fish, 1976, p. 483). Put more simply, members of interpretive communities share backgrounds and reading strategies that allow them to interact with a text and take from it the same meaning as other members of their interpretive community. Individuals who are not part of that interpretive community, or who are members of other interpretive communities, will apply different strategies to the act of reading a text and will therefore take from it different meanings. Fish also argued that interpretive communities are not inherently stable, but rather change over time, as the interpretive strategies and shared backgrounds they are based on also change.

Whereas early gaming research assumed that members of the same gender would interpret a game or situation in the same way, and that men and women would look for different aspects in their games, the theory of interpretive communities recognizes the power of readers to interpret texts similarly to those who share their interpretive strategies and differently from those who do not. Gender is thus not a determinant factor; players who have immersed themselves in gaming history and discourses around what games mean frequently possess similar interpretive strategies despite differences in gender, racial, or sexual identity, allowing them to read enjoyable meaning into texts and spaces that appear offensive or discriminatory to outsiders. For instance, while many women find it off-putting to see only sexualized female portrayals in games, it is still possible for at least some women to read against these conventions and find their own enjoyment, especially if the game offers other interesting content.

This is clear in media scholar Henry Jenkins's (1998) interviews with self-proclaimed "game grrlz," or female gamers who drew on the ethos of the Riot Grrl movement as a means for undermining gender expectations in gaming and in broader culture as well. These women modified traditionally masculine games to include female avatars or created female-friendly gaming groups that competed with male players on their own virtual "turf" through online multiplayer games. Rather than seeing the prevalence of objectified female characters as a barrier, the game grrlz made this trend part of their fun, overemphasizing femininity in order to subvert stereotypes. They used sexualized avatars and hyperfeminine screen names to rub in their victories over male opponents, claiming power for women by demonstrating that they could succeed in a male space. Players read enjoyment into games through competition, aggression, and dominance, despite the fact that these are typically masculine traits.

In other words, these gamers display what film theorist Linda Williams (1984) refers to as the "multiple and continuous female identity capable of fluidly shifting" between different identities and identifications (p. 9). In her analysis of the film *Stella Dallas*, Williams demonstrates how media address women in contradictory and fragmented ways, encouraging them to identify with many characters at once rather than offering a single, coherent subject position they can embrace fully. Because of this, she argues, women develop a specifically female reading competence based on flexible identification. More recent research demonstrates that the ability to identify with characters in multiple and diverse ways is not limited to women, but rather is embraced by many individuals who have been left out of media representations. Adrienne Shaw (2014b), for instance, provides excellent examples of marginalized gamers' diverse strategies for reading pleasure into texts that do not interpellate them through direct representation.

At the same time, identifying in multiple and fragmented ways, rather than through a single, coherent subject position, remains a popular strategy among female gamers. The game grrlz, for instance, flexibly prioritized their gamer identity and some aspects of their gender identity such as feminine appearances, to interpret texts in a female/gamer way and to perform this joint identity. At other times, players employ only their gender identity, or only their gamer identity, to read games in different ways and navigate gaming spaces.

This ability to prioritize different forms of identification indicates that the way forward for gaming may not be to offer distinct female and male subject positions, or "men's games" and "women's games," but rather to provide a diversity of positions from which players can explore different ways of being and experience identities and stories that are not their own. This aligns with women's earlier suggestions regarding well-crafted characters, which they felt would draw in both male and female players. A greater emphasis on the fun of embodying different identities and subject positions could open up gaming more broadly. It can also work to undermine limiting notions of gender identity more generally, illustrating how gender is a factor, but not the deciding factor, in how audiences relate to texts and characters.

Finally, women's interpretive repertoires and their ability to find pleasure in gaming also illuminate the pathway by which hegemonic notions of gaming can be subverted and altered towards a more equitable power structure. Although core is used to police existing hierarchies in gaming, women's detailed interpretive strategies show how they are, in many ways, already part of gaming's center. Emphasizing this in future discourses around gaming could help build a conscious affinity between "gamers" and others. In fact, women's ability to see themselves as gamers already allows them to feel connected to core game communities and culture even as they battle against marginalization.

The Pleasures of Gaming and Game Preferences

When interviewees discussed the aspects of gaming women enjoyed, it quickly became obvious that players' preferences were as diverse as their concerns about gaming and that most were not specifically gendered. For instance, women listed a wide variety of genres they enjoyed playing. These ranged from the heavily masculinized first-person shooter (FPS) genre, where players engage in firearms battles with opponents, to role-playing games (RPGs) like *World of Warcraft* or *Final Fantasy*, where players take on the role of an in-game character and guide them through a narrative storyline or a set of missions or quests. Even within a single genre, participants enjoyed an array of games. For instance, within the RPG genre, players enjoyed both games that had set characters with established backstories and identities and games that allow players to create their own character. Puzzle games, action-adventure games, fighting games, and more were all favorites of different interviewees. Players also turned to different games depending on what they were trying to accomplish with each individual play session.

The diversity of these preferences and the pleasures women found in games show that female gamers' play habits are deeply individual and contextual, reflective both of the gamer's play style and of the reasons they chose to play a game in the first place. Although the factors they enjoyed ranged from beautiful graphics to games that were critically acclaimed, participants expressed five main pleasures they found in gaming: sociability, relaxation, identity play, character customization, and competition. Past research explores all of these (e.g., Bartle, 1996, 2004; Yee, 2014), but the way women talk about them deserves further analysis and nuance. As new media researchers Jennifer Jenson and Suzanne de Castell (2010) demonstrate, women's reasons for play are "always negotiable [and] context dependent" (p. 56). At the same time, many conversations around gaming still attribute different preferences to male and female players, essentializing them according to their gender. Other dominant narratives assume that women are not naturally inclined to game and "must be specifically courted with 'female-friendly' games" (Bergstrom, 2019, p. 842). This perspective even occurs in casual game spaces, despite their greater openness to women (Chess, 2017). Therefore, further attention to the context and motivations for women's engagement with games, especially core games, is merited.

Assessing how women relate their gender to their gaming, and how they do not, shows unexpected results. Some feminine-gendered qualities like sociability were not actually related to women's gender identity, but rather their personal desires. Other qualities that are generally considered masculine, like competition, interviewees connected strongly to their gender identity. A deeper analysis of what women enjoy about gaming presents a multifaceted and ever-changing view of femininity, masculinity, and possible combinations of the two.

Sociability

One often-cited pleasure of gaming is its sociability. Not only are games an entertainment form that can be played with others in person, but they are frequently networked, allowing players to meet and interact with people from around the world. Therefore, they provide a platform through which individuals can connect. Researchers have extensively recognized the appeal of games' social aspects in the past and often consider sociability particularly appealing to female players (e.g., Graner Ray, 2004; Kafai, 1998; Laurel, 1998; Nardi, 2010; Taylor, 2003). This relates to longstanding gender stereotypes that posit women as social and relationship oriented. However, sociability can be an appealing aspect of traditionally masculine games as well as those targeted directly toward women.

In their ethnographic observations of *World of Warcraft* and *Everquest*, game studies scholars T. L. Taylor (2003) and Bonnie Nardi (2010) both found that the ability to interact with other players draws women to massively multiplayer online games (MMOs). The content structure of many MMOs encourages the development of social ties, as the games' higher levels consist of group-based missions called raids. *World of Warcraft* originally required groups of up to forty people to complete endgame content. Although that number has decreased to a minimum of ten through the game's expansions, the group structure of raids still represents a significant push for players to form social and working bonds. A player who lacks an in-game social network will never be one of the best and will also miss out on significant elements of the game's content.

Subsequent survey studies have found a multitude of reasons why players enjoy sociability in games. Some players keep in touch with real-life friends and family, playing with them across long distances to maintain offline relationships (Hussain and Griffiths, 2008) or using games as a shared interest in romantic relationships (Williams et al., 2009). Others use online friends to help them cope with careers or life situations that require them to move frequently, stating, "Online friends are always in the same place" (Hussain and Griffiths, 2008, p. 49). Games can also be a means for players to meet other people with similar interests, a particularly relevant element for women who frequently do not know other female players in person (Taylor, 2003; Axelsson and Regan, 2006; Sherry et al., 2006; Eklund, 2011). Through these various approaches, gamers use video games to account for social needs that offline interaction may not meet (Hussain and Griffiths, 2008).

Many of my participants appreciated the social aspects of gaming, as previous research would suggest. However, their specific approaches to sociability indicate that this preference is not a "natural" extension of gender, but rather a careful management of relationships and personal preferences. For some participants, games were useful at developing what social theorists refer to as "bridging ties" (Putnam, 2000, pp. 22–24), or broad-based connections across diverse social or geographic sectors. In other words, games helped interviewees meet people they would not have met in their day-to-day lives. This helped them manage social environments that they did not fit into or form new affinity groups based on shared interests rather than geographical similarities, among other things.

When Elayne first moved to college, she felt very disconnected from her new environment and found online games to be a saving grace for her social life. In her own words, "I graduated early from high school to go to Texas Tech, which is . . . yeah, well I was only there for a semester, but long story short, I was suddenly cut off from all my friends, and I guess I kind of found solace in *WoW*. [. . .] like I wasn't even living on campus because my parents moved with me, and so I literally had no one in Lubbock." While some might argue that turning to online games hindered her social life and her transition to college, Elayne's choice to leave Texas Tech after only one semester and her description of Lubbock, Texas, as "the most horrible, isolating place in West Texas" reveals the depth of loneliness she was dealing with. In this situation, being able to meet and play with friends online helped her cope. Other participants related less extreme experiences but found games equally useful for meeting new people. Online games were particularly helpful in developing bridging ties with others who shared their interest in video games. As Eva said, "In real life, I don't know anyone who plays video games. [. . .] For me to, you know, play with other people who share my interest in gaming, it was amazing. That's why I play co-op games or multiplayer games and everything like that now." Online, Eva could seek out people on the basis of a game they both enjoyed or even a shared love of games in general, rather than hoping people she met in her day-to-day life would happen to like games as well.

Players even found games particularly useful for meeting others because, they argued, games could overcome geographic distance and even some divides based on gender, race, or class. Katie Tyler compared online games to attending a club around a common interest, but celebrated the fact that "you meet people from all over the world: different countries, different states. And a lot of them are unique people who I don't feel that you'd meet otherwise because everyone is so different." She had even met up with some gaming friends in real life, translating online interactions into offline connections with people around the world.

Elizabeth elaborated further by pointing out how online games sometimes lowered barriers to connection by making the game itself the focus of early interactions. She argued, "It's just like . . . nice to be able to connect on that level and not have it really matter what you look like or, you know, how much money you earn or anything. It's just, 'hey, you enjoy this game, hey I enjoy this game too,' and you just get to bond and connect over that." Although some players have tells that can give away their gender, such as men's tendency to move their avatars more frequently than women do (Martey et al., 2014),[1] many of these are subtle. Without obvious gender cues (or class or race cues), players like Elizabeth felt that they could connect to people who might not otherwise reach out to them.[2]

Other participants saw games as a way to improve their existing relationships, through greater bonding (Putnam, 2000). Many described a preference for playing with family members or existing friends in person. They even adapted single-player games into group experiences, having one person play while others looked out for hidden passageways or helped develop strategies for beating difficult sections. Katie Tyler related an anecdote about playing the *Legend of Zelda* series with a friend, in which "one would read a guide if we got stuck and one would play, and then we would trade off playing so that way we both got to do it," while Jutte said that some of her best memories growing up came when her father played a game as she and her sister helped him find secret items or teased him when he missed them.

Chianna, who is a special education teacher, felt that party-style games, like those on the Wii, could contribute to important family bonding. Although many families no doubt still play board games, Chianna saw digital versions of these as more updated ways to encourage family time, something she argued was essential to child development. Other players simply saw games as more fun when played with others, because they simultaneously got to enjoy the games they loved and spend time with people they cared about. Helix put it quite simply: "It's a much more fun way to spend time with friends or my husband than just watching TV—there's more interaction."

The ability to increase connections and social interaction was a key pleasure of gaming, one that past research has recognized and one that players consistently pointed out as a reason to game. After all, competing against a computer character is often different from playing against another individual. Computers frequently have patterns that players can figure out and combat, while another human is more likely to change their strategy regularly and present a different type of challenge. Furthermore, the ability to chat with others about the progress of the game, both in competitive and in cooperative situations, is something a computer-controlled avatar cannot offer.

At the same time, gender does not determine how players will react to games or what they will enjoy, in contrast to the expectations of early game studies work and stereotypes that women are "naturally" more social than men (e.g., Cassell and Jenkins, 1998; Graner Ray, 2004; Kafai, 1996; Laurel, 1998). Depending on their individual needs and preferences, players were able to select games that met their desires for sociability, whether that was to connect to new people they might not have met otherwise or to deepen their existing connection with family and friends. Players who wanted to make new friends and connections largely played online, while players who wanted to bond more deeply with people they already knew could choose among single-player games, in-person multiplayer, and online multiplayer, as they could manipulate any of these forms into a social experience. Rather than simply seeking the ability to talk to others, or sociability for sociability's sake, they evaluated what they were looking for and how best to accomplish it. Unfortunately, gender-based stereotypes can still hold power, and greater attention to women's differences, and their frequent similarities to male players as well, is needed to continue undermining these.

It is true that sociability, especially in online circumstances, can default to trash-talk and harassment. Despite this, female gamers often found more benefits than downsides to social play, especially as they became more practiced at choosing the right environments and games for them over time. For instance, players who entered gaming spaces with friends were sometimes able to dismiss harassment more effectively than those who played alone. Therefore, players were willing to participate in a balancing act, entering into sexist spaces if the pleasures also available there were worth pursuing or if they had a means to defend themselves against negativity.

Relaxation and Control of Play Style and Pace

At other times, players sought out individual play and single-player games, which let them engage with a game in their own time or way. This increased their relaxation and gave them a feeling of control over their environment. Emily, for instance, recognized her preferred play style as a slower one. She said, "I like to go around and collect all the stuff and explore, and I know my brother sometimes is like, 'Who cares about that? You just have to get to the end of the game as quickly as possible. Then you can say you beat it and you won.' And I don't necessarily play [games] to win them as fast as possible but to kind of have fun playing them and hopefully beat it." At the same time, she felt she was less of a completionist than her fiancé and some of his friends, who would play through a game multiple times in order to master all its elements. Emily wanted to explore and find some of the game's secrets and side quests, but she rarely went back to a game she had already beaten. Single-player games allowed her to proceed how she wanted to, without pressure from friends or family members who approached games in different ways.

This lack of pressure also meant that many interviewees turned to single-player games when they wanted to relax or detox after a day of work. Individual play allowed them to fit gaming in between their other responsibilities, like work or school, without pressure to keep up with friends. For example, Alissa found that once she graduated from college with an art degree, she struggled to balance gaming with a hospitality job, her continued desire to pursue art, and a social life. Because of this, she moved away from games like *World of Warcraft*, where she had been part of a high-level raiding guild, due to the time these games demanded. Instead, she switched to a more individual approach. At the time of her interview, Alissa was playing through *Diablo III*, an action role-playing game that had a multiplayer component. She proceeded through the game primarily on her own, with friends from *WoW* joining her occasionally. However, she refused to let them hurry her through the game or demand more regular play than she could commit to. In this way, she used individual play to relax, to stay in touch with friends, and to keep gaming in her life despite her changing circumstances. Many other players also related enjoying the benefits of playing puzzles, completing quests, or pursuing in-game goals according to their own schedule.

Interviewees did not relate their desire for relaxing play specifically to gender, but given that women still face extensive challenges in balancing a career with the pressures of a second shift of housework (Hochschild and Machung, 1989; Schulte, 2014), they may find the ability to control their entertainment and environment especially significant. In this context, solo game play can be seen as a form of self-care that lets female gamers explore a game in the way they find most relaxing; they set the conditions for their own enjoyment. As with Janice Radway's romance readers, individual play is a means for female gamers to mark out space for themselves or to manage outside demands on their time. Radway found that the act of reading a romance novel mattered to her participants because it allowed them a mental escape. Because the women she spoke with primarily worked in their homes, taking care of their families and prioritizing the needs of others, they sometimes found it difficult to rest or recharge. A book served as a temporary shield from the things they had to get done and allowed them to focus on themselves. Similarly, and despite core games' masculinized status, my participants were able to mobilize game play as a means for relaxation and escape.

Recognizing the pleasures of solo game play is significant, as many past research studies have focused primarily on online or multiplayer gaming. These approaches may miss players who prefer single-player formats or who only play this way; I myself largely game on my own and have noticed that my reasons for doing so (e.g., controlling my progress and relaxing) are not always emphasized in existing work. This also matters because there is evidence that women's game play is more private than men's; although large-scale surveys indicate that women make up a significant portion of the gaming audience or that they game regularly (e.g., Lenhart et al., 2008; ESA 2004–2019), research in public gaming spaces like LANs and e-sports competitions finds that these spaces are dominated by men (Bryce and Rutter, 2002, 2003; Jansz and Martens, 2005; Taylor, Jenson, and de Castell, 2009; Taylor, 2012). Because public spaces are easier for researchers to access, they have been studied more than private gaming, which can hide women's presence and participation in gaming culture. This can then allow ideas of core as masculinized to perpetuate. Attention to the pleasures inherent in solo play can help address the gap between the masculinization of games' core and the deeply invested nature of female gamers. Despite the many sexist factors in core gaming, women do find a great deal to enjoy; these pleasures are just not always visible.

Transportation and Identity Play

Video games also offer numerous possible pleasures in exploring the feelings and experiences of another person or entity through a narrative storyline (Taylor, 2003; Frasca, 2003; Bryant and Davies, 2006; Shapiro, Pena-Herborn, and Hancock, 2006; Squire, 2006; Vorderer et al., 2006; Simons, 2007; Dubbelman, 2011; Gee, 2011). Narrative theorists consistently show that immersing oneself in a story allows one to experience situations from a new perspective (Simons, 2007). This is particularly relevant to the study of video games due to their unique interactive capabilities. Not only do video games create in-depth worlds and storylines for players to explore, but they also allow a high level of freedom regarding the particular order or means for that exploration (Frasca, 2003, p. 227). The openness of many video game worlds means that the player is not so much experiencing a story as they are living it in real time; they may therefore identify heavily with their character's experiences and emotions. Furthermore, video games can offer players fantasy scenarios, wherein they can battle dragons and ogres, save princesses, and more, but games can also offer facsimiles of real-life scenarios (Gee, 2011). For instance, although it relies on many damaging stereotypes, the *Grand Theft Auto* series may allow upper-class gamers to experience some of the challenges of low-income neighborhoods, while games like *Civilization* can introduce players to some of the many factors affecting national and international politics and historical development (Squire, 2006).

There are, of course, limitations to this; as digital media scholar Lisa Nakamura (2002) indicates through her concept of identity tourism, players who take on different identities in online or game spaces generally do not experience the liabilities of embodying that identity in offline spaces, and they often embody their new role in very stereotypical ways. This can reaffirm, rather than combat, inequality. These limitations are important to keep in mind, especially given players' concerns that video game characters were often flat or underdeveloped. These kinds of token characters may very well be stereotypical.

That being said, my interviews reflected existing work on narrative exploration, as players enjoyed experiencing storylines and environments that would be impossible in the real world, due to their fantasy or science-fiction nature, as well as trying to understand different characters, their motivations, and the choices they made within games. This also affected the games they chose, with many turning to single-player games for their deeper storylines. For instance, when Misty chose RPGs over FPS games, her overall favorite genre, she did so because she was looking to explore a narrative, while FPS games fulfilled her need for competition. She said, "I like the story and depth of RPGs. People always talk about the immersive quality of them, which I guess is kind of what it is. I can suspend reality for a bit and get really involved with the characters." Story-driven games allowed players to experience other perspectives on the world as well. Buttsvard described playing as "taking part in a fantasy. I can't always afford to go out and ride a horse around the desert. Or go out and kick someone's head off their neck. So, it's fun to pretend." The specific types of storylines participants referenced varied heavily, from the futuristic space adventures of *Mass Effect* or the historical fiction of *Assassin's Creed* to the campaign sections of *Halo* or *Call of Duty*, but the ability to put oneself in another's shoes for a time was widely appealing.

Enjoying narrative games because they immerse the player in different identities connects interviewees' experiences strongly to the concept of *transportation*, or "a distinct mental process, an integrative melding of attention, imagery, and feelings" (Green, Brock, and Kaufman, 2004, p. 312). Transportation is a theoretical construct used to describe both the process of a reader, viewer, or player getting immersed in a narrative media experience and the affective and cognitive impacts this immersion has on them. High levels of transportation can potentially increase one's enjoyment of a medium, can make the message a text is sending more persuasive, and can even alter the media users' opinions or beliefs by showing them different ways of considering an issue.

Most significantly to interviewees' experiences, transportation allows a media user to leave behind their self and instead see what it would be like to be someone else. This can help them escape from stress, self-doubt, and other negative emotional states, tying into players' use of games to relax and explore. Furthermore, transported players can experiment with different identities without facing the consequences or risks of trying to do so in their real lives. As social psychologists Melanie Green, Timothy Brock, and Geoff Kaufman (2004) argue, "A media viewer doesn't have to take the risk of changing jobs, spouses, or locales to experience another kind of life, but rather can vicariously experience such alternative life choices through the lives of the characters who inhabit the worlds to which he or she is transported" (p. 318). For instance, women are often socialized not to express anger, making it difficult for them to show frustration in daily life. Enacting calculated aggression within games can serve as a safe outlet for real-world feelings (Taylor, 2003). This also illuminates the ways in which role-playing games can appeal even when the main character has little in common with the female player; identification does not always depend on similarities, particularly when women are looking for an experience that differs from their real life. Each player brings their own needs, expectations, and individual readings of a character or situation to the text they are enjoying (Bryce and Rutter, 2002, 2003).

Traditionally, transportation theory applies largely or solely to narrative media, such as books or serial TV shows, and my participants often tied their transportation to narrative games. For example, many cited the 2010 game *Bayonetta* as a text they found transporting and in which they could explore different identities. In *Bayonetta*, players take on the role of the titular character, a witch who can shapeshift, summon demons, and fight using both magical attacks and traditional firearms. The gamer guides Bayonetta through a storyline in which she is pursuing a mystical object that is key to maintaining balance between light and dark magical forces, fighting off angels and other foes in order to proceed towards her goal. Participants enjoyed the experience of being Bayonetta due to her combination of over-the-top sexiness and both magical and physical power. In her interview, Nina started addressing game characters by describing how female characters who are hypersexualized or damsels in distress do not "offend" her, because overall, she supported normative gender roles and characteristics. However, she then described how much she loved the opportunity to play games as a character like Bayonetta, who combined a hyperfeminine appearance with hegemonically masculine aggression and power. Nina said, "I do like the way a lot of the stronger but very sexual characters are . . .

portrayed, like, I really like Bayonetta, I love Lara Croft, you know. They might be hypersexualized, but I actually really like them, and I would totally wanna be like them." Although she supported traditional gender norms in her offline life, the ability to subvert these through sexy, powerful characters was deeply enjoyable. This shows that she used transportation to play out and experiment with an identity that would perhaps be uncomfortable for her otherwise.

Buttsvard analyzed this experience even further. She specifically pointed out that playing as Bayonetta allowed her to be powerful and sexy, but in a way that was meant for her pleasure as a woman. She said, "I tried to get some male friends to play it but they all said it was too girly for them. So, that just reinforced, to me, that the sexiness of that game was absolutely not for the benefit of men." Bayonetta was thin, conventionally attractive, and dressed in extremely tight clothing, but the way she expressed her power in the game marked this appearance as something for women to enjoy; they could take on more power than would be possible in real life, and they could look good doing it. Bayonetta let players subvert or overcome traditional gender expectations without risking censure for doing so.

Participants also found and enjoyed opportunities for transportation and identity play in games that are not traditionally seen as narrative based, such as MMORPGs. In these large-scale games, players work their way through a loose story that takes place in a carefully crafted fantasy or science fiction world, but they do not have to progress through the game in the same way. They can complete missions, explore, or just spend their time fishing or learning to cook. There is no singular narrative experienced by all players. Despite this, many participants found the ability to create their own character to be particularly helpful to their transportation experiences. They could choose who and what they wanted their avatar to be, then make decisions through the lens of that chosen personality and role.

When able to select or create their characters, interviewees experimented heavily with personas that they were uncomfortable trying out offline or that simply did not fit into their lifestyle. For example, Angela specifically stated that she liked to play thief-style characters, "because it would be fun to be sneaky yet powerful in real life. [. . .] I also am pretty straight-laced in real life, so I like the thought of playing out the role of someone who is a little wilder and not afraid of breaking rules. I also seriously dislike being the center of attention, so playing a character who can win battles and then slip away quickly is appealing." Angela's attraction to thief-style characters was based on her own existing characteristics, such as disliking attention, as well as on characteristics she wished she could possess or wanted to try out. She liked to experiment with character appearance as well; when able to customize how her avatar looked, Angela tended towards "scars and tattoos and crazy haircuts" and towards characters that were tall and muscular, the opposite of her self-described "small and mousy" appearance. Some aspects of this, like height, were elements she physically could not possess outside of games, while others, like the tattoos and crazy haircuts, were appearance elements she may not have been able to try out without social or economic repercussions, as she was in the process of job hunting as an engineer. Games allowed her to mix what was possible and what was impossible in new ways.

This aligns with Shaw's (2014b) findings that players did not need to identify with their characters based on shared identity categories. Rather, they were often drawn to play characters who appeared very different from them on the surface, but who were dealing with problems similar to those the player had faced in real life. Transportation theory builds on Shaw's work by providing further explanation as to how and why players engaged with narratives or characters who had little in common with them. Such experiences allowed them to explore, in a low-cost, risk-free way, who they were, who they might want to be, and how they could respond to different social situations. As Green, Brock, and Kaufman (2004) describe it, "One reason transportation may lead to enjoyment [of media] is that it provides the opportunity for identity play. Transportation can open the doors to exploring and experimenting with other possible selves. Possible selves are those that individuals might become, wish to become, or fear becoming" (p. 318).

Another way in which participants took advantage of games' opportunities for transportation, identity play, and narrative exploration was that they combined traditionally masculine and traditionally feminine characteristics within their characters in order to subvert gender roles and norms. When able to create their own avatar, many participants opted to make their character conventionally attractive. Anna, for instance, made characters who were all traditionally pretty, but she played each differently. In her words, "I used to play the good character, all the time. No stealing, no being mean, not killing people if I could avoid it. I recently made a pretty evil *Skyrim* character that's been a lot of fun, though I end up feeling bad about stealing from people or assassinating them for no reason sometimes." Anna's choice to embody conventionally attractive avatars but then take on different personalities allowed her to experience different levels of power and varying moralities without needing to sacrifice her gender identity; she could be feminine while also seeing how it felt to be strong, good, evil, or any combination thereof. As with the players who enjoyed being Bayonetta, combining the traditionally masculine role of "hero" or "fighter" with a feminine appearance subverted "girl game" associations of femininity with domesticity, moved away from subject positions in which women were damsels in distress, and allowed players to be more flexible with their identifications.

Other interviewees found that taking on different characters helped them avoid the traditional limitations of femininity, such as when women are socialized to care for others or to be demure and passive. Bear, for instance, enjoyed playing destructive characters in games like *Team Fortress 2* because most of her spare time and her hobbies were devoted to building communities and relationships. She stated, "I work really hard to build community and mentor the people around me, and while it feels really valuable (and definitely is), there's a lot of responsibility. It's nice to just work off stress." Helping others build relationships, such as through her university e-sports club, made many demands on Bear's time and emotional energy. It was a form of *affective labor*, or work that produces intangible emotional products like "a feeling of ease, well-being, satisfaction, excitement, passion—even a sense of connectedness or community" (Hardt, 1999, p. 96). Affective labor is often necessary for communities to function effectively, but it can be draining for those who perform it. Furthermore, affective labor is often relegated to female community members, as it is associated with traditionally feminine gender expectations about care and nurturing. Although Bear did not connect her play habits to her gender specifically, she did find that playing a destructive and aggressive male game character eased the stress brought on by affective labor, freeing her at least for a time of the demands of community management.

Other participants also tended to make male characters when they wanted to be aggressive. This choice took advantage of hegemonic masculinity's association with violence, letting women play out their aggressive tendencies without being told that these were deviant. If they tried to do the same in the offline world, their female gender identity could potentially provoke more of a backlash, as femininity and passivity are conventionally linked. This is, of course, not to mention the other problems with being aggressive in the real world, such as legal concerns. Games offered relatively safe outlets to try out different emotions.

The relation of games and subject positions was both a barrier and a potential pleasure for players. On the one hand, players often struggled with the fact that games required them to embody masculine subject positions in order for the game content to make the fullest sense. They rebelled against characterizations that defined women as passive damsels in distress or that systematically linked their power to their sexuality. On the other hand, the ability to embody different subject positions was also enjoyable, provided the player was *opting* for that position. Mixing together different characteristics, exploring unique personas or subjectivities, and subverting traditional gender norms were pleasurable experiences in video gaming. Players did not object to being feminine and domestic as a rule; they objected to being told they could *only* be feminine or domestic when they wanted to be so much more.

Specifically Gendered Preferences

Although some of the pleasures listed above may be more salient for women than for men, such as when female gamers use transportation to explore expressing anger, my participants only described two of their frequently mentioned pleasures as significantly gendered. The first was customization. Women argued that their enjoyment of character customization was potentially greater than that men would experience. This was the case because it could alter the types of transportation they could experience but also because the option to play a character that matched their gender identity was rare. Such a choice on the part of the developers seemed like an invitation for women to be gamers. As Elayne stated, "I guess I feel kind of alienated or, uh, disregarded, dismissed, you know. So many, or so much of American culture, and media in general, especially media to be consumed, is just geared toward the white male as the default. [. . .] It's just really refreshing to play a female character, even if I may be in like, some crazy skimpy outfit." Players were even more enthusiastic about choice when customizing their character or character gender did not force them to play a different storyline or dress differently. Many referenced the *Mass Effect* series as one of their favorites because it allowed them to be a female character and because that female character possessed the same skills and storyline as her male counterpart. Players did not feel as though they were compromising by choosing "FemShep," and playing a strong, capable, female Special Forces soldier was a rare and enjoyable experience.

Speaking about games more broadly, Alissa felt that a choice of characters was an indication that the gaming industry and community recognized women as potential audiences. "The fact that you can choose a girl character, that is the gaming world's way of saying, 'We want you to play too. We want you to play the same games and here's how we want to show it to you. You can be a girl!'" Interviewees often felt that games defaulted to men, or, as Angela put it, "Right now it's mostly white and mostly male. It's weird to have four or five character options and all but one of them are white men." In such an environment, the ability to play as a female character stood out to players, and while it was not a requirement for enjoying a game, it was "nice when it happened" (Shaw, 2014b). For men, who almost always have an option to play a character that matches their preferred gender identity, such a choice would probably be less significant.

The other pleasure women related to their gender was competition. Although some past research marks competition as something men are more likely to enjoy than women (e.g., Graner Ray, 2004), that was not true among my participants, many of whom enjoyed testing their skills both against games themselves and against other players. T. L. Taylor, one of the first researchers to focus on women's pleasure in gaming, expressed this by saying, "The excitement over reaching a new level or getting out of a particularly bad one (a 'hell level') is not lost on any player including the women" (Taylor, 2003, p. 28). The sense of accomplishment that comes along with improving one's character or gear, learning a new skill, or defeating a new boss can be a powerful incentive for play. This appeal crosses game genres and consoles as well as both online and offline contexts, meaning that women can enjoy the process of mastery in almost any setting.

Mastery can also help women subvert the masculine-gendered expectations of gaming; although skill building is appealing to both men and women, "Succeeding in a male forum [can provide] a sense of achievement and respect and recognition" (Beavis, 2005). The possibility of beating the boys at their own games is an empowering one. Misty, for instance, found that shooting games appealed to her "competitive side. Especially when people get beat by a girl." Tinsel shared this perspective, stating, "FPS I loved initially because I was beating 'men,' lol."

Interestingly, both players followed these statements with a qualifier; Misty inserted a smiley face into her text-based interview, while Tinsel's "lol," or "laughing out loud" served a similar purpose. It is possible that these additions may have been a protective measure, allowing the speaker to argue that they were not being serious if the listener were to be offended by their specific targeting of male opponents. Because female players are numerically and culturally a minority in gaming spaces, such targeting could provoke a backlash. However, these statements and their modifiers also can be taken seriously as real expressions of enjoyment at in-game mastery and the players' ability to succeed in a typically male space and a typically male genre of games. As previous research has pointed out, beating men at their own game has been a pleasure for female players throughout game history (Jenkins, 1998; Beavis, 2005; Eklund, 2011).

The fact that women related so little of their pleasure in gaming to their gender probably connects to the fact that core games are heavily masculinized. Women rarely get to embrace both their gender identity and their gamer identity at the same time; they are given few female characters to play, and, as the previous chapter laid out, expressing their own gender identity in gaming spaces can result in harassment. Therefore, they have to focus on and embrace other pleasures in gaming, such as experiencing someone else's story or focusing on opportunities for socialization.

At the same time, the fact that they can and do enjoy these many elements of core games, and that their gender identity is not a defining factor in their gaming, also indicates how women have learned to prioritize different parts of their identity in order to make their experiences more positive. Rather than interpreting everything through the lens of gender, they interpret many games and experiences through the lens of a *gamer*, focusing on the experience of play or the exploration of a new environment. In this way, they express core characteristics, such as in-depth knowledge of games and a desire for competition. This works to break down associations of core and masculinity by showing that female-identified players can already be core; they share many interpretive strategies with their fellow core, male gamers.

Relationship to Previously Exclusionary Factors

The fact that interpretive strategies are often shared between male and female gamers also came through clearly when my participants discussed games that they disliked or avoided. When interviewing participants, I opened each discussion with a brief overview of the research project, discussing some of the past questions researchers have asked about games and gender and indicating what my main areas of focus were. Following this overview, interviews began with introductory questions, one of which was, "Are there any types of games you dislike?[3]" I asked these questions both to provide participants with an easy inauguration to the process of being interviewed and because past research has focused heavily on gender differences in what players like or dislike about games. I expected players' responses to reflect some of the elements previous studies of games and gender found exclusionary to women, such as core games' violence[4] or their hypersexualization of female characters.[5] While this latter concern did emerge as we talked, I found that these exclusionary factors were not the first things women thought of. Rather, their responses were in many ways identical to those any gamer would be likely to give, even when they had already been told that the research project focused specifically on *women's* experiences playing games.

Almost every participant emphatically stated that they avoided games they were "bad at"—ones where they struggled to complete game goals and make progress through levels or missions. This was their biggest concern when choosing what to play. As Adrianna stated, "If something is frustratingly hard for me to do, then I'm not going to have fun and . . . why play a video game if I'm just going to be miserable the whole time about how much I don't get it?" Although there are some games developers make so difficult that players must learn to take pleasure in even the smallest progress, like *Super Meat Boy*, *Rude Bear Resurrection*, or other masocore games, most gamers gravitate towards manageable challenges, games that may be difficult and require them to approach a scenario multiple times before they beat it successfully but that they know they can master. The fact that players were first and foremost concerned with the types of games they were good at is not a surprise.

What does deserve more attention is *how* skill affected players' game choices, as this differed among individual participants, subverting the expectation that women all tend to play casual games and avoid core ones. For some participants, fast-paced games that require constant attention were extremely difficult. They preferred games that allowed for a leisurely play style, where they could progress at their own pace, and they avoided games that lacked this option. For instance, Spinach did not play real-time games, which require the player to react continually to changes in their situation and to actions taken by their opponent. She stated, "I just can't think that fast, I can't click that fast." Instead, Spinach turned to choices like role-playing games (RPGs) in which, although battle elements were likely to be fast-paced, she could progress through other parts of the game as quickly or as slowly as she liked.

Helix expressed similar sentiments, arguing, "[First-person shooters or versus-style combat games] require you to react quickly and don't offer much downtime, as opposed to turn-based games where you can really think about your choices, or platformers, where you can focus intensely to get through a difficult sequence and then relax—maybe even set the controller down for a minute." In a turn-based game, players alternate who is in charge of the action. For instance, in the turn-based strategy game *XCOM: Enemy Unknown*, the player oversees a military operation combating an alien invasion. In a battle, the player will move all of their troops and give each commands, asking them to shoot aliens, heal their teammates, or save civilians. After this, the computer-controlled aliens will get a turn to move. While the player is taking their turn, the aliens cannot take any action, and vice versa. This means that the player can take as much time as they want during their turn without anything interrupting their plans. For gamers like Helix, who gravitated towards turn-based games and platformers, fast-paced elements were acceptable, but the game also had to offer breaks in which the player could recover and prepare for the next section in order for these participants to find it manageable and enjoyable.

Other players avoided different types of games. Rogue, like a few other participants, simply said, "I have no aim, I can't play anything that involves a gun." Because of this, she turned to RPGs or fantasy MMOs like *World of Warcraft* (*WoW*) while avoiding first- or third-person shooters. Some interviewees enjoyed puzzle games, but only ones that offered manageable challenges. If the puzzles were too hard, they would abandon the game. A few participants even avoided the types of games that are most frequently associated with female players—casual mobile games. Individual tastes and skill ranged widely across genres and play styles.

The second most common complaint about games had to do with their occasional shallowness—participants generally gravitated towards games with strong storylines, interesting or unique characters, and immersive environments. Participant Taylor Ryan summed up this perspective, stating, "I love interacting with [nonplayer characters or] NPCs[6] (they are doing such neat things with AI lately), becoming part of an intricate storyline, designing/crafting things in-game, affecting the game world in different ways, solving mysteries, figuring out puzzles . . . etc.!" Interviewees wanted games that would deeply engage them. Of course, as with individual skill sets, the particular genres or games they found engaging differed by individual.

Many found first-person shooters (FPSs), especially multiplayer ones in which their mission was simply to defeat another team, to be tedious. Marie said, "I find [first-person shooters] boring. I like to get engaged in the story and they don't exactly have a story most of the time." Some others were willing to play first-person shooters in single-player mode, in which missions are linked into an overarching plot.[7] This gave them their desired depth.

Players frequently avoided simplistic mobile games too. This was the case in part because of the way casual games are devalued within game culture; even interviewees who enjoyed casual games often defaulted to describing them as stupid or a waste of time. Therefore, players' dismissal of casual or mobile games cannot be fully divorced from broader discourses about casual games as not "real" games. However, players did also specifically reference the repetitive and uncomplicated mechanics of casual games as the problem; because they had invested so much time and effort into learning to play complicated core games, experienced players like DT found some mobile games too basic to be appealing.

Even MMORPGs, which tend to have larger female audiences than other genres, were not universally seen as immersive. Buttsvard was one of the participants who found them to be boring, describing them as "endless grinding," the slang term gamers use to describe repetitive actions a player can take within a game to build resources or experience.[8] Grinding can allow players to access harder levels or create better in-game items for their character, but many players find it extremely boring and time-consuming, making it a negative adjective when applied to the entirety of a game.

Finally, participants expressed concerns about elements like cost and accessibility, lamenting the decline of game rental locations like Blockbuster or the need to purchase multiple console, PC, or handheld systems in order to play every appealing game (as some are exclusive to specific platforms). These topics of discussion—skill, immersion, access, etc.—show that, despite being part of a study specifically focused on gender, female gamers often prioritize their self-identification as *gamers*. When simply asked about the types of games they prefer or avoid, female gamers are concerned with the individual experience of play, with meeting their personal preferences, and with doing so at a reasonable personal expense in terms of time and money. They focused on the factors that make gaming more or less enjoyable to themselves as players.

It was only after we talked further that players brought up elements like hypersexualized female characters or violence. And when they did so, their perspectives often contradicted past research that argues that these factors are off-putting for female players (e.g., Graner Ray, 2004; Kafai, 1998). For example, participants brought up in-game violence only three times within all thirty-seven interviews. Of these three instances, two spoke about violence negatively while one found it to be an amusing, cathartic pleasure, particularly if the violence was "gratuitous" and over the top (Bear, interview 1). This seems to indicate that, at least among women who have managed to find space for themselves within gaming, violence is not necessarily a salient negative for female gamers.

Interviewee Fiber Freak, for instance, argued that gore was the real problem, rather than violence. She loved fantasy-based games or *Star Wars* games, where she battled it out with swords and magic or blasters and lightsabers. If games contained only sanitized violence, as in *Star Wars*, or comic violence, as in the *Lego* game series, she could ignore it or even enjoy the mastery of defeating others. First-person shooters, on the other hand, she avoided like the plague, stating, "My boyfriend was trying to get me more into first-person shooting so he was trying to show me all these video games, and there's just something about first-person shooters, holding guns, and all the graphic blood spatter, just . . . I can't tolerate that kind of stuff." FPS games contain realistic graphics and high amounts of blood, for example using blood splattered across the screen to indicate when the player is being injured; Fiber Freak found this level of gore more upsetting than the actual acts of violence. The other participant who mentioned violence, Emily, specifically stated a distaste for violence against women, referencing *Grand Theft Auto* as a series she disliked because "it's like beat up women with a shovel." The context of violence in many ways mattered more than the act itself—how games portrayed violence and who it was directed against affected how participants interpreted it, adding a new perspective to previous work.

More Than Female Gamers

The preferences and issues described above represent only some of the many reasons female players choose or avoid certain types of games or play styles. Even as an abbreviated description of the benefits women find in gaming, however, they demonstrate that understanding "female gamers" as a singular market or entity unfairly limits players to a specific, often stereotypically feminine identity rather than allowing them the fluid and multiple identities they preferred. In terms of game selection, for instance, although interviewees often shared preferences or disliked similar aspects of games, there were always exceptions. Some turned to violent games for enjoyable catharsis while others found graphic violence unsettling. Some played only multiplayer, while others avoided it entirely or switched between solo play and group play depending on their circumstances. Their choices were always personally situated, contextual, and mutable, with many participants arguing that the games they enjoyed changed over time or with different stages of life.

Women's disparate preferences for games and their pursuit of individual pleasures can also be seen as feminist, although players did not generally refer to them as such. This is the case because the variety of women's preferences demonstrated how diverse they are, rather than categorizing them as a unit based on their gender identity. Given the many reasons why women socialized in games, it is clear that they enjoyed this approach not because of a natural female tendency to talk, but rather because of individual benefits they found in socializing. The same is true of players' enjoyment of both conventionally attractive female avatars and avatars that sported mohawks or tattoos.

Players used games to perform gender in a wide variety of ways, undermining essentialized stereotypes or expectations for what women should be or how they should act. This was evident, for example, in the way they frequently took pleasure in elements of games that allowed them to display power, especially feminized power that involved dominating men in competition or combining conventionally attractive avatars with extreme physical or magical force. Through these elements, and like the game grrlz Jenkins (1998) and Helen W. Kennedy (2006) studied, women undermined associations of femininity and passivity, instead linking femininity with strength, power, and competition. Their success in gaming and competition also subverts traditional expectations that men are better with technology than women by showing how women can also possess technical skill and mastery. Using skill to gain power in technological areas can have its downsides, as it makes unequal spaces appear to be meritocratic (Nakamura, 2017; Paul, 2018), but it can also allow women to take control of their environments and their femininity in new, powerful ways.

Finally, the deep knowledge about different games and genres women use to pursue experiences they will enjoy performs feminist action by showing how, despite the masculine connotations of core, women often already possess core characteristics. They are committed gamers, capable of prioritizing this part of their identity and using it to achieve individual goals like managing their time and environments or dominating their opponents. This illuminates the constructed nature of gaming's current power structures, the boundaries that police gaming's core, and the gendered hierarchies that go along with them. Highlighting women's existing core knowledge is therefore a step towards dismantling these inequalities.

The pleasures women find in games provide them with many individual benefits, such as stronger social ties, a feeling of accomplishment in competition, and practice identifying in diverse and fluid ways. These also matter on a broader, community-based scale, in that they show how female and male gamers share many interpretive strategies and a background in gaming that can tie them together. When looking at the same game, they have the potential to pull from it similar meanings. Many participants objectively recognized that games they did not like could qualify as *good* games—ones with interesting gameplay options, narratives, or mechanics. Only a small element of women's enjoyment of games was specifically gendered; the rest they felt was shared with men and with gaming communities more broadly.

This provides a potential pathway towards greater gender equality. Through an emphasis on their similarities, diverse gamers may be able to build a network of affinity strong enough to help dismantle uneven hierarchies of power based on the perceived differences between male and female players. As gender theorist Judith Butler pointed out when describing gender as performative, removing the requirement for all feminists to identify in the same way opened up new possibilities for political collaboration (1990, 1999). Other feminist theorists, including Donna Haraway and Chela Sandoval, pushed this argument further, contending that *any* movement that was tied to a specific identity was by definition exclusionary, as it would ignore individuals with intersectional identities. Haraway, quoting Sandoval, wrote, "The category 'woman' negated all non-white women; 'black' negated all non-black people, as well as all black women. But there was also no 'she,' no singularity, but a sea of differences among US women who have affirmed their historical identity as US women of color. This identity marks out a self-consciously constructed space that cannot affirm the capacity to act on the basis of natural identification, but only on the basis of conscious coalition, of affinity, of political kinship" (2000, p. 296). Here, Sandoval posits that politics require conscious recognition of similarities and shared goals, rather than reliance on identity and the visibility of that identity as a means for progress. Emphasizing the shared nature of men's and women's meaning-making strategies, and how these bind them into an interpretive community, may be one means for building this affinity.[9] That is, paying attention to the many ways in which women are already core could help negate core as an exclusionary category altogether.

Imagining a Gamer Community

Female gamers' deep connections to core gaming culture, and the many characteristics they share with other gamers, are also evident in the way many interviewees felt connected to the idea of an overall gaming community. As political scientist Benedict Anderson (1983, 1991, 2006) argues, given the scale and dispersed nature of modern society, a sense of nationhood or community is unlikely to be based solely on geographical proximity or boundaries. Instead, he presents the idea of imagined communities, in which individuals do not know each other personally but connect through an internal feeling of affinity. This comes from imagining others as engaged in the same activities, at the same time, in which the individuals themselves are involved. Anderson used this concept to explain nationalism and national identities, arguing that even in the smallest countries, individuals are unable to meet more than a tiny fraction of their fellow citizens. But through imagined communities, members of a nation feel connected to each other and to the state. This is due to shared characteristics of the nation, such as language, and moments of national pride, such as when a nation's athletes compete in the Olympics.

Although Anderson focuses on larger contexts, imagined community can also explain how individuals connect in smaller groups or feel an association with others they have not met based on shared interests. In the case of my interviewees, many saw themselves as part of an imagined gaming community, although they often envisioned it in different ways according to their personal experiences. Some players envisioned the "gaming community" very broadly, as a nebulous connection between people who played games. As Buttsvard stated, "To me, it's like asking if I consider myself part of the book reading community or movie viewing community. Yes, I am a human that takes part in media." Interviewees who took this stance saw themselves as somewhat connected to others via games and enjoyed knowing that others played the same games they did, but this connection did not necessarily impact their lives or self-identities in a meaningful way.

Others, however, took their connections to a gaming community further, and could outline both specific communities they felt they were part of and why. For instance, many players had individual games that they contributed to more frequently than others, which built greater affinity in that area. Bear was a fan of *Team Fortress 2* (*TF2*) and helped manage some online *TF2* forums. Because of this, she felt connected to people who played *TF2* more than she did to a broader game community. Contributing to game-related forums and fandoms and attending game-related events often helped players connect their personal experience to that of others and imagine themselves as related. Others linked "community" specifically to people they knew who also played games, both in person and online. By engaging in gaming with others or by connecting to people specifically through games, they felt as though they were a part of a larger experience. Arya, for example, felt linked to an overall gaming community because of her "friends who I have never met in real life. We catch up online and enjoy a game or two." She saw her social sphere as wider for having met people solely due to their shared love of a specific game.

Emotional affinity for games and experience playing them also kept many people connected to a broader imagined community. Interviewees like Harley, Alissa, and others felt that "I just love gaming in general" (Harley, interview 1) was more than enough of a reason to see themselves as part of a larger gaming community, and they frequently drew on their background in gaming to defend this connection. Harley, who was one of the oldest participants in the study, referenced the fact that she had played from "*Atari* all the way to what [gaming] is now." Her experience with the evolution of gaming, to her, made her intrinsically a part of the gaming community due to her role as a witness to its development.

Even more players referenced shared knowledge as a means for connecting to others. Chimera Soul enjoyed the fact that, when she found herself in one game talking to others about different games they have encountered, she generally understood what they were discussing. As she said, "If I haven't actually played it, I've heard of it, I have friends who play it." Being able to recognize and understand what other players were talking about was crucial to her, as she felt as though she was keeping up with gaming news. The same was true of DT, who read game news every day, even if she did not have time to play; keeping up with new developments was an essential part of community for her. Overall, having a history that allowed one to identify as a core gamer also frequently allowed interviewees to see themselves as part of something broader.

This is not to say that female gamers did not experience problems with their self-identification as both gamer and community member. At least a few participants said that they were hesitant to describe themselves as gamers, due to the longstanding ideological association of the term with straight white men. For instance, Eva played games extensively, and considered them one of her main hobbies. However, her struggle with the expectations of who qualified as a "gamer" were so strong that she actively hid her game playing from offline friends, referring to herself as a "closeted gamer." She felt that games and gamers were so heavily masculinized in society that her friends and family would judge her choice to play them, saying, "My friends, they're mostly girls, they would make fun of me for it and be like, 'Oh, that's for guys.' My mom would tell me that too." Interestingly, Eva described both her female friends and herself as very stereotypically girly; this is why she felt that they would not understand her choice to game, given core gaming's masculine connotations. However, her generally feminine self-presentation also made it easier for her to hide her gaming, as no one expected her to play core games.

Other players were not quite as firm about hiding their gaming habits, but many did feel a divide between society's perception of them and their own desire to talk about games, play games, and have others consider them a gamer. As interviewee Alissa said, "Any girl who's a gamer is a strong female. You have to be, because as I said before, [. . .] you're being told either right to your face or subconsciously that you're not good enough, that you shouldn't be doing this, get back in the kitchen and you know, make something or go sew something." Women faced a variety of forces, both overt and inferential, that worked to disconnect them from the identity of gamer. This is reflective of Shaw's 2012 work, in which she found that many marginalized game players avoided describing themselves as "gamers" due to the connotations of that term; as with her participants, some interviewees struggled with a conflict between enjoying games and wanting to disassociate from these characteristics. Furthermore, many negative stereotypes about gamers in general continue to circulate through popular culture (Kowert, Griffiths, and Oldmeadow, 2012), such as when shows like *South Park* and *The Big Bang Theory* portray players as obsessive, acne-ridden, and unkempt. This made participants concerned about whether or not friends, family, and acquaintances bought into these stereotypes and how that might reflect on them as players.

Finally, a small number of interviewees were not willing to consider themselves part of a gaming community. This was the case because they defined the concept narrowly, arguing that actual social interaction with other gamers while playing was a necessary component for a community, or because they felt that the gaming community excluded them. Jessica, for example, referred to herself as "a lone ranger" due to her affinity for solo play. She said that when she had previously played with friends or boyfriends, she felt connected to a gaming community, but as she shifted more towards solo play, this feeling diminished. Others felt as though the gaming community did not allow women to define themselves as part of it. They frequently found that other players assumed they were playing games as a way to get male attention, or they were marked out as "female gamers" rather than just regular members. Although most interviewees were able to dismiss these reactions and still get enjoyment out of games and game spaces, a few interviewees found that the narrow definition of "gamer" was too exclusionary, disconnecting them from gaming communities regardless of what games they played and how often. These limitations, along with many other factors, placed a barrier between interviewees and the community their experience and knowledge should have encouraged them to connect to.

Already Core

This outlining of players' different interpretations of community is not an attempt to dictate how players should see the gaming community. Rather, it is a recognition of the ways in which, despite their unanimous pleasure in games and gaming, women's relationship to games is still complicated by the persistent hegemonic presentation of core games as

masculinized and as exclusive to men. The fact that a portion of interviewees were unable to see themselves as connected to a broader gaming
community indicates how core ideas can force even committed players
into a paradoxical position where their enjoyment of games conflicts
with their desire to avoid being associated with "gamer" stereotypes.
Even players who rhapsodized about their enjoyment of core games,
and who demonstrated nuanced interpretive strategies for managing
their gaming experience, were sometimes hesitant to identify as part
of a broader gaming community, given the stereotypical characteristics
attached to it or other players' reactions to their presence. This undermined the internal feeling of affinity Anderson describes as essential to
an imagined community.

At the same time, the fact that many interviewees did still feel a deep
connection to gaming culture and communities and the fact that all participants were able to find pleasure in gaming cannot be overlooked, as it
highlights how women are, in many ways, already core. Because of this,
they break down some of the constructed barriers between gamer identity and a female gender identity, illuminating means through which the
exclusionary nature of core can be altered. Thinking again of the characteristics attached to core in gaming discourse, women's clear preferences and ability to express them through their knowledge of games *are*
core characteristics. Core requires commitment to gaming as a regular
hobby, extensive knowledge about games, highly developed skills as a
player, and the ability to play competitively. It also, as outlined earlier,
aligns with expectations of hegemonic masculinity, such as aggression
and dominance over others. While the interviewed players sometimes
avoided these latter characteristics, even when they played competitively, their ability to navigate games and gaming spaces demonstrated
core gamer identities. Each interviewee was able to point, without hesi-
tation, to games that did or did not fit their own personal characteristics
and play style. They had played widely enough and frequently enough
to have clear preferences. They also knew how to fit different styles of
games into their life depending on what their needs were at the time.
Players alternated social play with individual play, for instance, depending on whether they wanted to relax after work or connect with others.
All of these characteristics reflect in-depth commitment to and knowledge of games, key elements of being core. Women have invested time

and effort into core and casual gaming and developed extensive skill and familiarity with game tropes and offerings as a result.

Women's ability to take on these characteristics troubles the naturalization of core as a coherent concept. Because they adopt some aspects of core while rejecting others, such as its masculinization, they demonstrate the ways in which these characteristics are connected only by media coverage, industrial biases, longstanding discourses about who plays games and what games are, and players' resulting perceptions. Women also undermine the naturalized construction of core simply by identifying as female. Taking on other core characteristics without identifying as male subverts gendered constructions of men as core and women as casual.

It is true that at some moments, core gaming culture encourages women to take on or accept a masculinized subject position, such as when game content pushes them to objectify female characters or when they respond aggressively to potential competitors as a means of proving their skill. But interviewees also found that there were many times when they could happily inhabit both a female identity and a gamer identity; they just needed the ability to navigate game content and spaces in order to find the arenas that allowed for this. Women were not only willing to do the work needed to enter into an exclusionary space, but they were also highly capable of doing so. They can draw on their personal preferences and their experience with games in order to navigate offerings and prioritize a positive experience that will meet their individual, contextual needs. In turn, they then receive extensive pleasure from games, enjoying aspects such as sociability, meeting personal challenges, competing with others and with themselves, and more.

Players also were able to find places where, rather than having to embody a female/gamer position or a male/gamer position, they could embody an ungendered gamer position, escaping from the confines of "gamers'" masculine assumptions. This was evident in how clearly players expressed concerns about games that were not intimately linked to gender and in how they did not necessarily need to identify with the characters they played as in games. Interviewees expressed pleasure in different subject positions that rose above concerns about whether the characters' gender matched their own. Game culture, although it frequently pushes inhabitants towards masculinized positions and characteristics, does not do so all the time, allowing for moments of fracture and expansion when different core identities can be imagined and made possible.

Additionally, interviewees revealed both that they were able to embody fluid gender positions and that they enjoyed doing so, using elements like transportation to try out new combinations of traditionally masculine and traditionally feminine characteristics. Whether this meant physically dominating other characters while presenting an attractive, conventionally feminine appearance or seeing how one would be treated as a male character, an evil character, or even just an ostentatious character, interviewees pursued a wide variety of flexible experiences. Rather than wanting to be always female and always gamers, they desired the ability to identify in different ways based on context. This helped them, first, to manage the masculine subject positions games offered them and take on some characteristics while avoiding others. Furthermore, their drive for fluid identities and their ability to "construct a wide spectrum of negotiated positions" (Leblanc, 1999, p. 160) allowed them to take on what women's studies researcher Lauraine Leblanc (1999), in her study of punk women, termed "'trebled reflexivity': they challenge the norms of the dominant culture as well as the feminine norms of both culture and subculture" (p. 160). Women's embodying of masculine positions, their combination of masculine and feminine characteristics in their game characters, and their possession of core characteristics while being female helped them undermine the gender expectations both of gaming and of broader culture. Women acted against cultural expectations that define femininity as nonaggressive or noncompetitive, while also indicating that women could and did enjoy core games and game culture.

Players' ability to take on a female/gamer position, or to find their own negotiated position when offered only limited options, blurs the boundaries between gaming's central core and its margins, moving core from an industrial term back to a conceptual model. Many aspects of gaming culture, and in particular the construction of "hardcore" and casual, rest on the assumption that masculinity helps mark out what is central to gaming and gamers. Prioritizing women's experience shows that they are already part of gaming's core of invested players; they just have not been recognized as such due to an overemphasis on the significance of gender to what a "gamer" is. Therefore, a stronger recognition of how women already are central to gaming, and have been for a long time, can show that women are not just new, casual players drawn in by the casualized era. In doing so, it can address some of the sexism and inequality present in gaming.

First, such an approach will reemphasize Shaw's (2014b) point that diverse representations in games can be a benefit rather than a weakness. As developers have argued, they craft their games to target their main audience, who they assume are young, white men. However, not only do female players disprove this assumption, but the pleasure marginalized groups can take in characters that they do not identify with indicates that "gamers" can probably develop that same ability, learning to find pleasure in characters that are not straight, white, or male (Shaw, 2014b). In fact, many of them might already seek out characters who differ from them in terms of identity, and significant numbers of male players already gender swap when given the option (Martey et al., 2014; Stabile, 2014). Diversifying notions of core, and who gamers are or can be, does not mean removing hegemonic "gamers'" ability to enjoy games, but rather decreasing other players' challenges.

Second, attention to women as core or part of the core can help improve the interactions marginalized players have in gaming communities by divesting commitment to gaming from masculinity. When other players do not automatically assume that female-identified gamers are unusual, or gaming to get attention from men, women will be able to focus more clearly on the pleasures of gaming and less on defending their position. They will also probably be able to connect more strongly to an imagined community of gamers, developing the internal feeling of affinity necessary for this association. Through this, they could develop greater access to power over what gaming communities should look like, undermining their existing sexism and misogyny. Given that the casualized era is already working to redefine what gaming is and who gamers are, avoiding discourses that frame women as new or tangential to gaming and instead promoting ones that recognize their longstanding investment could be key to undermining gaming's sexism and instead developing a more equitable culture.

Hegemony and the forces policing it are strong opponents, particularly when the dominant group gives up all pretense of common sense and employs pure force, like harassment, in order to maintain its privileged position. However, women and other marginalized groups indicate that hegemony is not indomitable, by revealing its constructed nature and paths through which it can be subverted and changed.

5

Strategies for Play

Finding Space and Exercising Active Audience Power

Female players find much to enjoy about games, as well as many challenges. To help ensure that the positives outweigh the extensive potential negatives, female gamers have developed sophisticated strategies for choosing content and for managing their interactions with the gaming community. Exploring these strategies can allow developers, activists, and gamers who desire a more equitable gaming culture to proceed in ways that emerge from the needs of the community and are therefore more likely to be effective. After all, past attempts to open gaming up to more diverse audiences, such as the girls' games movement of the 1990s, all had good intentions, but most have been unsuccessful. This is the case in part because they did not account for what players were already doing and what they wanted.

Audiences are not passive recipients who watch or play anything that happens to be put in front of them; they actively choose and interpret the media they use. Whereas very early communication theory posited that media were a "hypodermic needle" injecting their messages directly and completely into the minds of media consumers, more modern work has forefronted audience power. Uses and gratifications research, for instance, has argued since the 1970s that people have specific needs, such as information gathering, and that they choose their media in order to fulfill those needs (Katz, Blumler, and Gurevitch, 1973). This resonates with my participants' detailed strategies for selecting which video games to play. Overall, they draw on four main resources to evaluate games and choose appropriate offerings. These are their personal skill set, their knowledge of developer or genre conventions, previews of game content, and social network recommendations. Collectively, these pieces of information help women decide whether or not to invest in a game, allowing them to find games that meet their personal preferences while also weeding out games likely to be offensive or unenjoyable to them.

Once players have selected their game, they display five further strategies for managing their playing experience and their marginalized position in core gaming spaces, particularly if they choose an online, multiplayer game. These strategies are leaving online gaming, avoiding playing with strangers, camouflaging their gender, deploying their skill and experience, or adopting an aggressive persona.[1] Players apply these different approaches contextually, responding to the situation they encounter or the strengths and weaknesses of their own personality. Through these strategies, they attempt to protect themselves from harassment or otherwise cope with the challenge of other gamers not seeing them as part of a core audience.

However, interview data also show that many of these strategies, both for game selection and for social environment management, have severe limitations. For instance, female gamers are well practiced at reading pleasure into games that seem sexist or exclusionary, and they have also developed a wide variety of methods for choosing which games they would like to play. At the same time, it is often clear that the core industry designs most games for men, rather than for women, and female gamers feel the force of that exclusion. Some participants referenced specific texts, like *Lollipop Chainsaw* or *Grand Theft Auto*, that they felt were too sexist to enjoy at all and that they just opted to avoid. Therefore, although players can choose which games to play, they often feel as though they are choosing from a pool of texts that is not meant for them and that is limited in distinctly gendered ways.

My participants encountered similar issues when managing their engagement with others, as they frequently ran into the perception that online gaming, and core gaming in general, were men's spaces and women were interlopers. This meant they often faced harassment or found that their best recourse was to hide their gender or choose to play single-player games. These choices, however, helped further the construction of online spaces as masculine by hiding women's contributions to and presence in gaming communities. But other approaches to avoiding harassment are exhausting, requiring the player to manage every element of their online identity carefully. Some strategies even have the potential to backfire and result in greater persecution, or they can be limited in effectiveness by game mechanics that give the player less control over how they interact with others.

Because of this, female players embody both the agency of an active audience and the limitations of a group marginalized by the hegemonic order. Interview participants consistently showed that they are capable of managing their media choices and online environments to make them as positive as possible. However, their discussions also revealed that they were often unable to access or affect real power structures in gaming. For that reason, they sometimes opted out of parts of core game culture, despite their deep investments in gaming, rather than suffer negative experiences.

Making the Best of Limited Choices: Strategies for Selecting What to Play

Although the gaming industry tends to group female players together, assuming that they prefer casual games to core games, each interviewee displayed strong personal preferences regarding their video games. As stated earlier, almost all participants avoided games they felt they were bad at, instead focusing on the specific genres and styles that allowed them to progress through the game effectively. In addition, they often played games for different reasons, such as competition or relaxation, and they came to gaming with different console, PC, handheld, or mobile systems and from different class or financial backgrounds. Because of this, each woman was looking for unique characteristics in her games and carefully sought out games that met her needs.

Even if they share some preferences, women take nuanced approaches to game selection. For example, interviewee Misty played a lot of first-person shooters like the *Call of Duty* series, and said, "Shooters I always just played with friends through high school and college, and it appeals to my competitive side. Especially when people get beat by a girl." Misty clearly looked for both social interaction and a competitive environment when playing multiplayer. On the other hand, interviewees like Jutte, who said she preferred "working with someone, rather than against someone," avoided heavy player-versus-player games and instead chose games with cooperative elements. Social interaction was as important to Jutte as to Misty, if not more so, but competition was something she avoided rather than sought out. They both enjoyed multiplayer games but looked for separate elements within those.

To choose games that meet their needs effectively, women must have detailed knowledge of their own preferences as well as the ability to sort through the video game industry's offerings to find those that will match with what they want to play. And interviewees displayed this ability, using their knowledge of genre conventions and developers, previews of games or reviews, and their social networks to find games that they would enjoy.[2]

Genre or Developer Conventions

When players found a genre of games they enjoyed, they often stayed with that type of text, exploring the different options available within that category. As Jutte explained, "We would mostly stick to the types of games that had worked for us before. Like first-person shooters were a tried and true thing for my household, we didn't bring in a lot of RPGs or anything like that." This made choosing a game much easier by providing set expectations for play style, content, and mechanics.

Frequently, players felt that certain genres worked well for certain play styles. For instance, game pace was a key consideration many players used to choose games. Players like Anna, who found it difficult to keep up with fast-paced action games, were more likely to tend towards RPGs or single-person story games. As she stated, "RPGs didn't punish you as much for being slower, so that made a huge difference." Her experience gaming was much more enjoyable when she could proceed at her own pace. On the other hand, Eva preferred shooting games or ones that had short missions and frequent save points, so that she could pick them up, play for an hour or so, and then put them down. Because of this, she avoided in-depth RPGs or MMOs, which are more time-consuming. Other players who preferred fast-paced games avoided turn-based games like *Civilization*, as waiting for their opponent to play tried their patience and lost their attention (Laine, interview 1).

Players also used a genre's expected content to choose what to play or avoid. Fiber Freak, for instance, described gory violence as "just not something I can do." This led her to avoid shooters and to prefer RPGs because, although they contained fighting or shooting mechanics, they presented this violence in sanitized ways. Shooting games, on the other hand, often revel in blood and guts, such as when *Call of Duty* games signal that a player's character is being shot by splattering blood across the screen. Other players enjoyed playing "games for the totally gratuitous violence (and sometimes totally gratuitous porn)" (Bear, interview 1). Bear chose games like *Team Fortress 2*, a shooting game with a strong element of comedy, to meet her needs in these areas, saying she selected games on the basis of their "humor, violence, [and] strategy." She was willing to play RPGs like *Skyrim* occasionally but found they did not hold her interest as well as more violent multiplayer games. Because Bear and Fiber Freak displayed completely opposite content preferences, they tended towards different genres as well.

Finally, interviewees frequently considered genre mechanics. When asked what she looked for when choosing a game, Angela declared, "Loot! I loooove having a wide variety of items to equip and use in a game. Honestly, plot is probably secondary to that for me. I love character building, and what you can equip or use is a huge part of that." Because of this preference, Angela and similar interviewees like Tinsel tended towards RPGs, which offer a lot of different forms of loot, or games known for their extensive weaponry, like the *Borderlands* series.

In addition to relying on genre conventions to help them pick games they would enjoy, players showed extensive knowledge regarding developers. As Anna said, "If I like a game from a particular developer or series, I'll usually look at other games related to it." The game company Bethesda, which is responsible for the *Elder Scrolls* series, was extremely popular with RPG fans or participants who wanted a deep storyline. BioWare, which has created numerous acclaimed series like *Baldur's Gate*, *Mass Effect*, and *Dragon Age*, was also seen as a company that paid attention to narrative. On top of that, participants felt Bioware games offered them positive female characters. Elayne said, "Bioware is, I guess, kind of unique in that they try to be pretty gender-neutral." For example, participants often commented on the enjoyment they received from playing the female version of Commander Shepard in the *Mass Effect* series, arguing that it was a relief to play a female character who was strong, self-sufficient, and clothed in reasonable armor. Because of this, they were willing to try other BioWare offerings. Similarly, if a producer was known for creating games that a participant had not enjoyed in the past, they were unlikely to explore that producer's newer options.

Previews of Game Content

Participants also reported using a variety of paratexts, or material related to but external from a game, such as marketing materials, cover art, or press coverage, in order to choose the video games they played. In particular, they relied heavily on online reviews and previews of game content. These included *Let's Play* videos, where another gamer films their progress through the game and provides commentary on their experience, official reviews from game magazines or websites, and community-based reviews on forums like Reddit. For example, DT took many steps in choosing a game. She said, "I check out YouTube for reviews (more than one), I look at what the comments say and go on Reddit and ask people whether I should go out and buy this game. Yeah, I do a lot of research before buying a game." By comparing multiple sources, she got a clear idea of what a game was like, whether it would fit her needs, and whether she should spend money on it. The source of the review also mattered. When looking at material from the game or reviews of it, participants were extremely discerning regarding what they considered or ignored. Bubble argued, "If someone who only plays RTS hated a FPS, it doesn't mean much to me . . . So, I'm pretty careful when reading reviews." She assessed a reviewer's history, compared it to her own tastes, and then decided whether that opinion was worthwhile or not.

Social Network Recommendations

In addition to their personal research, participants were willing to turn to their social networks and seek recommendations from friends. When Chimera Soul started playing *Team Fortress* 2 regularly and joined a set clan of players, they directed her to many new games. In her own words, "When I would be in the main chat, they would talk about other games, and I'd be like, 'Oh, well . . . you know, I'll give that a try.' Like something like *Left 4 Dead*, on my own, I probably never would have tried. [. . .] I had a gateway, starting with a clan." Because she and her clanmates shared a love of *Team Fortress 2*, Chimera Soul was willing to try other games they enjoyed even if these were out of her usual comfort zone. Numerous other participants, like Anna, Jasper, and Rogue, reported similar experiences, saying that they added to their "list of video games to buy" (Rogue, interview 1) when friends directed them to new material; they expected that friends would know their taste and would avoid directing them to anything they would dislike or find offensive.

Significance and Limitations

Although none of these strategies are revolutionary, and all of them are probably used by many other groups of gamers or media consumers,[3] they do provide evidence that women are active media users even when engaging with the traditionally masculinized medium of core gaming. They carefully choose what they want to play, displaying deep knowledge of game genres, developer histories, and gaming communities in order to do so. In addition, the care they put into choosing their video games combats the idea that women are a homogeneous bloc that only plays mobile or casual games or the perception that they are not deeply invested in game culture. These participants embody many facets of core and use these to sort through massive amounts of information and numerous review sources before spending their time and money on a game.

Multiple interviewees felt that they could not rely on industry marketing and advertising to help them select games, as the games developers offered "for women" often relied on limiting and outdated gender roles. Many were also targeted more clearly towards young audiences, rather than adult women; participants referenced games like *Nintendogs*, in which players care for virtual pets, or *Barbie* games as examples of these. My participants enjoyed many of these games, but they resented *only* being offered these texts when they wanted to engage with more core games as well. To do so, they had to move beyond industrial advertising in order to find good options.

Female players also struggled with choosing games due to the fact that they sometimes wanted to play casual titles but were concerned with how others would view this choice. Specifically, they were worried that playing casual games would ruin their ability to present themselves as core and that it would reaffirm negative, dismissive stereotypes about female gamers more generally. Feather, for instance, had just gotten a Nintendo 3DS prior to our first interview and was playing many games on that system. Although she appreciated that they were easy to fit into her busy schedule and was having fun, she also felt guilty about enjoying them. She said, "I'm kind of . . . not ashamed of the games I have been buying, but I'm not happy with myself at the games I've been buying. [. . .] I've played *Harvest Moon* a lot, it's a very girly game. I've got *Cooking Mama* and *Crafting* . . . I've got a lot of Mama games because they are short little blurbs of stuff. I don't know, I feel bad buying these as a woman because they are like little girl games to me, but they're kind of fun." Feather deeply enjoyed playing video games, finding time for them around many other commitments. However, the types of games that were easiest to fit in, ones she could carry around on her 3DS and play in short bursts, were ones that she felt would make people more likely to stereotype her and, through her, other female gamers. She also disliked reinforcing prevailing industry stereotypes about female gamers. Because of this, her relationship with casual games was an ambivalent mix of enjoyment and guilt.

For some players, the potential guilt was enough to keep them away from certain games entirely. Laine avoided playing *The Sims*, for instance, because of the "stigma attached to it," the expectation that it was a game only girls enjoyed. Similarly, other players spoke in dismissive terms about *Candy Crush Saga*, *Angry Birds*, and others, even though they often still played and enjoyed these. The game industry and community's treatment of casual games "as feminine, and therefore 'trivial'" (Vanderhoef, 2013) repeatedly made my interviewees loath to admit they played casual titles. This was especially true because they saw themselves, and wanted others to see them, as serious, core gamers, which meant they had to present their gamer identity in the right way.

Finally, female players had to choose how to deal with a game that was potentially exclusionary. For instance, they frequently found games that met their needs for storyline, pace, system compatibility, and price point, but then had to decide whether they wanted to invest in something that did not offer a female protagonist. In general, this appeared to be a compromise women were willing to make, if only to avoid limiting their game choices too heavily. When given the option, almost all said that they would choose a female character over a male character, but if the choice was not available, they would not automatically avoid that game. If the game had other characteristics that they felt they would enjoy, a lack of a female playable character was not a deal breaker for participants.

Offensive game themes or character representations were another story, and participants tended to avoid these tests or found ways to see what happened in them without having to buy them. When a game contained potentially offensive themes, such as a high level of violence toward women or a demeaning character presentation, female interviewees generally did not play them. This was true even if the game looked appealing for other reasons like game play.

One game players frequently said they avoided was *Lollipop Chainsaw*, a comedy horror hack-and-slash game released in 2012. In the game, players take on the character of teenage cheerleader/zombie hunter Juliet Starling, who fights against hordes of zombies using a rainbow-spewing chainsaw. When discussing *Lollipop Chainsaw*, Feather said, "I watched the complete game on play-through and it's just absolutely sexual innuendo and curse-words and pretty much just rampant sexualization of a minor. But it looked really fun. But I would never buy it because I would refuse to propagate that game play and that view of women but yet it looked fun. I watch my games that I don't want to visually buy." From the way she talked about the game, Feather's feelings on the matter were obviously very split, as she balanced a desire for fun against the need for games to treat women more seriously. Feather recognized the comedy elements of the game and felt that its hack-and-slash gameplay would be enjoyable. However, because of its problematic themes, like the sexualization of a near-minor (Juliet is just turning eighteen at the start of the game, which takes place on her birthday) and the abundance of cursing, she refuses to contribute monetarily to the developer. Other participants were similarly conflicted, balancing a love of games overall against specific cases that they considered demeaning.[4]

Because women in games are frequently marginalized or overly sexualized, particularly in core games, female players find an extra challenge in choosing games, often having to select from among a number of potentially negative options. In some cases, this has led them to develop interesting rules for selecting texts or characters. For instance, Buttsvard stated, "Basically here's my formula for female characters and their breast design: Does the character have more bosom than agency? If no, then awesome, if yes, then is there a larger context? Explore why. If there is no reason, then the game is probably terrible." She went on to support this statement with examples from some of her favorite games, contrasting Ashley, a *Resident Evil 4* character with "medium breasts, no agency," to Bonnie MacFarlane from *Red Dead Redemption*, a character she felt was "sweet and capable and tough." Because MacFarlane had an actual role in the game, rescuing the protagonist when he is wounded, Buttsvard remembered her for her personality and assistance, rather than for her figure. Ashley, on the other hand, she remembered for being pretty but useless.

Participants could not help but recognize that the core gaming industry focused primarily on games for men, treating women as an afterthought. And when they turned to casual games, they had to determine whether playing the game was worth potentially reinforcing negative stereotypes about themselves and about female gamers more generally. Because of this, they were always choosing games within an industrial and cultural system that significantly limited their options. At the same time, they carefully evaluated the extent to which potential texts fit into or were at odds with their values and belief systems and then chose whether to engage. At times, they even demonstrated their feelings by refusing to contribute monetarily to companies they find offensive, as Feather did when she chose to watch a play-through of *Lollipop Chainsaw* rather than purchase it. Women's strategies for choosing games show a balance between the constraints of a hegemonic culture that puts women on the margins and the ability of individual players to control their personal experiences.

"I Can Defend Myself": Mechanisms for Coping with Online Harassment

In addition to exercising their knowledge of games to choose texts that they are more likely to enjoy, female players also demonstrate impressive capacities for managing social environments in order to make them more pleasant. The current core gaming environment is toxic in many ways. Although statistics clearly show that "gamers" now make up only a portion of overall video game players (ESA, 2017, 2018, 2019), cultural perceptions of who plays core games have been slow to change accordingly, and nontraditional game players are still perceived as "outsiders." Because of this, more established audiences continue to target women, ethnic minorities, and/or LGBT players, for instance, for harassment. However, this treatment does not stop all individuals with these identities from enjoying games; many still play and have developed specific coping strategies they employ to avoid or respond to negativity.

Female players revealed five main strategies they use to manage their marginalized position in gaming spaces: leaving online gaming, avoiding playing with strangers, camouflaging their gender, deploying their skill and experience, or adopting an aggressive persona. A close examination of these strategies demonstrates how women regulate their media environment even though they are fighting an uphill battle against stereotypical ideas surrounding "gamers" and what gaming should look like. Women's outsider status may limit their power in the gaming environment, but they have developed creative approaches to help improve their situation, showing impressive capacity as active media managers.

Leaving Online Gaming

It's hard to make good alliances and to always have people to play with. So, multiplayer online games, they kind of force you to have friends and force you to play with other people, whereas when I play video games, I want to do it to have fun and enjoy myself, and I don't always enjoy myself when I'm trying multiplayer.
—Marie

I don't have a Live account. I used to play on my brother's account a bit, but then you get the nasty players. I used to play on my boyfriend's account, and then I got my own nasty players. So yeah, I don't really like the culture that's involved with multiplayer games.
—Feather

The first potential strategy women employ to deal with online harassment and manage their gaming environment is playing primarily single-player games. Because this project specifically targeted women who game, none of the interviewees avoided games entirely. However, many of them avoided online play, due to past negative experiences or even the perception that they were more likely to be harassed online. They saw single-player games or playing in person with friends as a safer alternative, staving off problems before they could start. As one player stated, "I don't play a lot of online games, so I don't really get harassed" (Buttsvard, interview 1).

While it is positive that women are able to enjoy games even when the multiplayer experience is unwelcoming, the fact that some committed gamers are driven away from online gaming helps contribute to the perception that core games are more for men than for women and normalizes gender harassment as a standard part of gaming spaces. Private gaming is naturally less visible than public, multiplayer gaming. Therefore, women who choose to play single-player or at-home multiplayer are often not counted among the ranks of gamers, even when they play frequently or have extensive experience. Because of this seeming absence, a great deal of previous research has tried to explain how game content may be driving women away from playing or how technology in general is oriented more towards men (e.g., Cassell and Jenkins, 1998; Kafai et al., 2008). However, newer research (Bryce and Rutter, 2002, 2003; Jansz and Martens, 2005; Jenson, de Castell, and Fisher, 2007; Jenson and de Castell, 2011) and interviewees' own responses show that it is frequently the social environments of gaming, rather than games themselves, that women find off-putting. They still game, but they do so in their own, private spaces, allowing the perception that gaming is a male pastime to continue unimpeded. This then results in higher levels of harassment directed at nonmale players, who are seen as outsiders, and restarts the cycle, driving more female players into private gaming or away from playing entirely. Overall, this allows gaming to continue functioning as a misogynistic space.

Although it is important to recognize women whose gaming is private, much can be learned from those who do participate in multiplayer arenas. These women overcome the perception that gaming is not for them and find creative ways to deal with potential barriers to participation.

Avoiding Strangers

I avoid them whenever possible. I don't like interacting with
strangers at all.
—Caddie

Among the women interviewed, not playing with strangers was one of the most common ways to avoid issues during multiplayer gaming. This strategy is popular because players assume that strangers are more likely to engage in harassment than friends are. For example, interviewees felt strangers reacted more poorly to mistakes committed while playing. As Angela said, "Strangers seem more likely to go off on you for not knowing something or playing in a way they don't like." Friends, on the other hand, were more likely to handle problems calmly, restrategize, and try again.

It is of course true that all players, not just women, enjoy playing with friends. However, women also found an extra benefit, in that friends would not subject them to unwanted advances. Interviewees frequently mentioned times when male players would flirt with them or make overtly sexual comments simply because of their gender. One interviewee, describing her experiences playing *World of Warcraft* (*WoW*) when she was in middle school, said that much older players frequently asked what color her underwear was (Katie Tyler, interview 1). Another summed up male players' reactions to her gender with the phrase, "Let me see your tits" (Alissa, interview 1). Female players saw these advances as both creepy and frustrating, as they took time and effort to fend off.

All interviewees recognized that there were always a few male gamers who were there just to play, and some had even become good friends. But many women spoke of how exhausting it was to wade through negativity in order to reach decent players. Feather said, for instance, "There are guys out there that I'm sure are fun and respectful and wonderful to play with, but I don't have the time or the energy to slog through it." Therefore, they stuck to playing with people they knew in real life or a handful of carefully vetted online friends.

From this strategy, it is clear that games that force players to engage with strangers are likely to be less popular among female players or within other marginalized groups. More welcoming games give players the option to work with friends, even in cases where they cannot avoid strangers entirely. For instance, although *League of Legends* (*LoL*) players can choose an AI opponent, the most common game type randomly matches teams against other players of their skill level. Therefore, one's opponents are almost always strangers, and strangers are sometimes needed to make up a full team of players. The *LoL* community is "pretty toxic" (Anna, interview 1), but research conducted by *LoL*'s parent company, Riot, found that "a team comprised of a group of friends was the most harmonious, followed by a group of friends who had been joined by some strangers" (Campbell, 2014). Playing with friends can be enough to overcome online harassment by helping players dismiss its impacts. As Kay stated, "I have someone who's here in the real world, who can say, 'No, don't listen to them,' and that's much more tangible to me than whatever those people say across the Internet."

Camouflaging Gender

I don't ever give my gender just out of the blue. If something comes up, I might say, but if someone calls me "he" in chat, I never correct it.
—Chimera Soul

My username doesn't really give away that I'm a girl, and there are times when I don't use my mic when I'm playing, so people don't really know that I'm a girl.
—Arya

Another popular method for preventing harassment is gender camouflage: carefully managing avatar attributes and the use of voice chat technology so that other players do not recognize one's offline gender identity. Almost all players who discussed their gaming screen names, for instance, spoke of how important it was that other players would perceive them as gender neutral or male. This was true even if they were playing as a female character; because a high proportion of men play female characters, avatar gender does not necessarily match offline gender (Stabile, 2014). Avatar name, however, seems to matter. Interviewee Angela stated, "I remember once playing *Team Fortress 2* with my ex with a Steam username that was feminine, and some random guy just started SCREAMING at me about being an attention whore. My ex thought it was hilarious, but I can't lie, I haven't used overtly feminine usernames since then." Despite the fact that her opponent did not know she was a girl, Angela's feminine username was enough to trigger a negative reaction.

Players also avoided using microphones and voice chat among groups they did not know, so that their voices would not reveal their gender. This not only headed off potential harassment but also protected the player from dealing with repetitive reactions. Even players who described the online experience as positive expressed frustration at the fact that, when they spoke up online, the person they were speaking with often ignored the content of their statement in favor of surprise about their gender (as described in chapter 3).

This not only repeatedly excludes women from the general gaming community by treating them as anomalies, but it is also frustrating because it defeats the purpose of using a microphone. The benefit of voice chat is that it is a faster means of communicating with team members and coordinating assistance, but for women, it does not always work that way. When they ask for help, their colleagues' surprise at hearing a girl sometimes delays assistance to the point where their character or their team can suffer a loss. Therefore, many women find it easier to avoid microphones entirely and sometimes even avoid game styles where being competitive requires voice chat. This allows them to "play as a gamer, instead of as a girl" (Bubble, interview 1), while demonstrating how these are culturally viewed as incompatible concepts.

Because "gamer" and "girl" were seen as very different identities, a few participants did play games under screen names that others would see as female or chose to use voice chat, treating these choices as a form of activism. Helix, for instance, said that she deliberately maintained a *LoL* account with a gender-neutral name and one that used the title "Lady" to mark it as female. Helix used the gender-neutral name most of the time, when her main goal was to play for fun. The feminine character she deployed more strategically, saying, "I sign on occasionally when playing, when I am feeling up to dealing with that kind of trash—because I feel like if women don't do anything to show, 'Hey, we're here, we're legitimate players, too!' that the atmosphere won't change."

Women like Helix and Emily, who also played under a feminine name deliberately, are willing to provoke harassment if it means making clear to other gamers that women play video games and can be very good at them. At the same time, they needed to balance this activist role with self-care; Helix only used her feminine username sometimes, and Emily often did not play the kinds of online games that are associated with the worst levels of harassment, such as *LoL* or first-person shooters. Simply asking all players to start declaring their gender identity in online gaming, to help demonstrate that audiences are more diverse than is stereotypically expected, would do a great deal to change gaming, but would also require players to cope with higher levels of harassment and employ different strategies for dealing with it, many of which also have limitations.

Deploying Skill and Experience

I always wanna make sure that people are wanting to play
with me because of my playing skills, not just because I'm a
chick.
—Elizabeth

I'm good at what I do, I taught myself, I'm not gonna do it
any differently and I'm not gonna try any less because you
feel insecure, I'll go find other people who appreciate it.
—Katie Tyler

When female gamers reveal that they are women, their strategies move from avoiding harassment to stopping it or finding ways to brush it off. For this purpose, many women rely on their skill and experience.

Some used skill aggressively; when players harassed them, they laughed it off as jealousy and pointed out how their history with games or their skill level surpassed that of the negative player. Alissa, for instance, defended herself against harassment in *WoW* by pointing out that she was the highest possible level in the game. She also stated that she "had been playing since vanilla," the slang term for the original it-eration of *WoW*. Alissa's long history with the game is a sign of skill and commitment that few other players have. By emphasizing this, she delegitimized other players' insults.

Other interviewees quietly ignored harassing players and simply fo-cused on the game. When the offending players found that the women and their allies were performing to a higher level, many of them stopped their negative behavior and apologized. Some even humbled themselves enough to ask for help. Helix stopped some extreme harassment from her guild members because she "was reasonably good at playing the game and extremely good at the sort of theorizing/strategizing/manage-ment needed to lead." Misty did the same with *Call of Duty*, stating that she "got good at *Call of Duty* out of spite [. . .] to shut anyone down who was tossing [her] aside on the sole basis of [her] gender."

Although emphasizing their skill or high level of experience with gaming was often enough to stave off harassment, this strategy did have its downsides. In addition to structuring equality and the right to avoid harassment as something to be earned rather than something inherent (Nakamura, 2017), relying on skill was a challenge. Many women strug-gled to keep up the skill level they needed in order to prevent negativity successfully, in both competitive and cooperative games. Alissa, one of the most aggressive interviewees when it came to using her skill level strategically, explained that as soon as she could not be one of the best, she stopped playing *WoW* despite her long-time commitment to it. She said, "It definitely was tough being in a situation where I don't want to have to compete, but I'm forced to and then forced to compete even farther just to make sure that I'm allowed to play." If she was not one of the best, Alissa felt that she did not have a safe place in the game, and it stopped being fun. Other players spoke of feeling similarly pressured, as if they had "to demonstrate [their] knowledge and prowess" (Jutte) in order to justify their status as a gamer.

A skill-based defense was also particularly difficult for female gam-ers, who have to display higher skill than male gamers to gain the same amount of power. This is the case because men's gender identity matches more clearly with a gamer identity. Games researcher Christopher Paul (2018) explains this through a case study of the popular professional *Overwatch* player Geguri. Geguri had not played professional games previously, but she quickly became a top competitor in *Overwatch*. Paul writes, "Geguri was extraordinarily successful in tournament play but was accused of cheating because other players thought her aiming was too good to be done without some sort of assistance" (2018, p. 46). Some professional players were so convinced she was cheating that they even agreed to quit playing if they were wrong. Geguri had to live-stream herself playing the game and be cleared by Blizzard, the company that produces *Overwatch*, before other players would accept her skill as authentic. Other (male) players who have been accused of cheating have not had to go to these lengths to prove themselves (Paul, 2018). This demonstrates how female players have to overcome a bigger hurdle to be seen as real, core gamers. Unless they had tangible proof of their skill, such as a position in a high-level raiding guild or difficult-to-obtain gear, female players were always doubted.

Aggressive Responses

I never acted the way they thought I would act, so I didn't cry and complain and be like, "OH MY GOD, YOU'RE SO MEAN!" I was a dick back to them. [. . .] A lot of guys are really surprised by that, but in a way, it's kind of earned me a lot of respect because they know I'm not a pushover. I'm not just gonna let them treat me a certain way just because I'm a girl. I fight for respect.
—Elizabeth

[Gaming] made me very sarcastic. It just gave me an edge over people cause I was either with them or it just went right over their heads and they were confused and just dropped it.
—Katie Tyler

Deliberately adopting aggressive personality traits is the last coping method interviewees relied on frequently. Participants like DT, Katie Tyler, and Elizabeth contended that showing men they could both take insults and dish them out earned them respect. When that occurred, insults stopped or changed from serious harassment to more joking banter. Deploying sarcasm had a similar result, garnering allies who found it funny while driving away harassers who did not get the joke. Taylor Ryan said, "I'm a big girl. I have a sharp tongue. I can defend myself and make them feel about two feet tall with a few sarcastic retorts."

Assuming more aggressive personalities to cope with harassment relies on making male players see that their female colleagues can stand up for themselves. For instance, when male players are overly chivalrous, treating women as if they need extra protection, gamers like Anna throw this behavior back into their face. As she said, "In game, usually guys will take the hint to back off from babysitting me when I start doing it back to them!" Like deploying skill, taking on aggressive qualities and returning insults in kind demonstrates to male players that women can be skillful gamers and can engage in trash-talk just as well as men can.

However, responding to harassment aggressively can be a double-edged sword. Women who chose this strategy sometimes faced accusations that they were "acting like an emotional female" (Laine, interview 1), with harassers drawing on the familiar trope of hysterical women to try to dismiss the player's response. As previous studies on online and game-related harassment have shown, women cannot always use the same rhetorical strategies as men, at least not without provoking further harassment or accusations that they are being overly sensitive to something that was not meant to be taken seriously (Gray, 2012, 2014; Herring, 1999; Nakamura, 2012; Salter and Blodgett, 2012). Interviewees employing this strategy felt that with confidence and a reasonable approach, it could be useful in many situations, but they carefully prepared alternative responses in case it backfired.

This approach also had the potential to turn women against each other to a degree, when those who were comfortable being aggressive would get frustrated with those who were not. Elizabeth described an incident in which a fellow female gamer had been harassed, and said, "I was just thinking to myself like, I would have not put up with that for more than two seconds, I would have told that guy off and messed with him in the game . . . I wouldn't have sat there and, you know, cried like a little girl and been like, 'You're mean! Why are you saying that?!'" Because Elizabeth stood up for herself and was able to brush off negativity, she did not understand why the other player took harassment so poorly and did not deal with it directly. Rather, she felt that the other player ended up making women look like "little girls," potentially negatively affecting the overall perception of female gamers. In some cases, therefore, confronting harassers head-on may have both short-term and long-term consequences and can even complicate women's relationship to one another, if they feel another female player is not confronting harassment in the "right" way.

Unpopular Alternatives

In addition to their favored coping strategies, interviewees referenced three other strategies that were less popular and far more controversial.

They used the first of these, employing technical solutions like blocking harassers, occasionally. Sophie, for instance, said, "I would either basically tell them to get lost or block them." But for many games, blocking a negative player came with a high disadvantage, "because you can't see what they type in-game, like if they sincerely tell you someone's coming your way" (Kay, interview 1). Not being able to see legitimate warnings or cries for help interfered with gamers' ability to win in multiplayer games and therefore was not a popular option. Technical solutions of this sort seemed to cause more problems than they solved for players, especially as many games make it easy for players to start a new character and resume harassment.

Relying on male assistance to drive off harassers was also an unpopular option. While some interviewees felt that playing with male friends or boyfriends may have decreased the harassment they faced, only one player, Elayne, specifically mentioned relying on her husband or male friends to help chase off people who were bothering her, and she only did so at in-person gaming events. Because her husband was physically present, this strategy worked; other players found that relying on men online did not always help. Helix, for instance, faced most of her harassment at the hands of her boyfriend's friends in *WoW*, even after he asked them to stop. This option therefore was ineffective in many situations, and it also seemed unpopular due to the independence of the interviewees. Most preferred to rely on themselves in order to deal with harassment, rather than needing assistance.

No interviewees employed the final strategy for coping with harassment, the calculated use of flirtation to win over male players. In fact, they largely looked down on others who chose to do so, finding this strategy to be an uncomfortable or counterproductive one. For example, when Elayne jokingly revealed her gender to a player who was trash-talking her, he immediately apologized and went from rude to flirtatious so quickly that she found it unnerving, describing it as "pathetic and ick." Other players spoke of how girls who flirted to get ahead in games changed overall expectations for female gamers. To quote Vickie again, "You'll hear some people talk about like . . . that was their impression of female gamers, that they always got something for free, or they did it to get help . . . I always tried to avoid having that connotation." Players like Vickie and Feather, who described encountering similar perceptions of "girl gamers," felt that flirting to get help encouraged harassment from men because it became the expected norm for female behavior. Men then saw women who flirted as behaving properly, which protected them from harassment, while those who did not flirt suffered. Helix agreed with this sentiment; although she was insulted on a regular basis while playing *WoW*, her female guild mates who flirted with everyone did not face harassment. Even though Helix was dating a fellow guild mate, other players still expected her to perform a particular, flirtatious role because of her gender.

The fact that participants only brought up this strategy in negative terms demonstrates the same value judgments they made about "girl gamers" or women who did not game in the "right" way. Because "girl gamers" were distinctly not core, my participants felt that they reaffirmed stereotypes that women were only casual gamers or that they were only interested in gaming to meet men. In doing so, participants argued, their behavior made it harder for core female gamers to be seen *as* core by other players. Therefore, interviewees judged and devalued these different approaches to play to protect their own investments in gaming spaces. Similarly, they judged and devalued using flirtation as a strategy to avoid harassment, despite the fact that they felt it could be effective, and argued that it was not an acceptable long-term solution to harassment. Instead, they felt it was part of the problem.

Significance and Limitations

In response to games' toxicity, many players have developed nuanced coping strategies for avoiding or managing harassment, as a means for protecting themselves. As matters stand, however, the majority of players' attempts to manage harassment or cope with its impacts while gaming are individual, based on personal efforts such as avoiding online games, not playing games with strangers, or hiding one's identity from others in game spaces (Nakamura, 2012; Cote, 2017).

While these are effective on a personal level, many of them create further problems by masking minority gamers' presence in game spaces, contributing to perceptions of games as masculinized and traditional "gamers" as dominant. As digital media and identity scholar Kishonna Gray (2014) points out, "Gamers can stay away from players they choose to avoid. However, this creates a problem in addressing meaningful solutions to verbal abuse within this space" (p. xxi). More specifically, coping mechanics are internal processes for managing harassment, and they therefore do little to undermine the hegemony of trash-talk. Relying on individuals to combat harassment also puts the onus of solving toxicity on the victims of it, forcing those who are already marginalized to try to make improvements. This is unlikely to be effective, as "groups unequal in power are correspondingly unequal in their ability to make their standpoint known to themselves and others" (Hill Collins, 1990, pp. 39–40).

Furthermore, it is equally clear that coping strategies require work. Women must constantly be aware of how others will interpret their behavior, username, voice, or skill, and they must carefully manage these aspects to ensure a positive gaming experience. Just as offline society requires women to defend themselves against sexual harassment or assault by managing their dress and behavior, the onus of online harassment management is put on the victim.

Finally, many of the strategies in use come with potential complications. Taking on an aggressive personality to stop harassers, for instance, can result in a negative backlash, but blocking harassers or hiding one's gender may further women's perceived absence in gaming and the association of games with men. In turn, this perpetuates the cycle of harassment.

Because of this, none of these approaches is a final solution; they are a "Band-Aid" on the problem rather than a cure (Emily, interview 1). Many participants were aware of this, and some took deliberate steps to try to change gaming, even if it meant further harassment. These women recognized that public gaming is necessary to changing women's treatment in the online environment. As Emily said, "My gamer names have always proudly referenced that I'm a girl gamer. And I refuse to change that. I feel hiding my gender would make me complicit in victim blaming; i.e., I need to work harder not to 'attract' harassment rather than the bully needs to stop acting horribly." At the same time, it is unfair to ask women to shoulder the entire burden of changing audience stereotypes and behaviors. Simply increasing their visibility and asking them to face the resultant harassment cannot be the only solution.

The rise of social, mobile, and casual games over the last decade has indicated to the games industry that its audiences do and should span beyond traditional "gamers," and that it is in their own interest to diversify. As chapter 1 showed, many developers have already been making strong overtures to nontraditional audiences. Activists therefore have an opportunity to take advantage of this moment, to push for greater social justice in gaming when developers are more likely to recognize its benefits. The question, of course, is what recommendations to developers should be.

Unfortunately, as interviewees indicated, gamers currently lack serious organizational support from developers and publishers. Companies frequently offer only tools for players to self-segregate, through blocking harassing players, for instance, rather than actually combating gaming culture's aggressive foundation. Others fall back on reporting mechanisms that do little to curb behavior, as many are not enforced or too easy to circumvent. Overall, these leave players feeling that developers are not taking seriously their needs and their desire to be equal members of the gaming community. Meaningful interventions into gaming culture require tools other than those currently available.

Drawing on Developers: Increasing Protections for Marginalized Gamers

Overall, problems with both game content and online environments can only be solved completely with a change to the hegemonic order of video games, whereby games designers and other players see women as essential to games' core rather than marginal or casual players. Because harassment is more common in male-dominated environments

(McDonald, 2012) or is used to "fix" the behavior of individuals who violate gender norms (Berdahl, 2007), making core gaming more diverse and normalizing women's presence should help decrease overall levels of misogyny. When diverse groups are accepted as members of the gaming community, the kind of exclusionary language required for trash-talk is likely to fall out of use, as harassment needs social norms to support it (Chui, 2014). Players would also then face fewer difficulties in finding games that avoid offensive representations or offer female protagonists.

Until that happens, however, it is important to prioritize other types of changes that could help marginalized gamers protect themselves. To this end, the remainder of this chapter analyzes some of the popular community-management strategies developers have relied on in the past, comparing these to players' stated preferences and challenges. It shows that successful interventions require attention to where players already are and how they want to manage their own communities, a step that many game companies have previously ignored. Finally, I suggest other short-term strategies developers could use to protect players during the slow process of cultural change.

Past Approaches to Community Management

As I have written about elsewhere (Cote, 2018a), many previous attempts to decrease toxicity in core gaming communities have been ineffective or have even met with serious resistance from players. In 2010, for instance, Blizzard Entertainment, the company behind the popular massively multiplayer online game (MMO) *World of Warcraft*, announced their RealID system, which would connect players' real names to their posts on official Blizzard forums. Blizzard's decision was based on evidence that anonymous players are more likely to harass others (Chisholm, 2006; Fox and Tang, 2014), but it led to a massive backlash. Forum posts on the issue argued that anonymity helps players feel safe communicating with strangers online. They also specifically referenced marginalized gamers, such as women, ethnic minorities, LGBT players, and/or disabled players, as those most threatened by the change, as revealing their identities could set these players up for increased, rather than decreased, harassment (Albrechtslund, 2011; Roinioti, 2011). This is reflective of what my participants related, as they relied heavily on the ability to manage when, how, and to whom they revealed their gender or their offline identity. Thus, although it was grounded in a logical assumption about the connections between harassment and anonymity, the RealID controversy shows that simply removing players' ability to be anonymous is not an acceptable approach to community management.

Other companies have relied on reputation systems, with varying levels of success. These approaches link a player's in-game behavior to an account reputation, which helps others decide whether they want to play with that individual. Reputation systems can even be connected to in-game penalties, where players are restricted or banned if their reputation drops too low. However, not all reputation systems are effective.

Evidence from Xbox Live's early reputation system, instituted shortly after the introduction of the Xbox 360, shows that just having a reputation system in place is not sufficient to prevent harassment (Cote, 2018a). The algorithms that governed this system often performed illogically, such as when they matched gamers with players they had asked to avoid (Orland, 2013) or even raised the ranking of players who were reported for bad behavior (Hinkley, 2010). Because Xbox Live reputations did not accurately reflect players' behavior patterns, they did little to curb harassment, as evidenced by Xbox's reputation as a potentially dangerous online space (Gray, 2014).

On the other hand, well-thought-out reputation systems have been effective in the past, at least to a degree. For instance, the community-management team at Riot Games has taken extensive steps to prevent harassment in the online *League of Legends* (*LoL*) community, which is notoriously toxic. Specifically, they have focused on protecting players from existing negativity, reforming or removing toxic players, and creating a culture focused on sportsmanship and positivity (Lin, 2013). To protect players, the company's Social System design team first made cross-team chat opt-in rather than opt-out; players had to choose to see what their opponents said, preventing them from accidental exposure to trash-talk. The design team also created a Tribunal System to evaluate player behavior. Players could report others' positive or negative actions, and community members could then vote on cases to determine whether that behavior was acceptable in *LoL* or not.[5] Unacceptable behaviors saw consequences, such as a warning e-mail or restricted chat abilities, while cases the community pardoned saw no punishment (Lin,

2013). Players who improved were given back their full chat abilities. Those who did not faced increasingly severe punishment, even if they were popular or professional players. For instance, two professional players were banned for six months in 2014 when they continued to abuse opponents even after their accounts were restricted (Farokhmanesh, 2014). This indicated that all players were to be held to the same standards.

Overall, this system led to a measurable decrease in negative behavior. According to Social System designer Jeffrey Lin, in the first three years of the Tribunal (2011–2014), "incidences of homophobia, sexism, and racism in *League of Legends* have fallen to a combined 2 percent of all games. Verbal abuse has dropped by more than 40 percent, and 91.6 percent of negative players change their act and never commit another offense after just one reported penalty" (Lin, 2015b).[6] Because my participants argued that harassment and toxicity made it difficult for them to enter game culture fully, these changes in *LoL*'s online environment are promising, as they help open up a space for all players to game with less risk.

Unfortunately, Riot retired the Tribunal in 2014, at first stating that it was retooling it to be more effective (Lin, 2014), then replacing it with a new Instant Feedback System (LeJacq, 2015; Lin, 2015a). Reports are now automatically reviewed by an algorithm that assesses the reported behavior and issues appropriate punishments alongside reform cards that detail why the player is being penalized (Lin, 2015a). Riot currently has no plans to reinstate the Tribunal, arguing that its new approach is more effective because it draws on Tribunal findings while working much faster (Forbes, 2018). At the same time, Riot recognizes the need for further improvement. Riot is also currently dealing with allegations that its industrial culture is sexist and exclusionary, indicating that player toxicity is not the only issue that needs to be addressed (D'Anastasio, 2018).

Despite this, even the moderate success of the Tribunal is important because it shows that change is possible. This has motivated further attempts on the part of developers to manage their communities. Blizzard, for instance, has implemented commendations for positive behavior in its popular online game *Overwatch*, while large game studio Ubisoft, which creates the *Assassin's Creed*, *Far Cry*, and *Tom Clancy's* series, among others, recently introduced automatic instant suspensions for players who try to type slurs into chat in *Rainbow Six Siege* (Castello, 2018). Perhaps most significantly, over ninety game companies recently signed on to the Fair Play Alliance, a collective effort "to collaborate on research and best practices that encourage fair play and healthy communities in online gaming" (Fair Play Alliance, 2018). Game companies are starting to prioritize more positive environments that make space for diverse players.

Further Suggestions from Interview Data

Unfortunately, encouraging overall cultural change through community management can take time, and players need more immediate tools for minimizing harassment while this change occurs. In their interviews, players expressed many preferences that developers can draw on to design more inclusive games. These include grouping mechanisms, new systems for displaying skill and experience, and different approaches to in-game chat.

My participants' strategy of playing with friends to avoid harassment meant that they were very fond of both short-term grouping mechanisms and long-term guilds or clans. These allowed players to choose whom they played with. For instance, interviewees enjoyed the ability to sign up for a *League of Legends* match as a team, ensuring that they were with at least a few friends. Blizzard's new *Overwatch* changes included the ability to sign up for matches in a group as well; between this and their commendation system, abusive chat has dropped between 15 and 30 percent (Castello, 2018). Similarly, Gray (2014) found that women of color playing Xbox Live games often grouped up to turn the tables on their harassers (p. 67). Gray's participants banded together to "grief" or intentionally irritate negative players as a means for resisting being marginalized (Gray 2014, p. 38). Playing with friends is a key coping mechanism for marginalized players, and developers should allow for this.

Guild or clan structures also allowed players to group with friends and provided information on where they could find safe spaces. Guilds that do not allow female members, for instance, are very up-front about that information, while groups that do not tolerate insults or profanity also make that clear. Game studies scholar Dmitri Williams and colleagues (2006) found, "Most players were keenly aware of the types of guilds and had ready, common labels for them (which we have used here, not created). For example, one player stated, 'We're a raid-oriented family friendly guild'" (pp. 345–46). Players could thus find groups that matched their socialization priorities and play style. Grouping mechanisms are already features of many multiplayer games and networked systems, so developers have a foundation for adding these capabilities in the future.

Other favored coping strategies require more creative design solutions. For instance, many interviewees used their skill or experience with games as a barrier against harassment; when they were harassed, they could laugh it off as jealousy from an opponent who was not as good a player. However, using skill as a means of protection requires players to commit large amounts of time and effort to continual improvement. Many players would quit a favorite game the moment they did not have time to excel at it, feeling as though they had lost their safe space. This is a particularly significant issue for women, who face the pressure of the "second shift," or the continued double burden of managing both work and a household (Hochschild and Machung, 1989; Schulte, 2014). The requirements of the second shift can deeply interfere with their ability to relax and find time for entertainment, including games.

Games thus need tools players can use to emphasize their high level of skill and experience. For example, game developers could provide badges or account histories so a player can display their past achievements or how long they have been playing. This does have limitations, as it supports the hegemony of core and the meritocratic idea that being *good enough* allows one to surmount harassment, but it would work as a short-term protective measure while broader cultural change occurs. New leveling systems could be another useful change. Once a player reaches the top levels of many games, such as MMOs, the time commitment required is enormous. A game in which players can continue to explore and progress without needing to play constantly would be ideal. *Guild Wars 2* allows for this using a dynamic level adjustment mechanic, which temporarily weakens a player whose level exceeds their current in-game zone. Therefore, players can return to old quests without finding them too simple, allowing them to develop further skills, defend their position in the game, and continue having fun without a massive time investment.

Developers could also help players manage their online identities effectively. Currently, players use linguistic markers, both verbal and typed, to distinguish who is a "gamer" and who is not; they then use these to direct harassment towards outsiders. The ability to avoid giving these cues in the first place could protect marginalized gamers. "As many women and people of color explain, [voice] creates the most havoc in their virtual lives—racial and gendered hatred based on how people sound" (Gray, 2014, p. 45). Although players can camouflage their gender or race by avoiding microphones, there are times when doing so interferes with multiplayer gaming, particularly in fast-paced games. Therefore, developers, if starting at the basic design level, may want to include some way to communicate quickly without using voice. One option could be including preprogrammed phrases or alerts linked to a short keystroke or mouse click, as *LoL* does with its "smart ping" system. At least some female players heavily rely on these pings to direct play and help the team succeed without provoking harassment due to their feminine voice (Ratan et al., 2015). Adding a similar system to other fast-paced games could decrease immediate issues with harassment. Such an offering would also help players avoid racial profiling via written communication, as players with poor grammar are often targets of harassment (Nakamura, 2009).

These suggestions provide short-term mechanisms for protection in the existing game environment but are unlikely to change gaming culture towards greater inclusivity and acceptance of diverse players. Therefore, they should be only one tool employed in addressing online harassment. However, their grounding in players' lived experiences demonstrates how understanding audience behavior can help developers create strategies and tools players will actually use.

Conclusions

In core gaming culture, minority players face high levels of negativity, including sexism, racism, homophobia, and other forms of discrimination. On top of this, players are primarily left to develop their own coping mechanisms, relying on individual strategies like avoidance or direct confrontation of harassers. This provides personal protection but does little to undermine the normalization of discrimination and a hegemonic structure that ostracizes many players.

At the same time, growing attention to these problems, and the fact that casual, social, and mobile games have made developers recognize that broad audiences play games, provide an opportunity for activists, players, and even interested game designers to push for greater change. Leveraging a desire for higher sales figures and bigger audiences, it may be possible to encourage developers to improve their game communities and increase the consequences players face if they choose to harass others. The question is what social justice–oriented game design looks like and how developers should institute it.

From the analysis above, it is clear that a combination of approaches is required. The strategies that gamers currently employ to protect themselves can continue to help them manage harassment, and developers can create new tools for immediate intervention. However, to foster overall cultural change and undermine gaming's exclusivity, developers need to push further. First, they need to prioritize the needs of minority players as much as those of their majority players, providing them with the power and tools needed to manage their environment and supporting them when others harass them. Second, they need to apply consistent consequences when players harass others, indicating that this behavior is unacceptable. Finally, they should avoid removing marginalized players' current means of self-protection, allowing them to play safely while cultural change occurs. Well-thought-out measures, like Riot Games' Tribunal, have the potential to curb toxic behavior, encourage players to reform, and thus undermine the cycle of aggression and violence that so heavily undergirds existing online game spaces.

This will benefit individual players, who will be able to enjoy games without discrimination, but it could also work to improve overall sociocultural trends. Although games are not the sole purveyors of sexism, racism, and homophobia in modern society, they are a widespread and popular entertainment medium. As such, their current status as a bastion of discrimination allows these attitudes to spread to other areas of popular culture and to affect individual lived experiences. Undermining them should therefore be a priority.

6

In the Aftermath

Women's Changing Views on Gaming and
Sexism Following #GamerGate

My first round of interviews clearly demonstrated that sexism structured many facets of female gamers' interactions with gaming communities and spaces and revealed that these challenges had not decreased due to casual's rise. If anything, women's struggles to be accepted as core gamers *increased*, as the rise of casual created an area within gaming that was seen as women's proper space. Thus, it was even more a violation of the norm for them to be core, and this, combined with anxieties about core changing or disappearing, led to high levels of harassment. Women were capable of handling these and finding enjoyment in gaming, but doing so required some work.

Shortly after I wrapped my interviews, however, matters became more complicated, as the Twitter movement known as #GamerGate occurred in 2014. GamerGate was motivated by the (later disproven) claim that female game developer Zoë Quinn had exchanged sexual favors with a journalist for positive coverage of her game *Depression Quest*. The movement was ostensibly about ethical concerns regarding games journalism. In practice, however, GamerGate played out in the form of gender-based harassment directed at female developers, players, and cultural critics, including Quinn, developer Brianna Wu, and Anita Sarkeesian (Massanari, 2015; Salter and Blodgett, 2017). These individuals were doxxed, meaning their personal information and home addresses were published in online spaces, they faced threats of rape and death, and some were even "swatted," which occurs when a harasser calls in a false crime report at the intended target's location, sending in SWAT teams to scare or injure them. Male developers or gaming community members who stood up for GamerGate victims also faced harassment. Because of its extreme nature, GamerGate rapidly became a topic for national news, with stories in the *Washington Post,* the *New York Times, Forbes,* the *New Yorker,* the *Guardian,* and more.

At the same time, many of these pieces, and much of the furor around GamerGate, focused on public-facing figures—cultural critics like Sarkeesian, developers like Quinn and Wu, and even academic members of the Digital Games Research Association (DiGRA) (Chess and Shaw, 2015). It was often unclear what impact GamerGate had—or continues to have—on female gamers' day-to-day engagement with gaming culture and communities. Was GamerGate a significant event for them? How did it affect their relationship with games and other gamers?

When I had the chance to reinterview my participants, these were some of my key questions. Surprisingly, they revealed that GamerGate was not a particularly significant event for them. Many dismissed GamerGate as just another instance of the sexism they already faced regularly, while others simply avoided GamerGate conversations entirely. The ways in which they discussed the movement, however, are still interesting. As we saw in earlier chapters, women's strategies for managing game spaces varied widely, with some, for instance, playing only with friends or hiding their gender to avoid harassment while others proudly proclaimed their female gamer identity in order to serve as activists. Participants also interpreted game communities and the term "gamer" in different ways, alternating between accepting the widely held belief that most gamers were male and pushing back against this to draw attention to game audiences' diversity and their own skill, experience, and knowledge of games. In these ways, the female gamers I interviewed both align with and undermine many existing beliefs about games and gamers, simultaneously embodying the characteristics of core while being separated from it due to their gender identity. This highlights the ways in which hegemonic and counterhegemonic forces are at play in defining the casualized era and its impacts.

Unsurprisingly, women's split identity as female/gamer also played out in diverse ways when they were confronted with an event like GamerGate, with some taking an explicitly feminist stance and others rejecting this in favor of more gamer-oriented interpretations of the event. Thus, their interpretations of GamerGate indicate the ways in which identity can be fragmented and negotiated differently even among individuals who share common characteristics. Their moments of agreement also matter, as despite their many disagreements, all wanted similar things for gaming's future. Their experiences again emphasize the casualized era's struggle between hegemonic and counterhegemonic forces, as some participants continued to support existent and exclusionary conceptions of core while others saw events like GamerGate as a chance to redefine these.

I also used my second round of interviews to investigate how women's gaming habits changed over time; given the costs incurred in being both female and a gamer, I wondered if this subject position was sustainable or if the work involved would drive women to stop gaming. As digital cultures scholar Kelly Bergstrom (2019) points out, researchers and other gamers generally assume people who do not play games are just not interested in them. But Bergstrom finds this is not the case; reasons not to participate in a subculture are far more complicated. My updated interviews therefore respond to her work by returning to the same players to evaluate whether, and under what circumstances, they might have left gaming in the five years since we first spoke.

This second round also helps contextualize women's play within their broader lives. As Mia Consalvo and Jason Begy (2015) point out, any study of gamers is assessing those players within particular contexts— contexts of game type, social environment, life stage, and more. Because of this, how a player describes their gaming habits at one moment may differ dramatically from how they describe them at a different date or if they are playing a different game. However, much of game studies has tended to treat players statically, tacitly assuming that a person who plays a certain way now will always play the same way. Consalvo and Begy push back against this essentialization, arguing, "We need better, more refined studies of the life courses of players to more adequately capture [players' changing game] activity" (Consalvo and Begy, 2015, p. 94). Follow-up interviews and other longitudinal methods are ways to address this concept of play lifecycle.

Thus, this chapter addresses two main questions. First, it assesses how female gamers interpret events such as GamerGate and whether these events affect them, their playing habits, or their attitude towards gaming and game culture. Second, it analyzes how players' gaming habits have changed more generally and what factors account for these changes. Through this approach, this chapter situates GamerGate within context, providing perspectives on it from individuals who have been involved in gaming since well before the movement and who, in many cases, still game despite it. Through their voices, it is possible to move beyond GamerGate by recognizing it for what it is—a symptom of deeper structures of sexism and backlash in gaming. The chapter also furthers our understanding of player lifecycle, showing how women's gaming changes in often surprising ways, but also how they continue to game despite the challenges in doing so.

Understanding GamerGate

As both a game studies scholar and a female gamer myself, I found Gamer-Gate to be unfortunate but not surprising. I was already involved in this project, and it was apparent that sexism in gaming was not a new thing. I also saw GamerGate as an expected outcome of core's crisis of authority; under the threat of losing their privileged position, of course core structures would lash out against perceived interlopers such as women. At the same time, I was thankfully not one of the academics who faced significant harassment from GamerGaters, and I was already largely removed from most multiplayer gaming spaces; studying games can unfortunately leave little time for playing them, and I spent my limited gaming hours on my favorite single-player games (e.g., *Assassin's Creed*, *Civilization*, and *Tomb Raider*) or *Candy Crush*. Because of this, I recognized that my perception of GamerGate might not reflect that of all or most female gamers. And if it was significant to them, this deserved to be addressed.

Furthermore, GamerGate has become de rigueur in conversations about sexism in gaming. As one participant stated, "Since then, every Slate.com article about some woman being harassed online, you get the one paragraph about GamerGate" (Spinach, interview 2). Given the extensive discussion of the movement in popular media and academic circles, it was unlikely that female gamers had avoided it entirely, especially if they were still playing regularly. Thus, I worked with my interviewees to build a more expansive view of the movement and what it meant.

Defining GamerGate

To lead off our conversations about GamerGate, I asked participants if they had heard of GamerGate and how they would describe it. Although a few simply referred to it as "a really broad term about harassment in the gaming community" (Marie, interview 2), many gave more in-depth descriptions that specifically linked GamerGate to questions of "gamer" stereotypes, core games' hegemonic masculinization, and increasing attention to counterhegemonic diversity and inclusion. Chianna, for instance, bluntly referred to GamerGaters as "a bunch of stuck-up white guys who can't get over the fact that . . . the world of gaming doesn't center around them." Elayne offered an expanded version of this statement, carefully explaining,

> Video games have for so long been like a safe spot or a safe area and really core to the identity of, you know, white males. Or like white male nerds who are already maybe kind of insecure in their masculinity, and they have this safe space and this thing that they are good at, and it's precious and really core to them. And then to have that, I guess, seemingly subverted by quote-unquote "forcing" diversity and the presence of female protagonists and basically people who did not look like them, to be not catered to after so long of being catered to, was kind of a shock. [. . .] I guess they felt really threatened, and so they just rose up to protect their identity.

Chianna, Elayne, and other interviewees like Emily describe GamerGate as a crisis of authority, in which the group that has been hegemonic sees its power shifting and reacts with force to prevent change due to the rise of counterhegemonic forces. In fact, Elayne even went on to refer to harassment and doxxing as hegemonic "gamers" "fighting back in all the ways that they could to protect this thing that they think exists." Interviewees saw GamerGate and other incidents of harassment as clear reactions to real or perceived diversification in gaming, citing examples such as *Dragon Age: Inquisition*, which featured a transgender character and same-sex romance options, as potential motivators for hegemonic "gamers'" concerns.

This aligns with the reaction game studies scholar Megan Condis (2015) found when studying BioWare's choice to add playable gay male characters to *Star Wars: The Old Republic* and *Dragon Age II*. Many "gamers" protested this decision, arguing that BioWare was forgetting about its "true" (straight, white, male) fans. As Condis elaborates,

"Gamers have been taught to desire (and to expect) a bodiless, apolitical experience within virtual worlds. In fact, many see that experience as the purpose for the existence of virtual worlds in the first place, the source of their entertainment value and of their potential as a refuge from the real world" (2015, p. 204). Thus, players saw the introduction of homosexual characters as a political incursion into their pure space of play, which was supposed to be about the game, not about identity. This is, of course, a stance one can only take when one's identity is *always already* included, as has been the case for men in games, but such privileges often become invisible to their bearers. Including others can then feel like *prioritizing* those others rather than fixing existing disparities (Kimmel, 2013).

Conflicts between diversification and existing privilege have been occurring in many traditionally masculinized areas, and my interviewees linked gaming's crisis of authority to similar issues in spaces such as comics. Laine, for instance, said GamerGate was "similar to the kind of pushback that's being seen in comic books as well with diversification of those characters and trying to limit the sexual nature of many characters." Although a full exploration of recent issues in comic book writing, publishing, and fan culture is beyond the scope of this book,[1] suffice it to say that this industry has faced its own challenges with gender and harassment, including a 2017 ComicsGate. ComicsGate began when a group of female Marvel Studios employees shared a photo of themselves going out for milkshakes to celebrate the life of Flo Steinberg, a groundbreaking female comics publisher who had been involved in the industry since the 1960s. This simple act of sharing ignited a tirade of abuse directed at the women in the photo, as well as female, person-of-color, and LGBT comic writers more generally. ComicsGate supporters argued that these individuals "were ruining comic books, and pushing out the views and voices of authentic fans" (Berlatsky, 2018). This online movement shares many similarities with GamerGate, both in terms of the harassment leveled at perceived outsiders and in terms of the existence of a narrowly defined, historically targeted group of consumers who fear losing their privileged status (Salter and Blodgett, 2017).[2]

Finally, interviewees linked all these issues, in games and other spaces, to the rise of the men's rights movement and to alt-right politics in the United States and worldwide. Emily, for instance, said, "I feel like GamerGate was a catalyst for like a men's rights movement that disguised itself as being about ethics and commercialization in gaming." That is, she believes the issue was never truly games at all; rather, it was about traditional spheres of masculine power, men who felt that these were being threatened, and how they reacted to this threat. Similarly, Taylor Ryan argued, "I do think that the world as a whole is going through a game-changing time at the moment, and when you see things like white nationalism coming to the forefront [. . .] I'm more shocked that such a huge culture, completely focused on intolerance and hatred, has emerged so abruptly. I suppose it's always been there, but it's become increasingly vocal and unashamed." These participants see games' traditionally masculinized power structures as representative of broader masculinized power structures, and GamerGate as a case study into what happens when these structures are faced with potential change. My interviewees are not alone in drawing these connections. In fact, supporters of movements like GamerGate and ComicsGate have explicitly stated that their goal is the reclamation of spaces they see as theirs and the reclamation of masculinity more generally (Berlatsky, 2018; Elbein, 2018). Therefore, issues in games can rightly be seen as reflective of broader politics and social trends (Condis, 2018; Lees, 2016).

With that being said, participants were not all in agreement about what GamerGate was or what it meant. While all of them agreed that there was never a cause for harassment, doxxing, or death threats, two of my interviewees did not see GamerGate as one-sided. Spinach, for instance, said, "It's one of those things where, yeah, like she probably did some things that weren't very good, but also people were harassing people and that's never good."[3] Feather presented a similar argument. She said, "GamerGate was awful, and I had friends on both sides of the fence, and I was very ambiguous because part of me felt what happened to [Quinn] is not acceptable. But she's not completely innocent either, at least with what I'm reading. Everyone's wrong. Everyone's wrong in this. There were no clean hands." Both rejected the intense harassment Quinn, and other female developers, gamers, and cultural critics like Sarkeesian, were subject to, but they also bought into the narrative that Quinn may have done something that started the problem in the first place.

GamerGate is therefore another circumstance in which the fragmented and contradictory nature of a female/gamer identity plays out in different ways for different individuals. Obviously, not all women are feminists or are likely to see GamerGate as a feminist issue. However, the fact that many of them did indicates that, even when they enter into a masculinized space or perhaps especially when they enter into a masculinized space, women's identity *as women* was salient. Participants often prioritized this part of themselves, supporting other female gamers, celebrating when they beat men at their own game, or proudly displaying their female/gamer identity in an activist way.

At the same time, women who have worked hard to attain a gamer identity and a high level of gaming capital may prioritize that part of their identity, especially when they know few other female gamers. On their own, it may be easier to interpret events like GamerGate in line with gaming's dominant ideologies, rather than taking a different stance based on one's identity as female. There is also social capital to be gained from being "one of the guys," as evidenced by female gamers who disliked meeting other women in game spaces. In these circumstances, it may be easier to take a middle-of-the-road position rather than risk alienating one's gamer friends.

Additionally, as insiders to game culture themselves, core female players may resent critiques that appear insufficiently grounded in gaming knowledge. Feather, for instance, transitioned smoothly from talking about Quinn to talking about Anita Sarkeesian and her work with the video series *Tropes vs. Women in Video Games*. Feather felt that Sarkeesian made some good points but that overall she was too critical of games because she was not a "real" gamer. Feather often took her own explicitly feminist stances towards games and game culture, wanting sexism in these areas to be critiqued and addressed. But she wanted these critiques to be on her terms as a gamer, and therefore as an insider to game culture. Women's differing prioritization of their gender or gaming identities deeply affected how they interpreted events like GamerGate.

Personal Impacts of GamerGate

Despite these differing interpretations of what GamerGate was, participants generally agreed that the movement had not affected them personally, in part because they were well practiced at avoiding sexism in game spaces. Additionally, some were already slightly removed from the online gaming communities that bore the brunt of GamerGate's harassment, while others deliberately avoided conversations about GamerGate because they did not think they could change participants' minds.

For Marie, GamerGate occurred as she was finishing a graduate degree, and the pressures of school and work kept her offline and out of the loop. She had also already decreased her online gaming, which meant she was less likely to be exposed to GamerGate issues in that sphere. Similarly, Misty avoided GamerGate largely without trying, as she felt it occurred primarily on Twitter, and she did not have a Twitter account. Other participants, like Adrianna, Emily, and Elayne, however, found that reading news about GamerGate was a "feel bad exercise" (Elayne, interview 2), which made them frustrated, angry, sad, or all of these at once. Because of this, they stayed away from news about what was happening.

Interviewees also took this avoidance approach because they thought nothing they said would make any difference. In Adrianna's case, she felt she was bad at arguing over issues she cared about, as she got too emotionally invested. Emily asked, "If I add my voice on it, is that really going to matter? . . . It just kind of felt like engaging them especially online is not going to make a difference, because they can hide behind the screen." She had previously been one of the strongest advocates for women in gaming, making sure that her gaming usernames always indicated that she was female and standing up for herself in online spaces. Now, however, she found herself limiting her activism. When I asked why, she said, "I might be more tired. Tired overall because I think there's a lot of . . . You know, especially with how things have changed since the election." The general political milieu, especially around issues like women's rights and healthcare coverage, required so much of her time and energy that the amount she had left for gaming advocacy was limited. Although she still shared her love for games when possible, she had reached the point where she sometimes opted out of difficult conversations if she felt her perspective would not make a difference.

This relates to how women coped with harassment online. As chapter 5 lays out, many women opted to avoid online gaming entirely, as this was one way to guarantee that other players would not harass them. Others played only with people they already knew. Although these types of actions potentially limited their play experiences, participants also felt that they were necessary measures for self-protection. Avoiding news stories about the harassment of other female gamers or about how women should not be gamers was useful for the exact same reason. Furthermore, although GamerGate itself did not affect participants too much, this does still indicate how gaming's overall sexist patterns can make it difficult for female gamers to be involved in the long term. Consistent exposure to sexist behaviors and beliefs, especially when combined with similar political and social trends, is exhausting. It is no surprise that (as the rest of this chapter explores) many female players find it easier to decrease their gaming, play in less social ways, or switch to in-person games rather than continue to battle exclusionary forces.

Cultural Impacts of GamerGate

One might expect that events like GamerGate, and the fact that much of what women faced had not dramatically improved between our first interview and our second, would drive female gamers to be less optimistic about the future of gaming. But to a woman, they all still felt that gaming was improving or could improve. In fact, many saw GamerGate as a good thing for gaming overall, despite its virulence. While mass media and nongamers were surprised by GamerGate's misogyny, interviewees felt that the movement was par for the course given that core gaming was "a pretty classic cesspool of sexism" (Adrianna, interview 2). In fact, some even said that an event like GamerGate was "bound to happen eventually" (Feather, interview 2). The scale of GamerGate, and the attention it got outside of gaming culture, however, was new.

Because of this attention, interviewees felt that GamerGate might actually provoke change. Adrianna, for instance, compared GamerGate to the #MeToo movement, arguing that just as sexism in Hollywood could not be addressed at all until it was made obvious, sexism in gaming could not be addressed until it was talked about. And just as the #MeToo movement was meant to give women in Hollywood a feeling of connectedness, participants argued that the negativity of GamerGate had encouraged the majority of gamers to band together against the small minority that was responsible for the movement.

Changing Gaming Patterns

Although GamerGate has not directly affected participants' experience with gaming, almost all did testify that their gaming habits and practices had changed significantly between our first and second interviews. Of the eleven interviewees I reconnected with, only two described their current gaming as similar to the way they had played five years earlier. The rest all played different amounts, prioritized different games, or played for different reasons. This was primarily due to greater responsibilities and demands on their time. However, they also attributed the difference to changing relationships, greater interest in or validation from other hobbies, and exhaustion with trying to keep up the skill level they needed to be seen as valid video gamers. This provides, as Consalvo and Begy (2015) suggest, strong evidence that players are not static entities, but rather that they are active and mutable, changing their gaming as needed to fit into their lives effectively.

Although some of my initial interviewees were older, the majority were in their early to midtwenties when I spoke to them in 2012–2013. They were recently out of college, often in their first "adult" jobs or attending graduate school, and had limited personal responsibilities, such as children or extended family members to care for. In 2017–2018, things looked very different. At the time of their follow-up interviews, all eleven participants were working full-time jobs in a variety of industries. Many had gotten married or moved from less serious relationships to more serious ones; some had young children while others had attained management positions at work, where they were responsible for other people as well as themselves. These changes had a strong influence on how players spent their leisure.

Decreased Gaming

Of the eleven interviewees who agreed to participate in a second interview, only two played as much as they had done at our first interview. One, Taylor Ryan, worked in the video game industry and therefore prioritized playing time as a necessity for her career, while the other, Emily, had a strong network of fellow players, including her husband, which made continued gaming an easy part of her overall social life.

The other nine participants stated that their gaming had decreased. Take, for instance, my participant Vickie. When we first talked, she was an involved PC gamer who was playing *Guild Wars 2* and *World of Warcraft* about ten hours/week, although she explained that was down from nearly forty hours/week. In between our first and second interviews, however, Vickie got married and had a son. Because of this, her play time decreased even further. She explained, "Now I get maybe . . . maybe five to six hours on average during a week and that's really cut down quite a bit, but usually you know, if I have time after I put my son to bed or time on the weekend or that. [. . .] And that's been pretty much since he was born." Fitting gaming around her son's schedule changed the amount of time she could dedicate to play.

The demands of a full-time career were also incompatible with the long hours and in-depth play expected of the core gamer. Participants related having less time for gaming as they had to wake up in the morning to go to work. While previously they would think nothing of long play hours and late-night gaming sessions, making that choice now could have a significant effect on their work performance. Feather, for example, said, "As we get older, I don't have the time anymore to stay up all night and play a bunch of console games." She was playing *Persona 5* when we spoke, which indicates that she does still fit in some longer games; it takes, on average, ninety-six hours to complete just the main storyline in *Persona 5* ("How long is *Persona 5*?" 2017). However, Feather generally reserved these titles for weekend binges, to avoid getting invested in a game, staying up all night, and underperforming at work.

Finally, many participants were in more serious relationships, which they prioritized over their gaming time. Elayne stated, "I'm five years older. I'm in a different place in life. I'm 28 now and I have a 40 hour a week job and then an awesome, wonderful relationship. Relationships are also full time so, yeah, it's like you can't just sit and veg for six to eight hours any given day. It's like a few snatches here and there." Whereas Elayne was previously a dedicated competitive gamer, even managing an e-sports team, her priorities had shifted over time. Now, she was more focused on work and spending quality time with her girlfriend.

Changing Play Habits

It would be easy to look at these preliminary results, especially the fact that women saw their own play habits as having decreased over time, as evidence that gaming is less important to older players or that a gamer identity is incompatible with increased responsibilities, serious relationships, and motherhood. When I looked at my interviewees' experiences more closely, however, it became evident that they still prioritize gaming. In fact, they had made many adjustments to their play style and the types of games they played to ensure that gaming could still be a part of their lives. This can be seen not only in how they adapted their video game play to fit their new realities but also in the fact that increasing numbers of women turned to nondigital games between our first and second interviews.

Vickie, for instance, continued to make gaming a priority even though she was able to fit in fewer hours of play. She did this by adjusting her play style. When we first spoke, Vickie was primarily playing *Guild Wars 2* (*GW2*), which was released around the time of our interview. At our second interview, she was still playing *GW2* but for different reasons and with a different pattern of play. Previously, *GW2* had attracted her because it was new, it was social, and it had good storyline elements; she could really get involved in her character and with other players. Now, however, *GW2* was like a favorite old sweatshirt; Vickie described it as "fun nostalgia." It was comfortable, relaxing, and did not require a lot of investment, as *GW2* is free to play. She also played it in a less social way, stating, "I don't interact as much. And a lot of that I think is just maybe me being older and not really wanting to interact with people unless it's on my terms or if I want to. And plus, I got used to, with my son when he was young, I'd have to maybe get up at a moment's notice and go check on him or go take care of him. And so, I didn't feel like I could [socialize]." This quotation indicates that Vickie's role as a mother directly affected her play habits by making more casual play, in which she could leave the game at any point, a necessity. But it also shows that she was willing to make these changes to remain playing. Furthermore, she kept gaming even though being older and being a mom made her feel like an outsider in *GW2*, where she felt most players were younger. She was unsure how they would react if she had to leave to care for her son and decided it would be easier just not to socialize at all; however, this feeling of not fitting in was not enough to keep her from the game.

Other participants, including Adrianna, Feather, Elayne, Spinach, and Vickie, found themselves turning towards less involved styles of video games, such as handheld, casual, mobile, or indie games. Not only were these games generally less expensive, making them easier to justify buying, but they were also shorter and less time intensive than traditional AAA console or PC games. Therefore, they could be more easily slotted into the gaps of time participants had between their responsibilities. Chianna and Laine similarly prioritized co-op or in-person gaming more, so that they could combine their need for socialization with their gaming, killing two birds with one stone. Laine in particular said that social games had become increasingly important, as she had started a new job as a professor. Gaming allowed her to network with new colleagues and develop strong social and working relationships simultaneously.

Dungeons and Dragons: The Analog Compromise

Finally, while the majority had previously been video gamers first, and other types of gamers second, several interviewees had decreased their commitment to video games in favor of in-person role-playing games like *Dungeons and Dragons* (*D&D*), live-action role-playing (LARP) games, board games, or even competitive pinball leagues. In particular, six of the eleven participants started playing *D&D* between our first and second conversations, at times in extremely in-depth ways. Because this diverged so heavily from their previous habits, and because analog games are in general understudied (Torner, Trammell, and Waldron, 2014), this change deserves further investigation.

This is especially true because the choice to play games like *D&D* seems at odds with women's primary reason for playing video games less—their lack of time. Because of the casualization of video games and their broad accessibility, from consoles to mobile phones, I expected that video games would be easier to fit into busy schedules than other forms of gaming. Pinball machines, *D&D*, and LARPs appeared to require more time or energy than video games, especially as many of these (barring, perhaps, pinball) are necessarily multiplayer events. Each requires players to find a small group of fellow players, schedule a time to meet in person, and prepare for that event in advance. Video games, on the other hand, could be picked up and played whenever one had the inclination.

To make matters more confusing, games like *D&D* and other tabletop role-playing games (TTRPGs) have a history of being exclusionary in the same way video games are. In one of the earliest studies of TTRPGs, sociologist Gary Alan Fine (1983) found that very few women played these games. Fine attributed this to how men and women are socialized towards different types of play, how RPG players were recruited through other masculinized interests or homosocial groups, how the games themselves were structured towards male players, and, finally, because he found that gaming environments were not welcoming to women. The players he interviewed and observed stated that female players were often subjected to sexual remarks and that this behavior was "considered standard, no big deal" (Fine, 1983, p. 68). Furthermore, male players often used fantasy-based games to demonstrate their character's sexual prowess, at times even through sexual assault. When the rare female player protested this, it became clear that the issue was not the player perpetuating fantasy rape, but rather the protester who interfered with that gamer's ability to perpetuate fantasy rape *comfortably*. As Fine sums it up, "In theory, female characters can be as powerful as males; in practice, they are often treated as chattels" (1983, p. 69).

Fine's work was completed in the 1980s, leaving games plenty of time to become more welcoming. However, work by an array of other researchers has found similar results, contending that TTRPGs are often specifically male fantasies and/or frequently contain sexist, racist, homophobic, or ableist traits (e.g., Henry, 2015; Jones, 2018; Stenros and Sihvonen, 2015; Stokes, 2017; Trammell, 2014, 2016). For instance, early *D&D* rulebooks positioned female characters with regards to male characters, with stats measured using phrases such as "man-1" or "man+1," and their skills and talents often emphasized appearance. As game studies scholar Aaron Trammell (2014) writes, "The system makes a consistent point: the bodies of women can only be understood when set in opposition to those of men, and within this realm they excel in abilities which foreground the importance of their beauty." Female characters also presented a variety of racial biases, with different in-game races (e.g., human, elf, gnome, etc.) ranked in a hierarchy according to existing beauty standards (Trammell,

2014). Tall, graceful, and exotic Elves had inherent appearance advantages over short, stocky Dwarves, or swarthy and heavily muscled Orcs. This ranking reaffirms "racial stereotypes that revere a pale and slight standard of beauty" (Trammell, 2014), while also reemphasizing the idea that women exist to be beautiful.

D&D has been similarly limited in terms of its representations of sexuality and disability. Explicitly queer characters have long been lacking from *D&D* and other fantasy-based RPGs, which have bracketed questions of sexuality out of game play even as other TTRPGs, such as those in the *World of Darkness* series, introduced LGBT characters (Stenros and Sihvonen, 2015; Stokes, 2017). Similarly missing are meaningful representations of disability (Henry, 2015; Jones, 2018; Stokes, 2017). Rather, disabilities are frequently used as mere descriptive characteristics (e.g., a villain with a limp) or as punishment for players' mistakes, in that players who suffer extensive amounts of damage can receive a variety of physical or mental "conditions" that limit their abilities for a set amount of turns (Jones, 2018). Although players can subvert the limitations of the game by opting to play disabled characters according to their preferences, this puts the burden of representation on them and is not a permanent solution because "inclusion means more than assuming that one is included, it means being named" (Henry, 2015).

These trends mark *D&D* as a potentially regressive space, which is at odds with the types of games that my participants enjoyed and that tend to draw in female audiences. For instance, participants who enjoyed the *Mass Effect* series specifically attributed this enjoyment to the series' progressive nature, where players could pick their character's gender and engage in same-sex relationships. Similarly, although most of my participants were white, they enjoyed and celebrated games that displayed racial diversity and actively expressed interest in expanding representations further. While Angela (interview 1) pointed out that games were "still mostly white and mostly male," Kay (interview 1) specifically called for "characters of more racial diversity than just mostly white people." These two and others recognized that diversity was inherently important to games, not only because it broadened the types of representations available within popular culture but also because it gave players more possible stories to explore.

More quantitative data shows similar priorities; studying the confluence of genre and gender indicates that games like *Dragon Age: Inquisition* and *Assassin's Creed: Syndicate* significantly outperform genre competitors in terms of their number of female players (Yee, 2017). This is probably the case because these games signal inclusivity; *Inquisition* features a transgender character and same-sex romance options, while *Syndicate* was the first main-storyline *Assassin's Creed* game with a playable female character. These games make themselves available to players who are not traditional "gamers" through diverse character and storyline options. *D&D*, evidence suggests, has not historically done this.

That said, some female *D&D* players have argued that even if game material is exclusionary or regressive, the act of playing can overcome this. Philosophy professor Shannon Mussett (2014) declared, "It is no secret that most who play tend to be boys and men, and there is little doubt that the world of *Dungeons and Dragons* is largely geared toward a masculine, rather than a feminine, fantasy. [. . .] And yet, for some of us who play, there seems to be something liberating in taking on the roles of both male and female characters in the world of *D&D*" (p. 190). Both Mussett (2014) and author/*D&D* aficionado Shelly Mazzanoble (2007) point out that male and female characters have similar abilities; although Trammell (2014) found that early rulebooks defined female characters differently from male ones, recent editions of the game have done away with sex-based stats. Therefore, one's in-game sex or gender identity does not change one's powers. Mussett takes this argument a step further, arguing that the level of imagination needed to play *D&D* effectively encourages similarly imaginative approaches to gender performance and identity, pushing players to question and rethink society's norms. She writes, "If we can stretch our minds beyond the limitations of our own imaginary bodies, as well as the bodies depicted in the books and miniatures, just think of where we can go to liberate ourselves from sexist representations" (Mussett, 2014, p. 197). This frames *D&D* as a potentially progressive space, depending on how one plays.

D&D has also undergone some recent changes, which include being portrayed more positively and accessibly in mass media and online. *D&D* has appeared in shows from the network sitcom *The Big Bang Theory* to the critically acclaimed Netflix series *Stranger Things*, and celebrities such as Vin Diesel and Joe Manganiello have become increasingly open about their tabletop game play. In 2017, for example, Manganiello participated in a weekly *D&D* Twitch stream along with a group of celebrity friends, including actress Deborah Ann Woll (*True Blood, Marvel's Daredevil*), actor Dylan Sprouse (*The Suite Life of Zach and Cody*), and actor/musician Utkarsh Ambudkar (*The Mindy Project, Pitch Perfect*). These changes have started to disconnect *D&D* from many embedded stereotypes about typical "gamers" and given it a more positive cultural cachet. The early 2000s have also seen a rise in podcasts and web series in which players stream their *D&D* games, which communications and culture student Alex Chalk (2018) refers to as "Actual Play" media. He argues that Actual Play media conduct "initiatory labor," modeling the game to new players and making it easier to start playing. Many streamed games also feature high numbers of female players (Chalk, 2018). Thus, *D&D* is not only being redefined as "cooler" than it has been in the past, but players can see some female models existing and thriving within this space.

Finally, and perhaps most importantly, the game itself has become more inclusive. The fifth edition (*D&D5e*) of the game, for instance, allows for nonbinary genders, encourages LGBT representations, and diversifies the games' portrayal of real-life races, including representing a black woman as the default image for the human race (Jones, 2018). While it still lacks strong representations of disability, this is a clear step towards the more progressive games female players seem to enjoy. Furthermore, *D&D5e* is less technical than previous offerings, moving away from complex systems for combat and towards smoother storytelling (Mappin, 2016). This allows new players to pick up the game faster and could contribute to the growing number of women who play. In fact, Elayne specifically referenced these changes in terms of her own gaming. She said, "Fifth Edition, it's brought in a lot of new people, myself included, because it's easy to pick up and it's not too convoluted. It's pretty new-player-friendly, and that's been awesome. It's been a really good influx of new people."

These elements signal broad cultural shifts that have opened *Dungeons and Dragons* to new audiences, but they do not account for all the reasons my interviewees chose to play. Specifically, interviewees prioritized in-person over online play as in-person gaming gave them control over whom they played with, resulted in more positive gaming experiences, and freed them from the labor involved in coping with online negativity. Given that all had only limited time available for playing, these choices made their gaming easier, more social, and more relaxing.

Elayne, for instance, had become more involved with *D&D* than any other participant. She was in two separate tabletop gaming groups and was also the Dungeon Master (DM), or the person who leads the game and controls its progression, for one of them. Elayne had previously been very involved in competitive video gaming, even managing an e-sports team. Now, her focus was *D&D*; she committed four to eight hours each Sunday to one group, a similar amount of time every other Saturday to another group, and eight or so hours per week preparing for her role as DM. When asked why she prioritized this gaming time, especially as she often reiterated how busy she was, Elayne gave many of the reasons she had previously given as to why she played video games—for the storytelling, the social aspect, and the fun of succeeding in beating game mechanics and challenges. She now turned to *D&D* for these, however, because "it definitely is nice being able to control the people that you game with. [. . .] Controlling the people that you game with mitigates the chances that you'll run into undesirables" (Elayne, interview 2). In other words, *D&D* met the same needs as video games without forcing her to deal with harassment or negativity.

Other participants expressed similar sentiments. Chianna refused to play online games at all but was heavily involved in a variety of tabletop games, board games, and live-action role-playing (LARP) games. In each of these venues, she was able to choose whom she interacted with and set the tone for their relationship. Misty, who also started playing *D&D* between our first and second interview, stated, "I think *D&D* is weird because it can be a lot nicer. But you're also actively role playing and sometimes you're not being very nice while you're doing that. [. . .] But the difference with that is that I know I'm still friends with these people, and it's like a role-playing thing, not a . . . the type of person they are sort of thing." Gaming face to face allowed female gamers to understand other players' motivations and choices and know that anything negative they said was simply part of the game. Because of this, issues were easier to dismiss and recover from.

Some players did have experience with negative tabletop groups. Although Elayne found her own groups supportive, she said many of her friends had "horror stories" about overly aggressive players, attention seekers, or "the creepy, leery, sexually-harassing-other-female-players guy" (Elayne). Feather also found herself questioning players' motivations when they invited her to game with them, wondering if they considered her a serious gamer or if they were including her because they were interested in dating her. Thus, in-person gaming can still require some careful navigation from female gamers. Most, however, easily found good people to play with and felt that their existing gaming groups were careful about screening new players, to avoid future issues. Some participants even stated that their *D&D* group had made participating in other areas of game culture easier, such as when Misty's fellow players stood up for her at a gaming convention when other people questioned why she was there or assumed that she was not a gamer.

Participants also indicated that tabletop gaming freed them from the coping mechanisms they had to employ when gaming online. Women who played games online often had to hide their gender, play with friends, clearly display high levels of skill and experience, or adopt aggressive personality traits to avoid or manage harassment from other players (see chapter 5). Each of these strategies required work, and many had a high potential to backfire, such as when trash-talking back to harassers spurred further negativity. Therefore, existing coping mechanisms were not a complete solution to online issues.

In-person gaming, however, did not share these challenges. Comparing her *D&D* play to her past competitive video game play, Laine said, "I miss the competition somewhat but not really. I was never great at games because I never had the time to fully immerse myself in them, so I never actually wanted to compete. It was a little too much pressure. I didn't want to be terrible because I felt as though that would reflect badly on my gender, not just my skills." While she had previously had to devote significant time and effort to building her skills before she was comfortable playing with others, Laine was now free of that pressure. Playing with friends who knew her as an individual made her mistakes hers alone, not reflective of her whole gender. This meant she was more comfortable trying something new, knowing her friends would support her even if she messed up. She also found that the cooperative nature of a *D&D* game, in which players work together for a common goal, helped her to relax and just have fun, rather than constantly fearing she was not good enough. As she became busier and could not maintain a high level of skill in online, competitive games, this less intense alternative was necessary.

Female Players' Lifecycles

Women's collective changes—from decreasing the amount of time they game to trying new play styles and genres—show clear evidence that players' life stage, responsibilities, and relationships can all affect their gaming habits and preferences. These effects range from how much they play to *why* they turn to games in the first place; while some expressed similar needs to those they gave in our first interview, others found that their use of games had changed, for instance from a social activity to simply relaxing or vice versa. This reaffirms Consalvo and Begy's argument that researchers need to account for player lifecycle and context. Although these results emerge from only a small number of interviews, and as a result may not be representative of all or even most female gamers' experiences, following up with the same participants revealed changing gaming patterns that otherwise may have been overlooked.

For instance, these findings suggest that the amount of work required to stay present in online gaming is not sustainable over the lifecycle of a female player. When I spoke with players during their first interview, many had already opted to leave online spaces due to past negative experiences; this number had increased by our second interview. Women either tire of managing harassment or have less patience for dealing with negative experiences as they grow older, perhaps due to increasing demands on their time. It also seems as if many strategies they had used previously were no longer as obtainable later in life. For example, as Laine pointed out, increasing responsibilities in other areas of a player's life decrease the time they have available to practice gaming, making it harder to avoid harassment using skill. Coordinating schedules with friends, so they are there for psychological protection in online spaces, may also be more difficult. This speaks to a continued need to find other solutions to harassment in gaming, as the current strategies women use place too much of the burden on them.

Analog games provide an alternative space in which gaming as a woman may be more sustainable. This is evidenced first by the fact that over half of the women I was able to follow up with had started playing *D&D* over the preceding five years, often at the expense of the video games they had previously played. Second, *D&D* was only one of the analog games they turned to. My participant Spinach, for instance, had become deeply involved in competitive pinball play and related that the pinball community was also more supportive than the online gaming community. Chianna found similar experiences in LARP games, as well as an array of non-*D&D* TTRPGs and other board games. In-person gaming generally provided more inclusive spaces than traditional video games.

While analog games can make gaming more welcoming for individual women by offering them safe spaces to play, however, they may not be a full solution to sexism and misogyny in gaming more generally. This is due to the lower visibility of analog games compared to digital ones. Not only are in-person gaming sessions generally smaller than online ones, meaning female gamers are seen by and normalized to fewer people, but games studies' existing focus on primarily digital games also works to conceal the significance of analog spaces.

Women's gaming may also become less visible over time if, like Vickie, they start to play in less social ways. As mentioned earlier, players who do not speak up regularly in game spaces are not counted among the ranks of gamers, even when they play frequently or have extensive experience. Their lower visibility then contributes to the perception that undergirds much of the harassment women face in gaming spaces, the perception that gaming is a male pastime and that women are outsiders.

The fact that women are offset to less visible and analog spaces illuminates the need for more diverse studies of games and methods of recruiting participants. If women increasingly turn to offline games as their solution to sexism, studying *video* games alone will not recognize this, making female gamers invisible and helping the gaming audience appear to be more male dominated than it is. Seeking out in-person gaming groups or conducting more longitudinal studies, so that players remain participants even if their gaming becomes less visible, are two possible solutions. Another possibility might be collaborating with game companies and using their player logs to ensure that researchers can reach less social players, who might not be paying attention to calls in general chat venues. Without making efforts like these, researchers may be contributing to the very structural inequalities and beliefs they are trying to break down.

At the same time, the ways in which participants managed their gaming, and the fact that all continued to game at least a little bit, show how these female gamers remained active, thoughtful consumers of video and analog games. It also indicates the value female gamers place on their identity as *gamers*. Women who have spent a significant amount of energy and time building a gamer identity and a corresponding level of gaming capital are generally not prepared to sacrifice that just because their schedules filled up. Rather, they used their knowledge to find other gaming outlets that met their needs. As Elayne's schedule displays, tabletop games still require a significant commitment. Similarly, Chianna devoted at least one full weekend per month to her LARP game and even more time to character creation, costume and makeup design, and other prep. Female gamers were willing to carve out this time, however, because the spaces they were gaming in gave back more than they required. Each interviewee carefully balanced their preferences, game offerings, and available resources to continue getting the most out of their play. They also had the skill and experience needed to choose appropriate games for their new contexts, such as when Vickie returned to an old favorite because she knew she could care for her son around playing or when Laine turned to social, rather than competitive, games to network in her new job. The fact that women know gaming well enough to make these choices demonstrates how they are, first and foremost, gamers.

All participants even continued to self-identify as gamers, although only a few claimed this identity with no reservations. Unsurprisingly, given her role as a game developer, Taylor Ryan was one of the two who enthusiastically claimed the title of gamer, which was also true during our first interview. Chianna was the other, and this was a slight change from when we first talked. She referred to herself as a casual gamer in our first interview, as she played primarily board or tabletop games and knew that these did not fit the stereotypical expectation of a "gamer." By our second interview, however, she felt that these games qualified as much as video games, if not more. She had also become more open about claiming a gamer identity in online spaces, often using the hashtag

#girlgamer on Facebook and Instagram posts about her play, and she received positive feedback to these posts. This made a strong gamer identity more attainable.

The rest of my participants tended to give some, or many, qualifications as to how or why they saw themselves as gamers. That is, women still simultaneously prioritized and struggled with their ability to possess a gamer identity, even with their changing gaming habits. They were aware, for instance, of "gamer" stereotypes that they wanted to avoid, as well as the fact that core gatekeepers might not see them as gamers. When asked if she considered herself a gamer, for example, Marie responded, "There's no reason not to consider myself one. I play games that I like, interact in some places and watch the news. Talk about games. Wrote about them. If anything, I'm more of a gamer than someone who just plays the newest *Call of Duty* online." This statement shows that she was willing to claim a gamer identity but felt the need to defend how and why that title applied to her. Other participants expressed similar, "Yes, but . . ." sentiments, simultaneously agreeing that they should count as gamers while also feeling pressure to support that claim.

This made some participants hesitant to express their gamer identity to others. Misty, for example, avoided conversations about popular games she had not played, while Laine said that revealing herself as a gamer often felt like taking a quiz, as others would immediately try to test her knowledge and disprove her claim to that title. She even pointed out that this was a particularly gendered behavior, arguing, "This isn't just in gaming. I have the same problem when I talk about liking comic books or cars. I don't know if I'm just more sensitive to it but I don't feel as though I get the same third degree when I talk about hobbies that are more common to my gender/age group/etc. like gardening or cooking." Entering masculinized spaces, like gaming, felt like a challenge to participants like Laine. They still laid claim to a gamer identity but recognized that this was not the same as a "gamer" identity, as their gender identity, play habits, and game choices did not align with core expectations.

At the same time, participants expressed a desire to reclaim the term "gamer" and make it more inclusive; they saw this term as a potential site of negotiation about who was or could be included in game culture. To illustrate, when asked if she would still identify as a gamer, Adrianna said, "I've got a bug up my butt about that particular label and the gatekeeping involved. I play video games sometimes, so I'm a gamer. I knit sometimes, so I'm a knitter. I'm also a nerd and a geek. You don't have to put exactly X amount of time in or have X amount of knowledge to be able to apply that label to yourself. I think it helps the stereotype of the basement-dwelling Mountain Dew-drinking gamer if more people just call themselves that." Adrianna felt that using the term "gamer," especially when others would not use that term for a specific player, helps apply it to a larger group of people and makes it more inclusive. Other participants (e.g., Emily, Laine, Misty, Elayne, Spinach) expressed similar sentiments, pointing out that, although many players felt as though one had to play a certain amount, engage with specific games and have specific preferences, or look a particular way in order to be a "gamer," the term itself really should just mean "anyone who plays games."

This was not a universal position. Feather and Vickie both at times employed their own gatekeeping around gamer identity, such as when Vickie said, "I kind of, I hate when people who like, play *Candy Crush*, are like, 'Oh, I'm a gamer!'" She similarly rejected the idea that players who only played casual games like *Bejeweled* could qualify as gamers. This was a particularly interesting statement, as it shows Vickie buying into some of the very narratives that work to ghettoize women to casual rather than core spaces. As new media researchers like Vanderhoef (2013) have pointed out, the feminization of casual games and their dismissal as less important than core games are strategic moves to maintain masculine power in gaming spheres. When pressed further, Vickie could not give clear reasons as to why she did not consider *Candy Crush* a game or *Candy Crush* players to be gamers. In fact, she said, "I don't really know why I wouldn't. I don't know the reasoning of why I don't really consider it a game. I guess it's because I don't think of it as something you have to put time and effort and I don't know. Yeah there's thought behind it but I don't know. Yeah. [laughs] I don't really know the reasoning of why I don't consider them to be games, but I just, I just can't" (Vickie). This quotation shows the ambivalence of her position. Earlier in our interview, Vickie strongly defended her own stance as a gamer, even though she played less. She even said that her inability to play as much did not at all relate to her ability to "qualify" as a gamer—she used air quotes around the term "qualify," as if to indicate that one should not have to qualify to be a gamer. At the same time, she employed her own set of standards as to what and who qualified or did not. And when pushed to explain these standards, she repeatedly said she did not know why she used them. This demonstrates the taken-for-granted nature of core norms, as they do not have to be understood in order to be employed. It also shows why exclusionary forces can be so difficult to break down, as participants who have overcome barriers may find themselves enjoying being part of the in-group.

Feather's gaming gatekeeping is interesting for similar reasons, as she turned exclusionary tactics back onto male players. Discussing the experience of dating as a female gamer, she said, "I've actually used [my gamer identity] to get rid of some guys. [. . .] I've literally pulled the gamer questions on them, like, 'What was the last game you played?' 'Oh, well, this.' I'm like, 'I'm sorry. I really don't feel like I can have anything to talk about with someone who hasn't played a game in the last decade.'" While women were normally the ones who had to demonstrate their history and skill with gaming in order to be accepted as gamers, Feather quizzed potential partners to ensure that they had sufficient shared interests. She recognized that this was "mean" behavior, as she herself had been subjected to the feeling that she did not belong in gaming spaces (see chapter 5). But she also found it somewhat empowering, as it was her turn to claim a gamer identity and decide who qualified and who did not.

Although these two interviewees were at odds with the majority of their peers, who wanted "gamer" to be defined as inclusively as possible, their experiences are significant as they indicate the continued strength of the hegemonic core in gaming and the ways in which women's negotiation with it can be fragmented and contradictory. Both Feather and Vickie countered the core ideals that interfered with their self-construction of a gamer identity, such as when they played less often (Vickie) or when they engaged with less traditional games (Feather). Feather, for instance, defended her play of feminized otome games, which are story-based games that involve developing a romance between the player's character and one or more in-game characters. But both simultaneously bought into and supported other core forces that did not negatively affect them or that could be used to gain special status as part of an in-group. If Vickie is a gamer, but players of casual games are not, she gets to access a subculture and a capital that others cannot. If Feather claims a gamer identity, but withholds this from male players, that identity might mean more. Exclusionary forces can be appealing, which makes them difficult to break down.

Nevertheless, She Persisted

Female gamers continued to face a wide array of challenges between our first and second interviews, of which GamerGate was only a small blip. As my interviews show, issues of sexism in gaming existed well before, and expand well beyond, GamerGate. Although this chapter has focused primarily on how women's gaming habits changed in line with their personal and professional lives, interviewees related many continuing concerns about harassment, hypersexualized female characters, and the games industry's attention to male audiences over female. They also still faced judgment from more traditional "gamers," who saw their gender identity as incompatible with a gamer identity. In many ways, GamerGate is emblematic of the broader paths through which sexism structures gaming practices and cultures. It is important to keep this in mind, as it is tempting to look at this movement as something that is over and that we have moved beyond. Doing so, however, artificially limits the impact of sexism to the past, when it is more accurately understood as ongoing.

Gaming sexism is also deeply linked to struggles in other areas, such as comics, and discussing each of these separately elides attempts to address their root causes simultaneously. Collectively, these events are about shifting power structures and the ways in which hegemony resists change; individuals who are used to being prioritized will actively defend this status through forceful means. This is not to blame every privileged gamer for the actions of a few, as many players welcome diverse characters, storylines, play styles, and gamers. There is, however, a vocal minority that has pinned their identity on being the only ones involved in geek spaces, and they will protect these against perceived incursions (Massanari, 2015).

This struggle is further complicated by the fact that at least some aspects of protecting gaming from outsiders can be appealing even to those who are generally excluded. As a few of my participants indicated, their status as core gamers, which they had fought for against numerous barriers, at times made them want to police gaming's boundaries themselves. This occurred when they felt critics did not have adequate knowledge about games to base their critiques on or when they felt other players were unfairly laying claim to the title of gamer without having earned it. These instances were similar to women's ambivalence around the "girl gamer" stereotype, discussed in chapter 3, wherein participants simultaneously rejected these stereotypes as meaningful and judged other players by them. Women's navigation of both gamer and female identities remains fragmented and contradictory, even around events that seem obviously antifeminist.

At the same time, women's love for games and gaming persisted unabated. It was for this reason—because games continued to matter to them—that they consistently wanted core games to be better. They still saw possibilities for more diversity in character representations, particularly in terms of race, gender, and sexuality. They still wanted developers to acknowledge that game audiences were more diverse than traditional "gamer" stereotypes would indicate. And they still wanted their fellow players to stop worrying about *who* was playing a character and just worry about *how* they were playing—to be judged by the same standard as anyone else.

Because of this, women continued to define themselves as gamers and to display many of the characteristics we associate with core. High levels of skill and experience, in-depth familiarity with an array of games, and knowledge of their own preferences are all key characteristics of being core. Unfortunately, given the offline or less social nature of many women's continued play, female gamers' identity as core gamers is likely to be overlooked. Game scholars and other interested parties may need to define "games" more broadly in order to account for their true diversity, while developers and community managers who want to build more inclusive spaces should also learn from women's choice to turn to analog spaces and the reasons they give for doing so. If video game creators want more inclusive online spaces, they need games that allow players to manage their time playing, to help them accommodate life changes, but they also need to offer games in which players can control whom they game with, as suggested earlier. Signaling that diverse gamers are important members of the community, as *D&D5e* has done through its inclusive rulebook changes, could help draw in more female players as well, as evidenced by the popularity of games like *Dragon Age: Inquisition* (Yee, 2017).

Conclusion

The Battle Continues

Shortly before I sat down to write this conclusion, Blizzard Entertainment announced that it was planning to introduce a mobile game, *Diablo: Immortal*, based on its popular *Diablo* series. The level of uproar this simple announcement provoked took the company by surprise; players accused the company of spitting in the face of gamers, urged others to boycott the game and the company, called for *Immortal* to be canceled, and even justified being disrespectful to Blizzard employees (Grayson, 2018; Horti, 2018). Some players had this extreme reaction because they were expecting Blizzard to announce another PC installment in the *Diablo* series, as the last had come out over six years earlier, while others were simply not impressed with early gameplay footage (McWhertor, 2018). Further players, however, accused Blizzard of forgetting who their real fans were and selling out to the mobile market. As games journalist Nathan Grayson wrote, rather sarcastically, for *Kotaku*, "People have decided that this is the ultimate betrayal, all because a single game isn't hyper-focused on the diehard PC and console crowd, and another wasn't officially announced to make up for it" (Grayson, 2018). Although Blizzard's creative team argued that they wanted the game to appeal to their "existing hardcore fans" alongside new players, those self-same hardcore fans felt that creating a mobile version of a popular core franchise was akin to ruining that franchise. Mobile games, like casual overall, are considered lesser than PC or console games.

This outcry over a simple mobile game illustrates how core and casual are still in the midst of their crisis of authority, and struggles over what counts in games and game spaces—and who counts as players—are not over. Many forces are still at work to maintain core as exclusionary. As a result, interventions to broaden that core are also still necessary.

Interestingly, one of the top comments on Blizzard's cinematic trailer for *Immortal* was posted by a user going by the name RedPill Shark (Horti, 2018). The term "red pill" originally comes from the 1999 film *The Matrix*, wherein protagonist Neo is offered a choice between a blue pill, which will leave him in the Matrix computer simulation, or a red pill, which will open his eyes to the reality of the world. This phrase has been appropriated by the men's rights movement, which uses the term to describe the moment members realize that men are being oppressed (Sharlet, 2014).

I bring this up not to claim that the negative reaction to *Immortal* is a vast, men's rights conspiracy (it is not), but rather to draw attention to the ways in which continued battles over video games and their meaning tie into broader sociopolitical issues. As I have worked on this project over the past eight years, we have seen significant moments in which marginalized groups have called for greater attention to their needs and greater access to power, from the Black Lives Matter movement and players kneeling at football games to the Women's March on Washington and beyond. But we have also seen significant pushbacks, such as growing white supremacy movements and increased restrictions on women's healthcare and abortion, such as the "Heartbeat Bill" recently passed in Ohio (Caron, 2018). As my participant Taylor Ryan pointed out in our discussion of GamerGate, "The world as a whole is going through a game-changing time at the moment, and when you see things like white nationalism coming to the forefront (not just in America, but here in Britain, with UKIP and the EDL), or Le Pen and her ties to fascism . . . In that sense, I A M surprised to be seeing attitudes that I associated with, say, Nazi Germany rising to the surface." Taylor Ryan felt, and many of my participants agreed, that issues in gaming were reflective of many broader struggles for power and identity. Ensuring that games continue to develop in progressive ways might not change the world completely for the better, but the odds are very good that doing so would help.

Hegemony is a pervasive force that can be difficult to undermine and change effectively, as interviewees' frequent conflicts and guilt about gaming displayed. In many ways, gaming's core remains a masculinized space, policed by exclusionary content trends, the direct harassment of female gamers and other "outsiders," surprise at diverse players' presence, and stereotypes about "girl gamers." This policing then encourages women and other marginalized players to buy into limiting notions of who gamers are and who games are for, continuing to perceive core as not for them even as they undermine this idea through their own presence. Because of this, sexism and misogyny in gaming are legitimated and even at times celebrated. From here, these forces can extend to affect other cultural areas as well, becoming one factor building up and contributing to the larger antifeminist culture the United States is currently experiencing.

At the same time, women and other marginalized players still choose to enter gaming culture for many reasons. They find a wide variety of pleasures both in game texts and in the act of play, including social connections, the ability to explore different identities and ways of being, and more. Even some elements previous research found to be off-putting, such as competition, can be enjoyable, as female gamers use these to express their power and skill, dominating male gamers in their own space.

Furthermore, as games scholar Adrienne Shaw (2014b) has previously discussed, "Gamer identity was mutable, shifted over time, and wove together complex relationships between media representation, consumption, and identification" (p. 151). Interviewees were differently connected to gender identity or gamer identity on the basis of context, history, and even personal preferences. Women took on fluid identities, alternately prioritizing their gender identity, their gamer identity, or both dependent on what characteristics they needed to use to navigate the spaces of gaming and the challenges they face within those spaces. In doing so, they both broke down the barriers of core as a meaningful category, revealing its constructed nature, and diversified conceptions about gender and femininity through varied performances of these identities.

Because of this, it is obvious that women are capable media managers who exert some degree of control over their environments and experiences to make these positive. Further, their presence in gaming and the interpretive repertoires they share with their male colleagues work to undermine ideas of core and its use to police an exclusive masculine sphere. By already embodying core in many ways, women mark themselves as similar to male gamers, showing how a stronger network of affinity could be developed between diverse types of players as a means for changing gaming's current patterns of sexism. As matters currently stand, women generally have to deal with gaming's misogyny on their own. They can use a wide variety of strategies to do so, such as avoiding online games, carefully screening the games they choose to play on the basis of reviews, or even proving that they are the best as a means for avoiding harassment. However, each of these strategies requires work and may prove to be an unsustainable means of protection, as evidenced by the number of players whose gaming decreased between our interviews.

Moving Forward

As mentioned in the introduction, many incredible movements to diversify games are already occurring, from the Pixelles and other female-targeted game-development incubators to the #INeedDiverseGames hashtag and nonprofit. But many of the women I spoke with did not know about efforts like these, or they had little interest in becoming game developers or creators and therefore were unaffected by these organizations. They also generally did not know other players like them, due to factors like women's tendency to hide their gender in online spaces. Therefore, while these interventions into the industry side of the issue need to continue, other interventions into player spaces are also necessary.

First, women's experiences showed that they were generally dealing with harassment and exclusion on their own; even though many participants were recruited from online forums specifically for female gamers, these existing connections between them were not particularly strong. Players still related knowing few other women who gamed. Furthermore, as participants expressed, forces like the "girl gamer" stereotype worked to keep women from relying on one another in gaming spaces. Thus, promoting and normalizing diverse play styles may be the first step towards change, as it would decrease value judgments about the "right" way to game or the "right" reason for being part of gaming communities. Casual gaming is already making some interventions into this area, but to aid its impact, discourses within gaming press, communities, and culture need to avoid marginalizing casual as less significant than core. Individuals and groups working to make games more inclusive also need to ensure that these efforts span both core and casual games, to avoid creating a marginal space that is open to all while gaming's core remains exclusionary.

Other means of promoting connections among female players, both with one another and with other gamers more broadly, could also help ease their individual stress through collective action. As players' experiences indicated, being able to game with friends was a key means for dealing with online harassment. This could occur through specifically targeted efforts, such as all-female gaming groups, but such an approach is likely to exclude players with intersectional identities. Therefore, it should not be the only approach players take to building community. As my interviewees stressed, games needed diversity on the basis of more than gender; therefore, building community through a shared love of specific games, or shared experiences of marginalization and strategies for coping, may be a way to connect players of diverse identities and build connections more widely. As feminist scholars like Butler, Haraway, and Sandoval argue, a conscious politics of affinity that does not rest on a specific identity can be the best way forward for political, social, and cultural movements.

Second, industry members and journalists need to be held more accountable for perpetuating discourses that make sexism both normal and acceptable in gaming spaces. Chief among these are discourses that treat female gamers as new or unusual, which mark them as "other," or discourses that assume all female gamers play in similar ways. Instead, recognizing that women have long been part of gaming culture, that they are both core and casual, and that they have diverse gaming preferences, most of which are not gendered, is essential. This will help female players become normalized, allowing them to build the connections they need to avoid feeling guilt about their hobby, to defend their choices to others, and to change perceptions of who gamers are. Increased attention to individual and analog play in both journalistic and academic work could also help achieve this, as women's play is frequently more private than men's. We need to draw out more clearly the interventions they are already making, especially given many players' turn to *Dungeons and Dragons* and other analog games.

Finally, as Shaw pointed out, developers should improve their focus on diversity in games, not because players need characters they can identify with or because diverse audience effectively *prove* that they are meaningful markets, but because players deeply enjoy experiencing different types of identification. When gaming, women took on a wide range of fluid identities and subject positions. They sought out games that allowed them to explore different ways of being and embody varied identities and affective states. Although dominant male audiences may not be used to having to identify in different ways while gaming, the enjoyment women found in doing so indicates that men will probably also be able to find pleasure in experiencing different stories and characters. Thus, there is no reason not to diversify games; telling diverse narratives can potentially increase all players' enjoyment of games while also signaling to marginalized players that they are important to developers and to culture more broadly.

Discussing recent incidents of sexism and exclusion in gaming culture, media studies scholar Sal Humphreys wrote, "Inclusivity is a constant project. Exclusions don't just 'happen' in games or in games studies research. [. . .] They are the product of active behavior on the part of those in power. If we want to have an inclusive society, culture, subculture, medium, or academic discipline, we have to work at it by pushing through the barriers of exclusionary behavior ourselves, or making sure we are not part of the snarling pack defending its territory from the 'threatening other'" (Humphreys, 2019, p. 829). Undermining the hegemonic structures that rank some forms of games and gamers over others is a key part of this process.

Limitations

Although this project provides an in-depth view of women's experiences in the casualized era, and assesses some of the ways in which they undermine expectations about both gamers and gender, it does have several limitations that future research projects could and should address. First, I can draw few conclusions about the experiences of other marginalized groups. The rise of casual games, which are heavily feminized, may be welcoming more women into gaming, but it is unclear from my targeted interviews what impact it might have on players of color and/or LGBT or disabled players. Greater attention to intersectionality could also be useful; although Eva recounted some experiences related to her intersectional identity as both female and Mexican, most of the participants for this study were white or spoke primarily about their experiences as women, rather than as intersectional, multiply identified individuals.

Being a gaming minority in multiple ways probably poses a new set of challenges that should be addressed.

Second, future projects should aim to pursue a deeper understanding of men's fears about industrial change. Although I propose some explanations why the casualized era may appear threatening and provoke a backlash against female players, and draw on outside work to support these, my participants all identified as female, and even did so in generally normative ways. Therefore, a project focusing on men could indicate what they find most significant about the casualized era and why they react to its changes in sexist ways. It could also break down different types of male gamers, as not all players harass women and as men frequently have their own internal hierarchies of power and privilege. Interviews with male gamers could indicate what drives some gamers to harass others, why others avoid this, and how this affects individual players' experiences. In particular, comparing sexist gamers to those who do not take on aggressive personas or who serve as allies to marginalized players can indicate how these more positive expressions could be encouraged.

Finally, future research should move outside of a Western context. Although interviewees for this study were recruited online to court diverse experiences, most of them were American, and those who were not primarily came from other Western countries. This limits the scope of possible conclusions to this area. However, places like Japan have extensive game cultures that differ in many ways from Western game culture. For instance, Japanese games often contain more androgynous characters than Western games do, focusing less on heavily muscled, hypermasculine men. Because of this, they may have different gender relations among players that could provide guidelines for change or greater equality in the US context or could present unique challenges of their own. These should be explored in order to provide a higher-level view of power structures and gender hierarchies in gaming and technological cultures more broadly.

Final Thoughts

Although the casualized era is not the first time when players, academics, or journalists have challenged the longstanding perception that all gamers are men, it is possibly the first time in game history when this questioning has been industry motivated and widely based. The proliferation of casual games and the deep changes occurring in the industry, such as the spread of new forms of funding and distribution, have decreased the power possessed by core forces and started to disperse this power more widely. This is not, or should not be, a surprise; focusing primarily on straight, white, young male audiences made sense as a risk-management strategy following the game industry's 1980s collapse, but it artificially limited developers' market (Fron et al., 2007). If anything has become obvious in the casualized era, it is that many different types of players exist. Because of this, it is highly unlikely that the games industry will revert back to its exclusionary focus on male gamers. To do so would sacrifice the extensive revenue to be gained from a broader consumer base.

At the same time, that reversion is still possible, as existing structures of power and value continue to affect when and how players could be understood as gamers. Gaming has long possessed sexist underpinnings, and the crisis of authority, in which power in gaming might shift, has only made these more salient. To ensure that we address them fully, we need to move beyond focusing on large, dramatic events like Gamer-Gate and maintain attention to the ways in which sexism permeates the everyday experiences of women who choose to enter masculinized spaces, as well as how they deal with it.

One large takeaway from this book can be expressed in a minimally modified quotation from literary and cultural scholar Janice Radway—"What is needed, I have come to feel, is a recognition that [female gamers] are themselves struggling with gender definitions and sexual politics on their own terms and that what they may need most from those of us struggling in other arenas is our support rather than our criticism or direction" (1991, p. 18). Women's experiences in the casualized era demonstrate that hegemonic structures of gaming, as in any other sphere, are pervasive and persistent, difficult to change quickly due to the forces that police them. At the same time, women and other marginalized gamers are using the flexibility and uncertainty of the casualized era to push for greater power in an area where they have long been marginalized. What can ensure that they succeed, instead of being overwhelmed by the forces and ideologies that try to return gaming to its masculinized roots, is greater recognition of their importance and help in expressing that more widely. A crisis of authority is an inherently uncertain moment. Change can occur, or the pure force the hegemonic class deploys can maintain that class's power. At the current moment, it is impossible to predict which direction the casualized era will end up taking, although, like my participants, I remain hopeful.

ACKNOWLEDGMENTS

The list of people who helped make this book a reality is extensive, and the thanks I can offer here will definitely not be proportional to the amount of support I have received while researching and writing it. Despite this, I will do my best to express my appreciation for some key contributors and ask that anyone I fail to thank in full will forgive the oversight.

First, to my participants, without whom this project could never have happened: Thank you for your enthusiasm, your humor, and your intelligent insights into the challenges and benefits of being a female gamer. I hope I have used your experiences in a way that resonates with your feelings about gaming. Special thanks to the eleven participants who responded to the call for second interviews; your continued eagerness to participate in this project fueled me through many rounds of updates and edits.

Second, thank you to the countless colleagues and mentors who helped me in navigating grad school, getting a job, doing that job, and writing a book. The first shoutout in this list goes to Susan Douglas, Megan Ankerson, Amanda Lotz, and Lisa Nakamura, who provided essential feedback on my early work. Your diverse perspectives and critiques made me a stronger researcher and writer. I am also deeply grateful to my grad school cohort (Lia, Timeka, Dam Hee, Sarah, Kitior, and Monique) and other fellow Michiganders, especially Sriram, Annemarie, Emily, Julia, Stewart, Caitlin, my GSIs, all the members of Media Studies Lab, and my conference buddy Cody Mejeur. All of you provided essential feedback, support, or happy hour breaks at critical moments throughout grad school and beyond. Further thanks to Siva Vaidhyanathan, who once told me I was "onto something with this video game thing," as well as Aswin Punathambekar, Sonya Dal Cin, Shira Chess, and many others for their support, their excellent and timely advice, and their willingness to answer frantic queries about how academia actually works. While writing this book, I started at the University of Oregon School of Journalism and Communication. Many faculty and staff made this transition possible and welcomed me to the Pacific Northwest; my gratitude goes out to all of you. Special thanks to the Franklin Five, who made the first year both manageable and fun.

Thank you to everyone I worked with at NYU Press, including Lisha Nadkarni, Dolma Ombadykow, Eric Zinner, and the production and co-pyediting staff, for putting your faith, time, and energy into this book. I am also grateful to Cathy Hannabach at Ideas on Fire, who turned a lot of ideas into a beautiful and usable index, as well as the anonymous reviewers whose feedback helped clarify many key points between the initial manuscript and the final copy. The excellent existing work in gender and game studies, especially that of Adrienne Shaw, Kishonna Gray, Kelly Bergstrom, T. L. Taylor, Anastasia Salter, Bridget Blodgett, Alison Harvey, and Mia Consalvo (among others), made this book possible by providing the solid foundation from which I could build. My wonderful research assistants, Alison O'Brien and Brandon Harris, are also responsible for moving this work forward and providing honest feedback on whether or not it was making sense. David Carter and Val Waldron's work at the UM Computer and Video Game Archive provided key resources, including most of the magazines analyzed in this book. Thank you to you all.

I am also deeply indebted to my friends and family for listening to me talk through ideas and complain about issues, for fielding late-night phone calls and extensive rants about games and feminism, and for making sure my work/life balance included sufficient life. You know who you are. Thanks to Mom and Dad for literally everything, to Jason and David for being my first and best fellow gamers, and to my extended family members, who are always up for a good game night. I love you! And finally, all my thanks and love to Eric for sticking with me despite the fact that I made you move to Oregon. The sacrifices you've made for my career, as well as your patience with my complaints, my tendency to edit out loud, and my continual requests that you read things over for me, have not gone unnoticed. I couldn't have done it without you, and I'm grateful for you every day.

APPENDIX

Research Methods

This appendix outlines the tenets of social constructivism and the ways in which this paradigm drove my decisions about research design and method, from magazine analysis to in-depth interviews to my use of grounded theory. Each of these components, and why I did what I did, will be explored below. Throughout, I draw heavily on the work of Drs. Yvonna S. Lincoln and Egon G. Guba (1985, 1986), who were among the first to put to paper the methods of naturalistic inquiry, and Dr. Robin Means Coleman (2000), whose methodology inspired many of the techniques and strategies I used. These authors' texts have been invaluable to the development of my work, due to their rigor and their clarity. Similarly, I hope this appendix will be useful not only for casual readers who want to know more about research but also for scholars who are interested in replicating my study or employing similar methods in other areas.

ASSUMPTIONS AND ORIENTATION

My work starts from a social constructivist, also called a naturalistic, background (Lincoln and Guba, 1985, 1986; Means Coleman, 2000). This paradigm argues that realities are multiple and constructed, and that they are unstable, changing over time and context (Lincoln and Guba, 1985). Put more simply, although there are real things that exist in the world, they are always understood through the lens of social and cultural institutions. Take the colors blue and pink. These terms refer to (most) humans' visual perception of different wavelengths of electromagnetic radiation bouncing off objects surrounding them. Within Western society, however, pink and blue are also more than this, as they are associated, respectively, with femininity and masculinity. These associations are reaffirmed through language, the fashion industry, parents' clothing choices for their children, gender reveal parties, and many other forces. Culture and social interactions give meaning to the colors blue and pink and then normalize these associations through repetition.

However, because these meanings are *given*, rather than natural or inherent, they are both multiple and unstable. Individuals from non-Western cultures, for instance, may not share the associations of pink and blue with femininity and masculinity or may associate them with completely different characteristics. The meaning of colors has also changed throughout Western history; in researching children's clothing, historian Jo Paoletti found that early 1900s ads promoted pink as the "more decided and stronger color," appropriate for boys, while "delicate and dainty" blue was considered more feminine (Maglaty, 2011). In a constructivist paradigm, therefore, there is no one single reality that can be understood completely and that persists forever. Rather, there exist multiple realities that differ on the basis of social and cultural context.

Social constructivism also argues that research cannot be something done *by* a researcher *to* a subject. Instead, it occurs in the interaction between researcher and participant. Furthermore, constructivists "argue that it is *impossible* to do research that is free of personal and political sympathies" (Means Coleman, 2000, pp. 267–68, emphasis original). Thus, my positionality is inherent to the work presented here. My background and identifications—female gamer, feminist, researcher, and more—help shape my research questions, my interviews, my analysis, and the way I write up my results. This was something I had to negotiate throughout the research process. For instance, it was at times useful for me to hide my own knowledge about a game. If someone didn't know that I had played *World of Warcraft*, their explanations of it were generally deeper and more detailed. This gave me better access to their worldview. At other times, revealing aspects of my female/gamer identity encouraged participants to talk more freely about uncomfortable topics, such as harassment or the difficulty of feeling as though they didn't belong in game-related spaces. My identities affected many parts of the research. In constructivist work, however, the researchers' job is to be reflexive about this influence, not to strive to remove themselves from the equation entirely (Means Coleman, 2000).

The goal of this project was thus never to find a set of facts that always hold true for all female gamers; a single truth about what it means to be a female gamer does not exist. Rather, the goal was to co-construct with participants a deeper understanding of the ways in which identifying as both female and gamer affected their lived experiences and what these effects meant with regard to broader social and cultural norms. The goal was also to recognize the ways in which these identities—female, gamer, and female gamer—were *not* the only factors influencing each individual's worldview, as evidenced by the many points in which participants disagreed with each other. Attention to these moments of fracture is meaningful, as they illustrate the multiplicity of experience that undergirds social constructivism. With these goals in mind, I turned to research methods that allowed for flexibility, nuance, and deep explorations of game culture and my participants' experiences, including discourse analysis and in-depth interviews.

RESEARCH DESIGN: MAGAZINE ANALYSIS

For my analysis of video game press, I began by compiling a list of popular video game publications using my personal knowledge and library and online catalogs. I also used a "snowball" approach, letting video-game-oriented publications direct me to other "essential reads" for gamers. I narrowed my list by removing company-specific publications (such as *Nintendo Power*), ones that contained only reviews, as they would not provide overall analysis of games' culture and industry, and ones that did not exist for the whole time period I was interested in. Originally, this was 2000–2010, but I later limited it to 2005–2008; given technology's relatively quick turnover time, works written in the early 2000s had little to no bearing on the mid-2000s. Instead, I focused on the years immediately prior to and immediately following the release of the Nintendo Wii, as it was a key moment in the rise of casual, social, and mobile games. Finally, I limited my analysis to publications for which I could actually access all or most of the issues published from January 2005 to December 2008.

As a result, I conducted a thematic discourse analysis of four magazines—*Game Developer*, *Edge* (the UK edition), *Game Informer*, and *Electronic Gaming Monthly*.[1] Thematic discourse analysis can be done using many different methods, but it takes as its primary concern questions of language and representation (Kirkpatrick, 2017). In this case, I focused on how the magazines discussed casual games, casual players, and changes to game culture or the gaming industry, and I used a grounded theory approach to analysis. Grounded theory generally begins with a question—e.g., "how do magazines frame the rise of casual games?" Rather than hypothesizing an answer, however, the researcher begins to collect data, categorize it according to the meaning of different sections (i.e., phrases or sentences), and organize these categories into patterns and themes (Glaser and Strauss, 1967; Lindlof and Taylor, 2002). Successful grounded theory develops from systematic analysis, and it is also iterative; when the researcher adds further data, they rethink and adjust patterns to account for new information. As communications professors Thomas R. Lindlof and Bryan C. Taylor (2002) explain, "Data from new experiences continue to alter the scope and terms of [the researcher's] analytic framework" (p. 218). The conclusions of the work thus emerge directly out of—are grounded in—the data itself. For this reason, grounded theory works well in a constructivist context, as it is flexible enough to account for multiple realities, including moments of disagreement or conflict, is firmly rooted in those realities, and is based on the interactions among researcher, participant, and data. It was also useful for understanding magazine discourses, as the focus on patterns and themes allowed me to pull out dominant messages that a typical consumer might be exposed to. This helps unveil the role of the press in constructing gaming culture.

RESEARCH DESIGN: INTERVIEWS

To explore female gamers' experiences, I turned to in-depth interviews. Their flexibility allowed me to assess multiple, often contradictory realities, as the conversation could change on the basis of each participant's unique experiences and what she found important that I may not have considered.[2] Interviews also yielded deep information, because I could follow up on interesting points and seek further explanation. I conducted interviews on two occasions. Initial interviews occurred in 2012–2013, while secondary interviews, conducted in 2017–2018, provide updated information on how female gamers play throughout different life stages and events within game culture.

During the initial round of data collection, I conducted thirty-seven in-depth interviews with self-identified female gamers, the majority of whom were recruited through online video game forums.[3] I wrote a general post explaining my project and asking interested parties to contact me for more details. The recruitment post study was deliberately vague; potential participants just had to identify as female and be older than eighteen, due to Institutional Review Board (IRB) restrictions. Similarly, the forums themselves were targeted towards female gamers, but not towards specific games or platforms. This broad approach is somewhat unusual for an interview-based study, as interviews tend to be useful in explaining specific, nuanced phenomena. For this study, however, a slightly more expansive form of purposive sampling was useful in order to account for the multiple realities of being a female gamer.

Women who game face a wide variety of issues, and people with different backgrounds are likely to face different barriers to core gaming, as the identity of a typical "gamer" is not only male but also white, straight, young, and middle-class. Gathering information from an array of people was meant to provide a similarly wide range of viewpoints on gaming's power structures and problems. This is also why I recruited participants online rather than in person; localized recruitment would have meant greater geographical similarity between participants, while the use of online forums meant that they could come from all over the United States and even from around the world.

When women responded to the initial recruitment post, I gave them more information about the study, the ability to ask questions, and a consent form[4] to sign electronically. Because recruitment occurred online, most interviews were also conducted this way. Participants selected their preferred chat software, as I wanted the process to be as easy as possible for them. After each interview was completed, I transcribed it, made minor grammatical edits for clarity, and removed participants' identifying information, substituting pseudonyms. Each participant chose their own pseudonym for the study, but was guided to choose a name that differed from any of their gaming identities, to safeguard their privacy. In line with expected standards for qualitative studies, I continued to conduct interviews until I reached a point of redundancy, where interviews started to yield no new information (Means Coleman, 2000).

At the end of each interview, I asked whether the participant was willing to be contacted again in the future. If they said yes, I saved their e-mail address. I used those e-mail addresses later to share the results of my work, seek women's feedback on it, and recruit members for follow-up interviews. During the second round of interviews, conducted roughly five years after the first, I reconnected with eleven of the original thirty-seven interviewees.

Participant Characteristics

Full participant details are included in tables A.3 and A.4 (found at the end of the appendix). As I hoped when I employed online recruitment, the women who responded to the call for participants did come from a few different backgrounds, although many shared some commonalities. First, they skewed somewhat young; the full sample ranged in age from nineteen to forty-five but averaged just over twenty-five. Only five participants were thirty or older.

They were also primarily white. Early interview guides did not ask about race, meaning four women did not identify their background. Of the thirty-three who gave information on ethnicity, twenty-five were non-Hispanic and white, while eight came from other ethnic backgrounds. Two define themselves as Arab, two as Mexican, and four as Korean, Chinese, or Asian American. I encouraged participants to describe themselves using whatever language worked best for them; this means that some participants changed how they described their ethnicity between interviews. Most participants were from various regions of the United States, but three were based in Canada, two in the UK, and one in Bahrain.

Participants are primarily college-educated, with many either holding or pursuing advanced degrees. At the time of their original interview, two participants defined themselves as having completed "some college," and two possessed associate's degrees. Nine were in the middle of their undergraduate study, and the rest all possessed at least a bachelor's degree. All the participants I reconnected with for a second interview had completed at least a bachelor's degree, and many held master's degrees or were in the process of pursuing them.

These demographic characteristics demonstrate that online recruitment came with some benefits and some limitations. For instance, I was able to recruit people from a few different backgrounds and talk to players across the United States. As US regions differ in terms of history, culture, and gender expectations, this probably broadened the types of experiences my participants had to relate. Furthermore, although the sample tended to be young, the inclusion of at least a few older participants helped provide a perspective on how gaming has changed over time, as well as whether age influences access to power or control. Because the goal of this study is broad exploration, rather than generalizability, even a small number of differences among participants was helpful in assessing their multiple experiences.

Online recruitment was, however, a likely factor in the similarities many participants share. Participants needed to have an economic background allowing them regular access to the Internet and the leisure time to play games, which could explain their high levels of education. They tended to be younger and white, which reflects both continued gaps in Internet access by age and race (Lenhart et al., 2010; US Census Bureau, 2017) and the tendency of Internet users who see themselves as outside the norm to hide their identity (as my participants often did while gaming). Because I recruited them online, participants also needed to be deeply involved in gaming, to the point where they would want to participate in online discussions about it. Therefore, my sample probably leaves out women who have chosen to quit the gaming community, although reconnecting with the same participants for updated interviews does try to account for this.

Finally, the self-selected nature of the recruitment process meant that women who play games but do not necessarily identify themselves as "gamers" may have opted not to participate. As game scholar Adrienne Shaw (2012) points out, this means that the sample is more likely to lack women who are gaming minorities in a number of ways—women who are also of color or queer, for instance—because the intersectionality of these characteristics further disassociates them from gamer identity and its stereotypical associations (white, male, young, etc.). Therefore, some perspectives may not be explored fully here. Future projects on gaming, gender, and identity will have to keep this in mind, and they may need to use offline recruitment techniques or find online forums that target minority gaming populations more specifically.

Data Analysis
Once I completed and transcribed each interview, I transferred it to NVivo, a qualitative software package, and analyzed the interviews using

the same grounded theory approach I applied to magazines. As mentioned earlier, grounded theory is useful in constructivist work due to its iterative nature and flexibility, which ensure that multiple realities are taken into account. Grounded theory's solid foundation within the data itself is also significant; in an interview context, this practice prioritizes the voices of participants as well as their interactions with the researcher, supporting co-constructed conclusions.

Quality Checks

Within a constructivist paradigm, well-done qualitative work achieves "trustworthiness" based on the following characteristics: credibility, transferability, confirmability, and dependability (Lincoln and Guba, 1985, 1986). These qualities parallel quantitative inquiry's values of internal validity, external validity, reliability, and objectivity. As these characteristics and their requirements have been laid out in detail in other sources (see, for instance, Lincoln and Guba [1986] or Means Coleman [2000]), I will not spend time repeating each here, although table A.1 summarizes each characteristic. Rigorous constructivist work also should achieve authenticity. That is, it should honor and value participants' rights and experiences, as well as their role in the co-construction of research (Means Coleman, 2000). Methodologists Yvonna S. Lincoln and Egon G. Guba (1985, 1986) propose five measures of authenticity: fairness, ontological authenticity, educative authenticity, catalytic authenticity, and tactical authenticity. I have created table A.2 to summarize each of these.

TABLE A.1. Trustworthiness Criteria, table created by the author drawing on Means Coleman (2000) and Lincoln and Guba (1985, 1986)

Trustworthiness Criteria	Quantitative Parallel	What it Means
Credibility	Internal Validity	Do the results fairly reflect the truths of your participants and context?
Transferability	External Validity	Have you provided enough detail that a reader can apply your conclusions to other circumstances?
Confirmability	Reliability	Can someone reconstruct your results from your data?
Dependability	Objectivity	Is your research process clear and thoroughly explained?

TABLE A.2. Authenticity Criteria, table created by the author drawing on Means Coleman (2000) and Lincoln and Guba (1985, 1986)

Authenticity Criteria	What it Means
Fairness	Were all possible truths fairly and evenly exposed and evaluated?
Ontological Authenticity	Have the involved individuals' and groups' knowledge and experiencing of the world improved as a result of the research?
Educative Authenticity	Do involved parties have an increased understanding for other points of view?
Catalytic Authenticity	Has the research encouraged people to take action?
Tactical Authenticity	Have participants been empowered by the research?

Throughout the research process, I sought to achieve the criteria of trustworthiness through an array of methods. For instance, I verified the credibility of my work through member checks, in which I shared preliminary writing with my participants for their feedback. This ensured that my conclusions correctly reflected their experiences and feelings. I also completed follow-up interviews with many participants. Careful attention to and documentation of my research process contributed to confirmability and dependability. For instance, I have recorded and acknowledged times when my participants' input altered the questions in my interview guide. As stated above, I originally neglected to ask participants about their racial or ethnic background; thankfully, they pointed out that this was meaningful to their experiences, and I adjusted accordingly. At other times, I have tried to recognize and contextualize my a priori assumptions about what would matter to participants, as well as to show how I changed my views when these assumptions were not supported.

In terms of authenticity, it is much harder to establish whether one has achieved these goals or not, as many can only occur towards the end of the research process. Some of the suggestions I make throughout this book, for instance, are meant to serve the purpose of catalytic and tactical authenticity. For the measures that can be evaluated, such as fairness, however, I have relied on standard methods such as informed consent, open discussion, and member checks, to ensure participants felt heard and were able to share freely even views that did not align with

TABLE A.3. Participant Demographic Characteristics at Interview One

Participant	Age	Race	Location	Educational Background	Major	Career
Adrianna	26	White	Southern US	Grad school—MFA	Creative writing	Receptionist/office manager
Alissa	24	White	Northeastern US	Bachelor's	Art	Hotel supervisor, artist
Angela	30	White	West/Central US	In college	Electrical engineering	Student
Anna	20	White	Northeastern US	In grad school	Media and tech	Grad student
Arya	28	Korean	Western US	Bachelor's	Art history	TV producer
Bear	23	White	Mid-Atlantic US	In grad school	Epidemiology	Grad student
Bubble	24	White	Northwestern US	Bachelor's	Computer science	IT
Buttsvard	30	White	Northeastern US	Bachelor's	Painting	Illustration and design
Caddie	24		Mid-Atlantic US	Law school	Current student	Law student
Chianna	25	White	Northeastern US	Bachelor's	Special education and theater/ creative writing	Teacher
Chimera Soul	35	White	Northeastern US	Associate's degree	Applied science	Stay-at-home mom (formerly R&D)
Doopdoop9000	21	Chinese/ Japanese	Canada	Bachelor's	Psychology	Social media company admin
DT	23	Arab	Bahrain	Bachelor's	Early childhood education	Preschool English teacher
Elayne	24	White	Southern US	In college	Sociology	Student
Elizabeth	20	Mexican	Southern US	In college	Psychology	Student
Emily	24	White	North central US	Bachelor's	Writing, politics, and Italian	Nonprofit fundraising
Eva	22	Mexican	Southern US	In college	Dermatology	Student
Feather	25	White	Mid-Atlantic US	Bachelor's	Psychology	Administrative work

Name	Age	Race/Ethnicity	Region	Education	Field of study	Occupation
Fiber Freak	25	White	Southern US	Bachelor's	Liberal arts	Screenwriting
Harley	35	White	Northeastern US	Some college	Liberal science	Kitchen work and PC repair
Helix	27	White	Southern US	Bachelor's	Web design and English	Website content writer
Jasper	24	Asian	Mid-Atlantic US	Bachelor's	Economics	Accounting
Jessica	24	White	Central US	Associate's degree	Applied science	Internet marketing and web design
Jutte	24	White	Central US	In college	Anthropology and sociology	Student
Katie Tyler	19		Northeastern US	In college	Biomedical engineering	Student
Kay	21	White	Central US	In grad school	English and creative writing	Student
Laine	25	White	Central US	In grad school	Neuroscience	Student
Lee	20	White	Mid-Atlantic US	In college	History and computer science	Student
Marie	21		Canada	In college	Aviation	Student and part-time worker w/ military
Misty	25	Arab	Northeastern US	Master's	Architecture	Architect
Nina	23	Asian	Mid-Atlantic US	Bachelor's	Systems engineering	Technology consultant
Rogue	24	White	Northeastern US	Master's	Literacy, special ed, and elementary ed	Special education teacher
Sophie	24		Canada	In college	Social work	Student and horse & carriage driver
Spinach	21	White	Mid-Atlantic US	In college	Psychology	Student
Taylor Ryan	26	White	UK	In grad school	Game development	Grad student
Tinsel	45	White	UK	Bachelor's	Personnel and employee development	Currently unemployed (health concerns)
Vickie	28	White	Mid-Atlantic US	Bachelor's	History	IT

TABLE A.4. Participant Demographic Characteristics at Interview Two

Participant	Age	Race	Marital Status	Sexual Orientation	Career
Adrianna	31	White	Single	Heterosexual	Health sciences librarian
Chianna	29	White	Married	Asexual	Special ed teacher
Elayne	28	White	In a relationship	Bisexual	Healthcare accounting
Emily	29	White	Married	Heterosexual	Fundraising
Feather	29	White	Single	Heterosexual	Office/project manager
Laine	29	White	Married	Heterosexual	University professor
Marie	26	White	Married	Bisexual	Flight dispatcher
Misty	30	Mixed	In a relationship	Heterosexual	Architect
Spinach	25	White	Single	Queer	Graduate student
Taylor Ryan	31	White/ Latina	In a relationship	Heterosexual	Game designer
Vickie	33	White	Married	Heterosexual	Telecommunication engineering

my own. Member checks were also helpful in other areas, such as onto-logical and educative authenticity, as they exposed participants not only to their own views but also to those of other interviewees. For many of them, this was a rare experience; as games researcher Lina Eklund (2011) points out, and as I similarly found, women generally don't know many other female gamers. Being able to see others, even if their experiences and perspectives differed, was refreshing. To quote Feather's second interview—"There's validation in knowing you're not alone."

GAMEOGRAPHY

Games referenced throughout the book are listed below in alphabetical order by title. For the sake of brevity, many are grouped by series and credited to their original or primary publisher/developers although different companies may have contributed throughout their history. Readers interested in further details on particular games can find that information on individual game websites or sources like Wikipedia.

Angry Birds [mobile game]. (2009). Developed and published by Rovio Entertainment.
Assassin's Creed [series]. (2007–2018). Developed and published by Ubisoft.
Baldur's Gate [series]. (1998–2016). Originally developed by BioWare and published by Interplay Entertainment. Later installments have various developers/publishers.
Battlefield V [computer and console game]. (2018). Developed by EA DICE, published by Electronic Arts.
Bayonetta [console game]. (2009). Developed by PlatinumGames, published by Nintendo.
Bayonetta 2 [console game]. (2014). Developed by PlatinumGames, published by Nintendo.
Bejeweled [web browser game]. (2001). Developed and published by PopCap Games, Inc.
Bioshock [series]. (2007–2013). Originally developed by 2K Boston and 2K Australia, published by 2K Games, Inc. Later installations are developed by Irrational Games and 2K Marin.
Borderlands [series]. (2009–2015). Originally developed by Gearbox Software, published by 2K Games, Inc. Later installations have various developers.
Call of Duty [series]. (2003–2019). Originally developed by Infinity Ward and published by Activision Publishing, Inc. Later installments have various developers.
Candy Crush Saga [mobile game]. (2012). Developed and published by King.
Civilization [series]. (1991–2019). Originally developed by MPS Labs and published by MicroProse. Later installments have various developers.
Clash of Clans [mobile game]. (2012). Developed and published by Supercell.
Club Penguin [browser game]. (2005). Developed and published by New Horizon Interactive.
Cooking Mama [series]. (2006–2017). Originally developed by Office Create and published by Majesco (North America). Later installments developed by Cooking Mama Limited.

Crafting Mama [DS game]. (2010). Developed by Cooking Mama Limited, published by Majesco (North America).

Depression Quest [browser game]. (2013). Developed and published by Zoë Quinn.

Diablo III [computer game]. (2012). Developed and published by Blizzard Entertainment.

Diablo: Immortal [mobile game]. (Forthcoming). Developed by NetEast and Blizzard Entertainment, published by Blizzard Entertainment.

Donkey Kong [series]. (1981–2018). Originally developed and published by Nintendo. Later installments have various developers.

Doom [series]. (1993–2020). Originally developed and published by id Software. Later installments have various developers.

Dragon Age [series]. (2009–2014). Developed by BioWare, published by Electronic Arts.

Dungeons and Dragons [tabletop role-playing game series]. (1974–2014). Originally designed by Gary Gygax and Dave Arneson, published by Tactical Studies Rules, Inc. Now designed and published by Wizards of the Coast.

Dungeons of Dredmor [computer game]. (2011). Developed and published by Gaslamp Games.

Dynasty Warriors [series]. (1997–2018). Developed by Omega Force and published by Koei.

The Elder Scrolls [series]. (1994–2019). Primarily developed and published by Bethesda Softworks, although some series installments have been out-of-house productions.

The End Is Nigh [computer and console game]. (2017). Developed and published by Edmund McMillen and Tyler Glaiel.

Everquest [computer game]. (2009). Developed by Verant Interactive and 989 Studios, published by Sony Online Entertainment (North America).

Fallout [series]. (1997–2018). Originally developed and published by Interplay Entertainment. Later installments have various developers.

Far Cry [series]. (2004–2019). Originally developed by Crytek and published by Ubisoft. Now developed by Ubisoft.

Farmville [Facebook game]. (2009). Developed and published by Zynga.

Faunasphere [browser game]. (2010). Developed and published by Big Fish Games.

Fez [console and computer game]. (2012). Developed by Polytron Corporation and published by Trapdoor.

Final Fantasy [series]. (1987–2019). Developed and published by Square (now Square Enix).

Flower [console and mobile game]. (2009). Developed by thatgamecompany, published by Sony Computer Entertainment and Annapurna Interactive.

Gears of War [series]. (2006–2019). Developed by Epic Games and The Coalition, published by Microsoft Studios.

Gone Home [computer game]. (2013). Developed and published by The Fullbright Company. Later published on other platforms by Majesco and Annapurna Entertainment.

Grand Theft Auto [series]. (1997–2013). Originally developed by DMA Design and published by various companies. Now developed and published by Rockstar Games.

Guild Wars 2 [computer game]. (2012). Developed by ArenaNet and published by NCSOFT.

Halo [series]. (2001–2017). Originally developed by Bungie and Gearbox Software, published by Microsoft Game Studios. Later installations have various developers.

Harvest Moon [series]. (2007–2017). Originally developed by Platinum Egg, Inc., and published by Natsume (North America). Now developed by Appci Corporation.

Her Story [computer and mobile game]. (2015). Developed and published by Sam Barlow.

Horn [mobile game]. (2012). Developed by Phosphor Games Studio and published by Zynga.

Injustice: Gods among Us [console and mobile game]. (2013). Developed by Nether-Realm Studio and published by Warner Bros. Interactive Entertainment.

Journey [computer and console game]. (2012). Developed by thatgamecompany and published by Sony Computer Entertainment.

Just Dance [series]. (2009–2019). Developed and published by Ubisoft.

The Last of Us [console game]. (2013). Developed by Naughty Dog and published by Sony Computer Entertainment.

League of Legends [computer game]. (2009). Developed and published by Riot Games.

Left 4 Dead [computer and console game]. (2008). Developed and published by Valve.

Left 4 Dead 2 [computer and console game]. (2009). Developed and published by Valve.

Legend of Zelda [series]. (1986–2018). Originally developed and published by Nintendo. Some installments have been developed out-of-house.

Lollipop Chainsaw [console game]. (2012). Developed by Grasshopper Manufacture, published by Warner Bros. Interactive Entertainment.

Mass Effect [series]. (2007–2017). Originally developed by BioWare and published by Microsoft Studios and Electronic Arts. Later installments have various developers.

Microsoft Solitaire [computer game]. (1990). Developed by Wes Cherry and published by Microsoft.

Minecraft [computer game]. (2011). Developed and published by Mojang.

Minesweeper [computer game]. (1992). Developed by Curt Johnson and published by Microsoft.

Nintendogs [DS game]. (2005). Developed and published by Nintendo.

Overwatch [computer and console game]. (2016). Developed and published by Blizzard Entertainment.

Papers, Please [computer and mobile game]. (2014). Developed and published by 3909 LLC.

Persona [series]. (1996–2020). Developed and published by Atlus.

Pokémon [series]. (1996–2019). Developed by Game Freak, published by Nintendo and The Pokémon Company.

Portal [computer and console game]. (2007). Developed and published by Valve.

Red Dead Redemption [console game]. (2010). Developed and published by Rockstar Games.

Resident Evil 4 [computer and console game]. (2005). Developed and published by Capcom.

Rust [computer game]. (2013). Developed and published by Facepunch Studios.

The Sims [series]. (2000–2019). Developed by Maxis and The Sims Studio, published by Electronic Arts.

Sonic the Hedgehog [series]. (1991–2017). Originally developed by Sonic Team and published by Sega. Later installments have various developers.

Star Wars: Knights of the Old Republic [series]. (2003–2019). Originally developed by BioWare and published by LucasArts. Later installments have various developers/publishers.

Super Mario [series]. (1985–2019). Developed and published by Nintendo.

Super Meat Boy [computer and console game]. (2010). Developed and published by Team Meat.

Team Fortress 2 [computer and console game]. (2007). Developed and published by Valve Corporation.

Tom Clancy's [series]. (1987–2020). Originally developed and published by Red Storm Entertainment. Now primarily developed and published by Ubisoft, although different installments have various contributors.

Tomb Raider [series]. (1996–2018). Originally developed by Core Design and published by Eidos Interactive. The rebooted series (2013–2018) is developed by Crystal Dynamics and Eidos Montreal and published by Square Enix.

Wii Sports [console game]. (2006). Developed and published by Nintendo.

Words with Friends [mobile game]. (2009). Developed and published by Zynga.

World of Darkness/Chronicles of Darkness [tabletop role-playing game series]. (1991–2016). Primarily developed and published by White Wolf Gaming Studio.

World of Warcraft [computer game]. (2004). Developed and published by Blizzard Entertainment.

XCOM [series]. (1994–2017). Originally developed by Mythos Games and MicroProse and published by MicroProse. Recent installments are developed by Firaxis and published by 2K games.

NOTES

INTRODUCTION

1 I use this terminology not to imply that all games are now casual, but to highlight the extreme impact that casual, social, and mobile games have had on game industry and culture since the mid-2000s.

2 The concepts of core and casual, although previewed here, will be explored in greater depth in chapter 1.

3 Because the term "gamer" comes with many stereotypes regarding identity and behavior—e.g., straight, white, male, and cisgender, as well as isolated, socially awkward, and potentially aggressive (Shaw, 2012)— I use "gamer" in quotation marks to refer to the stereotypical identity. I refer to all other gamers as gamers or players, without quotation marks, interchanging these terms as needed for better readability.

4 Social, casual, and mobile games are frequently distinguished on the basis of their platforms and mechanics, but my overall argument focuses on the differences between traditional "core" video games and casual/mobile/social games. Therefore, I refer to these three types simultaneously as "casual games," drawing on their similarities rather than their differences.

5 Other forms of exclusion—transphobia, homophobia, ableism, and racism, for instance—have also been prominent. All of these need to be addressed, but for the sake of keeping this book manageable in length, it will focus primarily on issues of gender and sexism.

6 See Kiesler, Sproull, and Eccles 1985; Kent 2001; Dyer-Witheford and dePeuter 2009; Kirkpatrick 2015; Kocurek 2015; Cote 2017.

7 Gramsci developed his ideas about hegemony and the crisis of authority in reference to major sociopolitical shifts, such as the rise of fascism in Italy, rather than smaller-stakes changes within an entertainment area. However, his analysis and theoretical framework map strongly onto gaming's current issues, providing a useful structure despite the differences in scope.

8 E.g., "Watching *Dallas*" (Ang, 1985), "Defining Women" (D'Acci, 1994), "Reading Celebrity Gossip Magazines" (McDonnell, 2014), and "Cupcakes, Pinterest, and Ladyporn" (Levine, 2015).

9 Full details on the study's methods, including participant demographics, are in the appendix.

CHAPTER 1. CORE AND THE VIDEO GAME INDUSTRY

1 Readers may recognize that my descriptions here are leaving out a key segment—indie games. This is because indie games do not necessarily act either as hegemonic or counterhegemonic forces (Fisher and Harvey, 2013; Harvey and Shepherd, 2017). Therefore, while I will discuss individual indie games when relevant, I am hesitant to group all of indie into core or casual. I encourage interested readers to check out the work of Stephanie Fisher, Alison Harvey, and Tamara Shepherd for a deeper analysis of indie games.

2 Full methodological details for the magazine analysis are in the appendix.

3 Platform games or "platformers" require the player to maneuver a character through an environment by jumping across suspended platforms, over obstacles, or both. The famous *Super Mario Bros.* series is an example of a platform-style franchise.

4 Female gamers encounter similar challenges to their authenticity through "girl gamer" stereotypes, which posit that women only play video games in order to meet and attract men.

5 For a visual breakdown of expected casual/core values and actual, measured casual/core play habits, see Juul 2010, figures 2.1 (p. 29), 2.2 (p. 30), 2.15 (p. 51), and 2.16 (p. 52).

6 *Injustice: Gods Among Us Mobile* (2013) is a trading-card-based fighting game, where players collect cards showing different DC Comics characters and use these to battle other players or computer opponents. The game draws from the conventions of analog trading card games and therefore relies on a high degree of player knowledge and experience.

7 *Horn* (2012) is a mobile action-adventure game. It draws on fantasy themes and English mythology to offer an immersive environment, hours-long quests for players to complete, and many other trappings traditionally associated with core rather than casual games.

8 A full description of my methodology is in the appendix.

9 This is another illustration of why I have not included indie games in my core/casual divide, as some follow traditional core expectations, with enormous budgets and graphics, and others do not.

10 iPod games existed at this time, and the iPhone and AppStore came out in 2008.

11 Again, many indie games do still follow core expectations; therefore, each should be addressed individually to see what it accomplishes and how.

CHAPTER 2. TITS, TOKENISM, AND TRASH-TALK

1 These include high levels of violence (Children Now, 2001; Dietz, 1998; Graner Ray, 2004; Haninger and Thompson, 2004; Smith, Lachlan, and Tamborini, 2003), low numbers of female characters and a high proportion of sexualized female characters (Beasley and Standley, 2002; Behm-Morawitz, 2017; Burgess, Stermer, and Burgess, 2007; Dill and Thill, 2007; Downs and Smith, 2010; Ivory,

2006; Jansz and Martis, 2007; Miller and Summers, 2007; Scharrer, 2004; Waddell et al., 2014), and general social forces that separate girls from technology (Gilmour, 1999; Schott and Horrell, 2000; Bryce and Rutter, 2003; Jenson, de Castell, and Fisher, 2007; Jenson and de Castell, 2011). Gaming spaces are also frequently masculinized (Bryce and Rutter, 2002, 2003; Jansz and Martens, 2005; Taylor, Jenson, and de Castell, 2009; Taylor, 2012), and the games industry can be unwelcoming to women as well (Blodgett and Salter, 2014; Huntemann, 2013; Johnson, 2011).

2 Players also face the same limitations in terms of sexuality or race, where games often presume a player is heterosexual, cisgender, or white. These assumptions have provided interesting opportunities for players to deliberately queer games (unfortunately not a focus of this project), but they also demonstrate how narrowly developers define "gamers."

3 *Assassin's Creed: Syndicate* (October 2015) was the first main-storyline game to feature a female character, although she is one of two protagonists, alongside her twin brother. This has since become standard for the franchise.

4 Casual games again offer an alternative space where female characters are not sexualized (Wohn, 2011).

5 This is again simplifying the impact of race and sexuality to maintain a focus on gender. Most video game characters are white and heterosexual, complicating identification and enjoyment on the part of players who identify as nonwhite, LGBT, and/or both.

6 Participants also linked problems with women's representation in games to overall diversity issues, making statements like, "It would be cool if there was more diversity in games. Right now, it's still mostly white and mostly male. It's weird to have four or five character options and all but one of them are white men" (Angela, interview 1). While their main focus was on the representation of women, both due to the goals of the study and their status as female gamers, players recognized that issues spread well beyond gender alone, affecting racial and sexual representations as well.

CHAPTER 3. GIRLY GAMES AND GIRL GAMERS

1 Sorry, bro. But at least this way I'll know you read my book!

CHAPTER 4. ALREADY CORE

1 Rosa Mikeal Martey and colleagues (2014) collected data within the game *World of Warcraft* in order to assess how players of different gender identities varied in terms of chat, movement, and appearance. The researchers found that men were more likely to direct action verbally and to move their character around, even when movement was unnecessary. Women, on the other hand, used more emotional phrases, emoticons, and exclamation points. Interestingly, men who gender-switched, or played a female avatar but identified as male, generally showed a mix of these behavioral patterns (pp. 293–94). The researchers

associated these differences with the way men and women are socialized to ideal gender roles.

2 At other times, of course, anonymity is a burden on players, as anonymous players can harass others with fewer consequences. However, Elizabeth's statements show that anonymity is not necessarily a bad thing, and players have a complicated relationship with it.

3 For more details about interview construction, see Cote and Raz 2015.

4 E.g. Children Now 2001; Dietz 1998; Graner Ray 2004; Haninger and Thompson 2004; Smith et al. 2003.

5 E.g., Beasley and Standley 2002; Behm-Morawitz 2017; Burgess, Stermer, and Burgess 2007; Dill and Thill 2007; Downs and Smith 2010; Ivory 2006; Jansz and Martis 2007; Miller and Summers 2007; Scharrer 2004; Waddell et al. 2014.

6 NPCs are nonplayer characters, or avatars controlled by the game itself. They act as allies or enemies, allow the player to buy or sell items, and reveal new parts of the storyline, among many other tasks.

7 Although players discussed their issues with first-person shooters' storylines separately from their issues with harassment, it is important to note that FPSs tend to have toxic communities and high levels of trash-talk because of their competitive game play and masculinized, aggressive content. Some players opted to avoid multiplayer FPS games for this reason rather than due to their storyline, demonstrating that both individual preferences for game characteristics and community aspects can matter to the games players choose to engage with.

8 Examples of grinding include circling a low-level area killing easy enemies to collect small amounts of experience points en masse or sitting at a lake fishing for a few hours specifically to raise one's "fishing" skill.

9 Obviously, such an approach is likely to be more complicated than it sounds; as this book emphasizes, there are many existing barriers in the way of easy affinity. This approach also should not rest entirely on the efforts of marginalized gamers, requiring assistance from journalists, developers, and majority gamers. However, it remains one possible path towards decreased discrimination.

CHAPTER 5. STRATEGIES FOR PLAY

1 Although this work cannot draw quantitative conclusions or make claims that are representative of female gamers as a whole, due to the semistructured nature of the interviews and the limited number of participants, these strategies are listed and discussed in order of popularity. More women practiced various avoidance strategies (e.g., not playing online) than directly combated harassment through skill or aggressive responses.

2 It is likely that male gamers as well as female gamers use these different approaches to choosing games, as many are significant investments of both time and money. Core games cost fifty to sixty dollars each, or more for special editions, and take at a minimum several hours to play. Gamers have a vested interest, therefore, in choosing games they will like. However, female gamers have to find

games that are both enjoyable and inoffensive, and they may find their offerings more limited than men do because of this.

3 For example, there are many similarities between the interviewees for this study and the romance readers Radway spoke with. Romance readers, like gamers, had clear preferences for what made a "good" or "bad" text. They generally avoided novels that included rape or multiple sexual relationships, preferring novels that had happy endings and a monogamous relationship between the heroine and the hero. These fit their expectations for love and their own life situations, in which most were married. Both Radway's readers and my participants worked to ensure that they engaged only with texts that fit their preferences, as they often had limited time or money to invest in their chosen medium.

4 Although a number of interviewees spoke about *Lollipop Chainsaw* in negative terms, Nina expressed an interest in playing it, treating it as a parody of how sexualized women are in games rather than as an offensive text. This again demonstrates that women cannot be treated as "just a homogenous bloc that react badly to sexualized images" (Buttsvard, interview 1). Each makes individual decisions regarding how she will react to certain texts and why.

5 Although such a strategy could backfire if unwelcoming players flood the system with positive reports for negative behavior, this did not happen in *LoL*, where Tribunal decisions matched developer judgments "80% of the time" (Cross, 2014, p. 15). Demographic statistics regarding Tribunal participation could not be found. However, Riot player statistics at the time showed that over 90 percent of *LoL* players were young men (Lyons, 2012). This reflects the overall demographics of the game industry and could partially explain the high level of agreement between players and developers.

6 This is not to argue that *LoL* has solved all its problems. Negativity is still extremely common, and it is likely that reports address only obvious harassment, rather than more subtle exclusionary tactics and micro-aggressions. But even if the Tribunal System has only resulted in marginal improvement, it can still serve as a useful foundation from which to encourage community-level change.

CHAPTER 6. IN THE AFTERMATH

1 Interested parties can read chapter 5 of Salter and Blodgett's (2017) *Toxic Geek Masculinity* for an overview.

2 Interestingly, ComicsGate and similar movements have occurred even though the history of comics *is* diverse, with famed creators like Stan Lee deliberately representing many groups of people through comics like *Black Panther* and the X-Men series (Ostroff, 2016; Dern, 2017).

3 Spinach did not specify who "she" was in this circumstance, but given the context, she was discussing either Quinn or Sarkeesian. I didn't notice during the conversation that she hadn't explicitly named a subject, and therefore failed to follow up and ask for specifics.

APPENDIX

1 I analyzed every issue of *Game Developer, Edge,* and *Game Informer.* For *Electronic Gaming Monthly,* I only had access to the issues from 2007 to 2008.

2 See Cote and Raz (2015) for further details on the strengths and weaknesses of in-depth interviews.

3 I describe these generally, rather than listing the specific forums, in the interests of guarding participants' anonymity. This is also why I have opted not to include my specific recruitment call in this appendix; although I have deleted all posts to further safeguard participant identities, the often-archived nature of the Internet means that a search using the exact language of the original post could still find something that might direct back to respondents.

4 Due to the interactive nature of constructivist research, it is essential to give participants ample information about the study, what their participation means, and what their rights are as contributors. For more on informed consent, especially in online contexts, see Cote and Raz 2015, pp. 97–98.

BIBLIOGRAPHY

"About." I Need Diverse Games (n.d.). Retrieved from https://ineeddiversegames.org/about/.

Agnello, A. J. (2013). Naughty Dog demanded *The Last of Us* be focus tested with women. *Digital Trends*, April 25. Retrieved from: www.digitaltrends.com/.

Albrechtslund, A.-M. (2011). Online identity crisis: Real ID on the *World of Warcraft* forums. *First Monday, 16(7)*.

Anable, A. (2018). *Playing with feelings: Video games and affect*. Minneapolis: University of Minnesota Press.

Anderson, B. R. O'G. (1983). *Imagined communities: Reflections on the origin and spread of nationalism*. London: Verso.

———. (1991). *Imagined communities: Reflections on the origin and spread of nationalism*. Rev. and extended ed., 2nd ed. London: Verso.

———. (2006). *Imagined communities: Reflections on the origin and spread of nationalism*. Rev. ed. London: Verso.

Anderson, S. (2012). Just one more game . . . *Angry Birds, Farmville*, and other hyper-addictive "stupid games." *New York Times Magazine*, April 4. Retrieved from: www.nytimes.com/.

Ang, I. (1985). *Watching Dallas: Soap opera and the melodramatic imagination*. London: Methuen.

Anthony, S. (2013). Can you build a gaming PC better than the PS4 for $400? *ExtremeTech*, November 18. Retrieved from www.extremetech.com/.

Auerbach, D. (2014). Letter to a young male gamer. *Slate*, August 27. Retrieved from www.slate.com/.

Axelsson, A., and Regan, T. (2006). Playing online. In P. Vorderer and J. Bryant (eds.), *Playing video games: Motives, responses, and consequences* (pp. 291–306). Mahwah, NJ: Erlbaum.

Bartle, R. (1996). Hearts, clubs, diamonds, spades: Players who suit MUDs. *Journal of MUD Research, 1(1)*. Retrieved from http://mud.co.uk/.

———. (2004). *Designing virtual worlds*. Indianapolis, IN: New Riders.

Beasley, B., and Standley, T. C. (2002). Shirts vs. skins: Clothing as an indicator of gender role stereotyping in video games. *Mass Communication & Society, 5(3)*, 279–93.

Beavis, C. (2005). Pretty good for a girl: Gender, identity, and computer games. Paper presented at DiGRA 2005: Changing Views—Worlds in Play. Vancouver, British Columbia, Canada.

Behm-Morawitz, E. (2017). Examining the intersection of race and gender in video game advertising. *Journal of Marketing Communications, 23(3)*, 220–39.

Berdahl, J. L. (2007). The sexual harassment of uppity women. *Journal of Applied Psychology, 92*, 425–37.

Bergstrom, K. (2019). Barriers to play: Accounting for non-participation in digital game play. *Feminist Media Studies, 19(6)*, 841–857.

Berlatsky, N. (2018). The ComicsGate movement isn't defending free speech. It's suppressing it. *Washington Post*, September 13. Retrieved from www.washingtonpost.com/.

Blodgett, B., and Salter, A. (2014). #1ReasonWhy: Game communities and the invisible woman. *Proceedings of the 9th International Conference on the Foundations of Digital Games*. Foundations of Digital Games, Liberty of the Seas, Caribbean Cruise, April 3–7.

Blush, S. (2010). *American hardcore: A tribal history.* Los Angeles: Feral House.

Braithwaite, A. (2016). It's about ethics in games journalism? GamerGaters and geek masculinity. *Social Media + Society 2(4)*, 1–10. https://doi .org/10.1177/2056305116672484.

Bramwell, T. (2012). EuroGamer's game of the year. *EuroGamer*, December 30. Retrieved from www.eurogamer.net/.

Brod, H. (ed.). (1987). *The making of masculinities: The new men's studies.* Boston: Allen & Unwin.

Bryant, J., and Davies, J. (2006). Selective exposure to video games. In P. Vorderer and J. Bryant (eds.), *Playing video games: Motives, responses, and consequences* (pp. 181–95). Mahwah, NJ: Erlbaum.

Bryce, J., and Rutter, J. (2002). Killing like a girl: Gendered gaming and girl gamers' visibility. Paper presented at Computer Games and Digital Cultures Conference, Tampere, Finland. In F. Mäyrä (ed.), *Computer Games and Digital Cultures Conference Proceedings* (pp. 243–55). Tampere, Finland.

———. (2003). The gendering of computer gaming: Experience and space. In S. Fleming and I. Jones (eds.), *Leisure cultures: Investigations in sport, media, and technology* (pp. 3–22). Great Britain: Leisure Cultures Association.

Burgess, M. C. R., Stermer, S. P., and Burgess, S. R. (2007). Sex, lies, and video games: The portrayal of male and female characters on video game covers. *Sex Roles, 57(5–6)*, 419–33.

Burrill, D. A. (2008). *Die tryin': Videogames, masculinity, culture.* New York: Peter Lang.

Butler, J. (1990). *Gender trouble.* New York: Routledge.

———. (1999). *Gender trouble.* London: Routledge.

Campbell, C. (2014). Sarkeesian driven out of home by online abuse and death threats. *Polygon*, August 27. Retrieved from www.polygon.com/.

———. (2018). In *Assassin's Creed Odyssey*, Kassandra is better than Alexios. *Polygon*, October 9. Retrieved from www.polygon.com/.

Caron, C. (2018). Ohio House passes bill to criminalize abortions of fetuses with a heartbeat. *New York Times*, November 16. Retrieved from www.nytimes.com/.

Cassell, J., and Jenkins, H. (1998). Chess for girls? Feminism and computer games. In J. Cassell and H. Jenkins (eds.), *From Barbie to* Mortal Kombat: *Gender and computer games* (pp. 2–45). Danbury, CT: NetLibrary.

Castello, J. (2018). Foul play: Tackling toxicity and abuse in online video games. *Guardian*, August 17. Retrieved from www.theguardian.com/.

Caumont, A. (2013). Who's not online? 5 factors tied to the digital divide. *Pew Research Center*, November 8. Retrieved from www.pewresearch.org/.

Chalk, A. (2018). A chronology of *Dungeons & Dragons* in popular media. *Analog Game Studies, 5(2)*. Retrieved from http://analoggamestudies.org/.

Chasteen, A. L. (2001). Constructing rape: Feminism, change, and women's everyday understandings of sexual assault. *Sociological Spectrum, 21*, 101–39.

Chess, S. (2014). The politics of casual: Situating casual play in a hardcore industry. Paper presented at the Annual International Academic Conference on Meaningful Play, East Lansing, MI, October.

———. (2017). *Ready Player Two: Women gamers and designed identity*. Minneapolis: University of Minnesota Press.

Chess, S., and Shaw, A. (2015). A conspiracy of fishes, or, how we learned to stop worrying about #GamerGate and embrace hegemonic masculinity. *Journal of Broadcasting & Electronic Media, 59(1)*, 208–20.

Children Now. (2001). Children and the media. Retrieved from www.childrennow.org/.

Chisholm, J. F. (2006). Cyberspace violence against girls and adolescent females. *Annals of the New York Academy of Sciences, 1087*, 74–89.

Chui, R. (2014). A multi-faceted approach to anonymity online: Examining the relations between anonymity and antisocial behavior. *Journal of Virtual Worlds Research, 7(2)*. Retrieved from https://journals.tdl.org/jvwr/.

Condis, M. (2015). No homosexuals in *Star Wars*? BioWare, "gamer" identity, and the politics of privilege in a convergence culture. *Convergence, 21(2)*, 198–212.

———. (2018). *Gaming masculinity: Trolls, fake geeks, and the gendered battle for online culture*. Iowa City: University of Iowa Press.

Connell, R. W. (2000). *The men and the boys*. Berkeley: University of California Press.

Connell, R. W., and Messerschmidt, J. W. (2005). Hegemonic masculinity: Rethinking the concept. *Gender & Society, 19(6)*, 829–59.

Consalvo, M. (2009). Hardcore casual: Game culture return(s) to *Ravenhearst*. In *Proceedings of the 4th International Conference on Foundations of Digital Games* (pp. 50–54). Orlando, FL.

———. (2012). Confronting toxic gamer culture: A challenge for feminist game studies scholars. *Ada: A Journal of Gender, New Media, and Technology, 1*. doi:10.7264/N33X84KH.

Consalvo, M., and Begy, J. (2015). *Players and their pets: Gaming communities from Beta to Sunset*. Minneapolis: University of Minnesota Press.

Cote, A., and Raz, J. (2015). In-depth interviews for games studies. In P. Lankoski and S. Bjork (eds.), *Game Studies Research Methods* (pp. 93–116). Pittsburgh, PA: ETC Press.

Cote, A. C. (2017). "I can defend myself": Women's strategies for coping with harassment while gaming online. *Games and Culture, 12(2)*, 136–55.

———. (2018a). Curate your culture: A call for social justice–oriented game development and community management. In K. L. Gray and D. J. Leonard (eds.), *Woke gaming: Digital challenges to oppression and social injustice* (pp. 193–212). Seattle: University of Washington Press.

———. (2018b). Writing "gamers": The gendered construction of gamer identity in *Nintendo Power* (1994–1999). *Games and Culture, 13(5)*, 479–503.

Cross, K. A. (2014). Ethics for cyborgs: On real harassment in an "unreal" place. *Loading . . . The Journal of the Canadian Game Studies Association, 8(13)*, 4–21.

D'Acci, J. (1994). *Defining women: Television and the case of* Cagney & Lacey. Chapel Hill: University of North Carolina Press.

D'Anastasio, C. (2018). Inside the culture of sexism at riot games. *Kotaku*, August 7. Retrieved from https://kotaku.com/.

Dern, Z. (2017). Diversity in comics: What's been done and what needs to come. *Huffington Post*, June 4. Retrieved from www.huffingtonpost.com/.

Dietz, T. (1998). An examination of violence and gender role portrayals in video games: Implications for gender socialization and aggressive behavior. *Sex Roles, 38(5–6)*, 425–42.

Dill, K. E., and Thill, K. P. (2007). Video game characters and the socialization of gender roles: Young people's perceptions mirror sexist media depictions. *Sex Roles, 57(11–12)*, 851–64.

Douglas, S. J. (2010). *The rise of enlightened sexism: How pop culture took us from "Girl Power" to "Girls Gone Wild."* New York: St. Martin's.

Downs, E., and Smith, S. L. (2010). Keeping abreast of hypersexuality: A video game character content analysis. *Sex Roles, 62(11)*, 721–33.

Dredge, S. (2015). *Candy Crush Saga* players spent £865m on the game in 2014 alone. *Guardian*, February 13. Retrieved from www.theguardian.com/.

Dubbelman, T. (2011). Playing the hero: How games take the concept of storytelling from representation to presentation. *Journal of Media Practice, 12(2)*, 157–72.

Dyer-Witheford, N., and dePeuter, G. (2009). *Games of empire: Global capitalism and video games*. Minneapolis: University of Minnesota Press.

Eklund, L. (2011). Doing gender in cyberspace: The performance of gender by female *World of Warcraft* players. *Convergence, 17(3)*, 323–42.

Elbein, A. (2018). #ComicsGate: How an anti-diversity harassment campaign in comics got ugly—and profitable. *Daily Beast*, April 2. Retrieved from www.thedailybeast.com/.

ESA (Entertainment Software Association). (2004–2019). Essential facts about the computer and video game industry [Press release]. Retrieved from www.theesa.com/.

Escoffier, J. (2009). *Bigger than life: The history of gay porn cinema from beefcake to hardcore*. Philadelphia: Running Press.

Fair Play Alliance. (2018). Retrieved from www.fairplayalliance.org/.

Faludi, S. (2006). *Backlash: The undeclared war against American women*. 15th anniversary edition. New York: Three Rivers Press.

Farley, C. J. (2011). *The Last Airbender: Legend of Korra*; The creators speak. *Wall Street Journal*, March 8. Retrieved from: http://blogs.wsj.com/.

Farokhmanesh, M. (2014). Riot continues to crack down on "toxic" *League of Legends* pro players. *Polygon*, June 2. Retrieved from www.polygon.com/.

———. (2018a). *Battlefield V* fans who failed history are mad that the game has women in it. *Verge*, May 24. Retrieved from www.theverge.com/.

———. (2018b). *Battlefield V*'s creators: Female characters are "here to stay." *Verge*, May 25. Retrieved from www.theverge.com/.

Fenster, M. (1993). Queer punk fanzines: Identity, community, and the articulation of homosexuality and hardcore. *Journal of Communication Inquiry, 17(1)*, 73–94.

Fine, G. A. (1983). *Shared fantasy: Role-playing games as social worlds*. Chicago: University of Chicago Press.

Fish, S. (1976). Interpreting the "Variorum." *Critical Inquiry, 2(3)*, 465–85.

Fisher, S., and Harvey, A. (2013). Intervention for inclusivity: Gender politics and indie game development. *Loading . . . The Journal of the Canadian Game Studies Association, 7(11)*, 25–40.

Fiske, J. (1996). *Media matters: Race and gender in U.S. politics*. Minneapolis: University of Minnesota Press.

Forbes, B. (2018). Ask Riot: Will *Tribunal* return? Retrieved from https://nexus.leagueoflegends.com/.

Foucault, M. (1970). *The order of things*. London: Tavistock.

———. (1982). The subject and power. *Critical Inquiry, 8(4)*, 777–95.

Fox, J., and Tang, W. Y. (2014). Sexism in online video games: The role of conformity to masculine norms and social dominance orientation. *Computers in Human Behavior, 33*, 314–20.

Frasca, G. (2003). Simulation versus narrative: Introduction to ludology. In M. J. P. Wolf and B. Perron (eds.), *The video game theory reader* (pp. 221–35). New York: Routledge.

Fron, J., Fullerton, T., Morie, J. F., and Pearce, C. (2007). The hegemony of play. In *Situated play: Proceedings of DiGRA 2007 Conference* (pp. 1–10). Tokyo, Japan.

Gaynor, S. (2014). Why is *Gone Home* a game? Game Developer's Conference Presentation, San Francisco, CA, March 20. Retrieved from www.gdcvault.com/.

Gee, J. P. (2011). Stories, probes, and games. *Narrative Inquiry, 21(2)*, 353–57.

Gilmour, H. (1999). What girls want: The intersections of leisure and power in female computer game play. In M. Kinder (ed.), *Kids' media culture* (pp. 263–92). Durham, NC: Duke University Press.

Glaser, B. G., and Strauss, A. L. (1967). *The discovery of grounded theory: Strategies for qualitative research*. Chicago: Aldine.

Gramsci, A., and Hoare, Q. (1971). *Selections from the prison notebooks of Antonio Gramsci*. London: Lawrence & Wishart.

Graner Ray, S. (2004). *Gender inclusive game design: Expanding the market*. Hingham, MA: Charles River Media.

Grant, C. (2014). Polygon's 2013 game of the year: *Gone Home. Polygon*, January 15. Retrieved from www.polygon.com/.

Gray, A. (1992). *Video playtime: The gendering of a leisure technology*. London: Routledge.

Gray, K. (2015). Week in gaming: When is a game not really a game? *TechRadar*, July 25. Retrieved from www.techradar.com/.

Gray, K. L. (2012). Intersecting oppressions and online communities. *Information, Communication & Society, 15(3)*, 411–28.

———. (2014). *Race, gender, and deviance in Xbox Live: Theoretical perspectives from the virtual margins*. Waltham, MA: Elsevier.

Grayson, N. (2018). Riot, Blizzard, and Twitch are teaming up to fight toxic gaming behavior. *Kotaku*, March 12. Retrieved from https://kotaku.com/.

Green, M. C., Brock, T. C., and Kaufman, G. F. (2004). Understanding media enjoyment: The role of transportation into narrative worlds. *Communication Theory, 14*, 311–27.

Hachman, M. (2013). Game consoles are already dead—and developers know it. *ReadWrite*, March 4. Retrieved from http://readwrite.com/.

Hall, S. (1995). The whites of their eyes: Racist ideologies and the media. In G. Dines and J. M. Humez (eds.), *Gender, race, and class in media* (pp. 18–22). Thousand Oaks, CA: Sage.

———. (1996a). Gramsci's relevance for the study of race and ethnicity. In K. Chen and D. Morley (eds.), *Stuart Hall: Critical dialogues in cultural studies* (pp. 411–40). London: Routledge.

———. (1996b). The question of cultural identity. In S. Hall, D. Held, D. Hubert, and K. Thompson (eds.), *Modernity: An introduction to modern societies* (pp. 596–632). Boston: Blackwell.

———. (1996c). Who needs identity? In S. Hall, and P. du Gay (eds.), *Questions of cultural identity* (pp. 1–18). London: Sage.

———. (1997). The work of representation. In S. Hall (ed.), *Representation: Cultural representations and signifying practices* (pp. 13–74). London: Sage.

Haninger, K., and Thompson, K. M. (2004). Content and ratings of teen-rated video games. *Journal of the American Medical Association, 291(7)*, 856–65.

Hanke, R. (1992). Redesigning men: Hegemonic masculinity in transition. In S. Craig (ed.), *Men, masculinity, and the media* (pp. 185–98). Newbury Park, CA: Sage.

Haraway, D. (2000). A cyborg manifesto: Science, technology, and socialist-feminism in the late twentieth century. In D. Bell and B. M. Kennedy (eds.), *The cybercultures reader* (pp. 291–329). London: Routledge.

Hardcore. [Def. 1]. (2018). In *Merriam Webster Online*, retrieved June 2, 2016, from www.merriam-webster.com/.

Hardt, M. (1999). Affective labor. *Boundary 2, 26(2)*, 89–100.

Harvey, A., and Fisher, S. (2015). "Everyone can make games!": The post-feminist context of women in digital game production. *Feminist Media Studies, 15(4)*, 576–92.

Harvey, A., and Shepherd, T. (2017). When passion isn't enough: Gender, affect, and credibility in digital games design. *International Journal of Cultural Studies, 20(5)*, 492–508.

Henry, E. S. (2015). Reimagining disability in role-playing games. *Analog Game Studies, 2(2)*. Retrieved from http://analoggamestudies.org/.

Herring, S. C. (1999). The rhetorical dynamics of gender harassment on-line. *Information Society, 15*, 151–67.

Hill Collins, P. (1990). *Black feminist thought: Knowledge, consciousness, and the politics of empowerment*. New York: Routledge.

Hinkley, A. (2010). *Xbox LIVE* reputation does not work. *Examiner.com*, September 20. Retrieved from www.examiner.com/.

Hirdman, A. (2007). (In)visibility and the display of gendered desire: Masculinity in mainstream soft- and hardcore pornography. *Nordic Journal of Feminist and Gender Research, 15(2–3)*, 158–71.

Hiscott, R. (2014). Why indie game devs thrive without big publishers. *Mashable*, March 8. Retrieved from http://mashable.com/.

Hochschild, A. R., and Machung, A. (1989). *The second shift*. New York: Penguin.

Holmes, M. R., and St. Lawrence, J. S. (1983). Treatment of rape-induced trauma: Proposed behavioral conceptualization and review of the literature. *Clinical Psychology Review, 3*, 417–33.

Horti, S. (2018). Blizzard was expecting backlash for *Diablo Immortal*, but "not to this degree." *PC Gamer*, November 4. Retrieved from www.pcgamer.com/.

How long is *Persona 5*? (2017). Retrieved from https://howlongtobeat.com/.

Humphreys, S. (2019). On being a feminist in games studies. *Games and Culture, 14(7)*, 825–42. https://doi.org/10.1177/1555412017737637.

Huntemann, N. (2013). Women in video games: The case of hardware production and promotion. In B. Aslinger and N. Huntemann (eds.), *Gaming globally: Production, play, and place* (pp. 41–57). New York: Palgrave Macmillan.

Hussain, Z., and Griffiths, M. D. (2008). Gender swapping and socializing in cyberspace: An exploratory study. *CyberPsychology & Behavior, 11(1)*, 47–53.

Independent Games Festival. (2012). 14th annual IGF announces winners: *Fez* gets grand prize, *Dear Esther, Spelunky, Antichamber* win awards. *UBM Tech*. Retrieved from http://igf.com/.

Ivory, A. H., Ivory, J. D., Wu, W., Limperos, A. M., Andrew, N., and Sesler, B. S. (2017). Harsh words and deeds: Systematic content analyses of offensive user behavior in the virtual environments of online first-person shooter games. *Journal of Virtual Worlds Research, 10(2)*. Retrieved from https://journals.tdl.org/jvwr/.

Ivory, J. D. (2006). Still a man's game: Gender representations in online reviews of video games. *Mass Communication & Society, 9(1)*, 103–14.

Jackson, L. (2012). Aisha Tyler responds to criticism with "Dear Gamers" letter. *G4tv.com*. Retrieved from www.g4tv.com/.

James, D. (1988). Hardcore: Cultural resistance in the postmodern. *Film Quarterly,* *42(2),* 31–39.

Jansz, J., and Martens, L. (2005). Gaming at a LAN event: The social context of playing video games. *New Media & Society, 7(3),* 333–55.

Jansz, J., and Martis, R. G. (2007). The Lara phenomenon: Powerful female characters in video games. *Sex Roles, 56(3–4),* 141–48.

Jenkins, H. (1998). Voices from the combat zone: Game grrlz talk back. In J. Cassell and H. Jenkins (eds.), *From Barbie to* Mortal Kombat: *Gender and computer games* (pp. 328–41). Danbury, CT: NetLibrary.

Jenson, J., and de Castell, S. (2010). Gender, simulation, and gaming: Research review and redirections. *Simulation & Gaming, 41(1),* 51–71.

———. (2011). Girls@Play: An ethnographic study of gender and digital gameplay. *Feminist Media Studies, 11(2),* 167–79.

Jenson, J., de Castell, S., and Fisher, S. (2007). Girls playing games: Rethinking stereotypes. *FuturePlay,* November 15–17.

Johnson, R. (2011). Play-determined men: Reproducing masculine work and play in the video game industry. Paper presented at the annual meeting of the International Communication Association, Boston, MA, May 25.

Jones, S. (2018). Blinded by the roll: The critical fail of disability in *D&D. Analog Game Studies, 5(1).* Retrieved from http://analoggamestudies.org/.

Juul, J. (2010). *A casual revolution: Reinventing video games and their players.* Cambridge, MA: MIT Press.

Kafai, Y. (1996). Differences in children's constructions of video games. In P. Greenfield and R. Cocking (eds.), *Interacting with video* (pp. 39–66). Norwood, NJ: Ablex.

———. (1998). Video game designs by girls and boys: Variability and consistency of gender differences. In J. Cassell and H. Jenkins (eds.), *From Barbie to* Mortal Kombat: *Gender and computer games* (pp. 90–117). Danbury, CT: NetLibrary.

Kafai, Y., Heeter, C., Denner, J., and Sun, J. Y. (2008). Preface: Pink, purple, casual, or mainstream games. In Y. Kafai, C. Heeter, J. Denner, and J. Y. Sun (eds.), *Beyond Barbie and* Mortal Kombat: *Gender and computer games* (pp. xi–xxv). Cambridge, MA: MIT Press.

Kain, E. (2018). Kassandra vs. Alexios: Which *Assassin's Creed Odyssey* character is best to play as? *Forbes,* October 4. Retrieved from www.forbes.com/.

Katz, E., Blumler, J., and Gurevitch, M. (1973). Uses and gratifications research. *Public Opinion Quarterly, 37(4),* 509–23.

Kauz, A. (2009). Love/hate: A plea to play as a female Shepard. *Destructoid,* December 16. Retrieved from www.destructoid.com/.

Kennedy, H. W. (2006). Illegitimate, monstrous, and out there: Female *Quake* players and inappropriate pleasures. In J. Hallows and R. Mosley (eds.), *Feminism in popular culture* (pp. 183–201). London: Berg.

Kent, S. L. (2001). *The ultimate history of video games: From* Pong *to* Pokemon, *the story behind the craze that touched our lives and changed the world.* Roseville, CA: Prima.

Kerr, A. (2003). Girls/women just want to have fun: A study of adult female players of digital games. *Proceedings from the Level Up Conference 2003*. Utrecht, The Netherlands.

———. (2017). *Global games: Production, circulation, and policy in the networked era*. New York: Routledge.

Kiesler, S., Sproull, L., and Eccles, J. S. (1985). Pools halls, chips, and war games: Women in the culture of computing. *Psychology of Women Quarterly 9*, 451–62.

Kim, R. (2008). E3: *Nintendo Wii* pulls ahead of *Xbox 360* in console sales. *SF Gate*, July 17. Retrieved from http://blog.sfgate.com/.

Kimmel, M. S. (2013). *Angry white men: American masculinity at the end of an era*. New York: Nation Books.

King, J. (2018). *Assassin's Creed Odyssey* review. *Trusted Reviews*, October 18. Retrieved from www.trustedreviews.com/.

Kirkpatrick, G. (2012). Constitutive tensions of gaming's field: UK gaming magazines and the formation of gaming culture, 1981–1995. *Game Studies, 12(1)*. Retrieved from http://gamestudies.org/.

———. (2015). *The formation of gaming culture: UK gaming magazines, 1981–1995*. New York: Palgrave MacMillan.

———. (2017). How gaming became sexist: A study of UK gaming magazines, 1981–1995. *Media, Culture & Society, 39(4)*, 453–68.

Kocurek, C. A. (2015). *Coin-operated Americans: Rebooting boyhood at the video game arcade*. Minneapolis: University of Minnesota Press.

Kohler, C. (2013). *Gone Home*: A video game without all that pesky video game in the way. *Wired*, August 15. Retrieved from www.wired.com/.

Kowert, R., Griffiths, M. D., and Oldmeadow, J. A. (2012). Geek or chic? Emerging Stereotypes of online gamers. *Bulletin of Science, Technology & Society, 32(6)*, 471–79.

Kubik, E. (2009). From girlfriend to gamer: Negotiating place in the hardcore/casual divide of online video game communities. Doctoral dissertation, Bowling Green State University. Retrieved from https://etd.ohiolink.edu/.

Kuchera, B. (2007). *Nintendo* the big winner, PS3 dead last for the first half of 2007. *Ars Technica*, July 24. Retrieved from: http://arstechnica.com/.

Kuittinen, J., Kultima, A., Niemelä, J., and Paavilainen, J. (2007). Casual games discussion. In *Proceedings of the 2007 Conference on Future Play* (pp. 105–12). Toronto, Canada.

Kultima, A. (2009). Casual game design values. In *Proceedings of the 13th International MindTrek Conference: Everyday life in the ubiquitous era* (pp. 58–65). Tampere, Finland.

Laurel, B. (1998). Brenda Laurel on games for girls. *TED*, March 2009. Retrieved from www.ted.com/.

Leblanc, L. (1999). *Pretty in punk: Girls' gender resistance in a boys' subculture*. New Brunswick, NJ: Rutgers University Press.

Lees, M. (2016). What GamerGate should have taught us about the "alt-right." *Guardian*, December 1. Retrieved from www.theguardian.com/.

LeJacq, Y. (2015). *League of Legends* is bringing back an old system to deal with jerks. *Kotaku*, May 4. Retrieved from https://kotaku.com/.

Lenhart, A., Kahne, J., Middaugh, E., Macgill, A. R., Evans, C., and Vitak, J. (2008). Teens, video games, and civics: Teens' gaming experiences are diverse and include significant social interaction and civic engagement. *Pew Internet & American Life Project*. Retrieved from https://www.pewresearch.org/.

Lenhart, A., Purcell, K., Smith, A., and Zickuhr, K. (2010). Social media and mobile internet use among teens and young adults. Washington, DC: Pew Internet & American Life Project. Retrieved from http://www.pewinternet.org/.

Levine, E. (ed). (2015). *Cupcakes, Pinterest, and ladyporn: Feminized popular culture in the early twenty-first century*. Urbana: University of Illinois Press.

Lin, J. (2013). The science behind shaping player behavior in online games. Presented at the annual Game Developers Conference 2013, San Francisco, CA, March 26. Retrieved from http://gdcvault.com/.

———. (2014). Upgrading the Tribunal. *League of Legends* game updates, May 16. Retrieved from https://na.leagueoflegends.com/.

———. (2015a). New player reform system heads into testing. *League of Legends* game updates, May 20. Retrieved from https://na.leagueoflegends.com/.

———. (2015b). Doing something about the "impossible problem" of abuse in online games. *Re/code*, July 7. Retrieved from http://recode.net/.

Lincoln, Y. S., and Guba, E. G. (1985). *Naturalistic inquiry*. Newbury Park, CA: Sage.

———. (1986). But is it rigorous? Trustworthiness and authenticity in naturalistic evaluation. *New Directions for Program Evaluation, 1986(30)*, 73–84.

Lindlof, T. R., and Taylor, B. C. (2002). *Qualitative communication research methods*. Thousand Oaks, CA: Sage.

Lipkin, N. (2013). Examining indie's independence: The meaning of "indie" games, the politics of production, and mainstream co-optation. *Loading . . . , 7(11)*, 8–24.

Lipman-Blumen, J. (1976). Toward a homosocial theory of sex roles: An explanation of the sex segregation of social institutions. *Signs, 1(3)*, 15–31.

Lomas, N. (2014). The console market is in crisis. *TechCrunch*, March 9. Retrieved from http://techcrunch.com/.

Lotz, A. (2014). *Cable guys: Television and masculinities in the 21st century*. New York: NYU Press.

Lynch, T., Tompkins, J. E., van Driel, I. I., and Fritz, N. (2016). Sexy, strong, and secondary: A content analysis of female characters in video games across 31 years. *Journal of Communication, 66(4)*, 564–84.

Lyons, S. A. (2012). *League of Legends* has 32 million monthly active players. *Destructoid*, October 12. Retrieved from www.destructoid.com/.

Maclean, E. (2016). Girls, guys, and games: How news media perpetuate stereotypes of male and female gamers. *Press Start, 3(1)*. Retrieved from www.press-start.gla.ac.uk/.

Maglaty, J. (2011). When did girls start wearing pink? *Smithsonian Magazine*, April 7. Retrieved from www.smithsonianmag.com/.

Maiberg, E. (2014). Phil Fish selling rights to *Fez* after being hacked. *GameSpot*, August 23. Retrieved from www.gamespot.com/.

Mappin, D. (2016). Reviewed: *Dungeons & Dragons* 5th edition. *Ars Technica*, February 6. Retrieved from https://arstechnica.com/.

Martey, R. M., Stromer-Galley, J., Banks, J., Wu, J., and Consalvo, M. (2014). The strategic female: Gender-switching and player behavior in online games. *Information, Communication & Society, 17(3)*, 286–300.

Massanari, A. (2015). #GamerGate and The Fappening: How Reddit's algorithm, governance, and culture support toxic technocultures. *New Media & Society, 19(3)*, 329–46.

Mazzanoble, S. (2007). *Confessions of a part-time sorceress: A girl's guide to* Dungeons & Dragons *game*. Renton, WA: Wizards of the Coast.

McDonald, P. (2012). Workplace sexual harassment 30 years on: A review of the literature. *International Journal of Management Reviews, 14*, 1–17.

McDonnell, A. M. (2014). *Reading celebrity gossip magazines*. Cambridge, UK: Polity Press.

McRobbie, A. (2009). *The aftermath of feminism: Gender, culture, and social change*. London: Sage.

McWhertor, M. (2018). *Blizzard* responds to *Diablo*: Immortal backlash. *Polygon*, November 3. Retrieved from www.polygon.com/.

Means Coleman, R. (2000). *African American viewers and the black situation comedy: Situating racial humor*. New York: Garland.

Mejia, Z. (2018). Just 24 female CEOs lead the companies on the 2018 Fortune 500—fewer than last year. *CNBC*, May 21. Retrieved from www.cnbc.com.

Miller, M. K., and Summers, A. (2007). Gender differences in video game characters' roles, appearances, and attire as portrayed in video game magazines. *Sex Roles, 57(9–10)*, 733–42.

Mullaney, J. L. (2007). "Unity admirable but not necessarily heeded": Going rates and gender boundaries in the straight edge hardcore music scene. *Gender and Society, 21(3)*, 384–408.

Mussett, S. M. (2014). Berserker in a skirt. In Dungeons & Dragons *and Philosophy* (pp. 189–201). Chichester, UK: Wiley.

Nakamura, L. (2002). *Cybertypes: Race, ethnicity, and identity on the Internet*. New York: Routledge.

———. (2009). Don't hate the player, hate the game: The racialization of labor in *World of Warcraft*. *Critical Studies in Media Communication, 26(2)*, 128–44.

———. (2012). "It's a ***** in here! Kill the *****!": User-generated media campaigns against racism, sexism, and homophobia in digital games. In A. Valdivia (ed.), *The international encyclopedia of media studies* (vol. 5, pp. 2–15). Malden, MA: Blackwell.

———. (2017). Racism, sexism, and gaming's cruel optimism. In J. Malkowski and T. M. Russworm (eds.), *Gaming representation: Race, gender, and sexuality in video games* (pp. 245–50). Bloomington: Indiana University Press.

Narcisse, E. (2012). Aisha Tyler rants "I've been a gamer since before you could read." *Kotaku*, June 13. Retrieved from http://kotaku.com/.

Nardi, B. (2010). *My life as a nightelf priest: An anthropological account of* World of Warcraft. Ann Arbor: University of Michigan Press.

Newman, G. (2016). Why my videogame chooses your character's race and gender for you. *Guardian*, April 13. Retrieved from www.theguardian.com/.

Newman, M. Z. (2017). Atari *age: The emergence of video games in America*. Boston, MA: MIT Press.

Nieborg, D. B. (2015). Crushing candy: The free-to-play game in its connective commodity form. *Social Media + Society, 1(2)*. https://doi.org/10.1177/2056305115621932.

Nylund, D. (2004). When in Rome: Heterosexism, homophobia, and sports talk radio. *Journal of Sport and Social Issues, 28(2)*, 136–68.

O'Leary, A. (2012). In virtual play, sex harassment is all too real. *New York Times*, August 1. Retrieved from www.nytimes.com/.

Orland, K. (2013). Microsoft gives a damn 'bout your bad reputation on Xbox One. *Ars Technica*, July 31. Retrieved from http://arstechnica.com/.

Ostroff, J. (2016). Superhero diversity takes flight as comic books fight for gender, race, and LGBT balance. *Huffington Post*, May 26. Retrieved from www.huffington post.ca/.

Paul, C. A. (2018). *The toxic meritocracy of video games: Why gaming culture is the worst*. Minneapolis: University of Minnesota Press.

Phillips, W. (2015). *This is why we can't have nice things: Mapping the relationship between online trolling and mainstream culture*. Cambridge, MA: MIT Press.

Polo, S. (2012). Props: How to apologize on the Internet for a gender-related mishap. *Mary Sue*, April 19. Retrieved from www.themarysue.com/.

Polygon Staff. (2012a). The state of games: State of AAA. *Polygon*, July 2. Retrieved from www.polygon.com/.

———. (2012b). The state of games: State of indies. *Polygon*, July 3. Retrieved from www.polygon.com/.

Potok, M., and Schlatter, E. (2012). Men's rights movement spreads false claims about women. *Southern Poverty Law Center Intelligence Report 145*. Retrieved from www.splcenter.org/.

Putnam, R. D. (2000). *Bowling alone: The collapse and revival of American community*. New York: Simon & Schuster.

Radway, J. (1984). *Reading the romance*. Chapel Hill: University of North Carolina Press.

———. (1991). *Reading the romance*. Chapel Hill: University of North Carolina Press.

Ratan, R. A., Taylor, N., Hogan, J., Kennedy, T., and Williams, D. (2015). Stand by your man: An examination of gender disparity in *League of Legends*. *Games and Culture, 10(5)*, 438–62.

Rayna, T., and Striukova, L. (2014). "Few to many": Change of business model paradigm in the video game industry. *Communications & Strategies, (94)*, 61–81, 154–55.

Rohlinger, D. A. (2016). The far-reaching consequences of the Supreme Court abortion rights challenge. *American Prospect*, March 1. Retrieved from http://prospect.org/.

Roinioti, E. (2011). Blizzard will soon display your real name: Identity and governance in *WoW*. Paper presented at the Philosophy of Computer Games Conference, Athens, Greece, April.

Rosin. H. (2010). The end of men. *Atlantic*, July/August. Retrieved from: www.theatlantic.com/.

———. (2012). *The end of men: And the rise of women.* New York: Penguin.

Rosmarin, R. (2006). *Nintendo*'s new look. *Forbes*, February 7. Retrieved from www.forbes.com/.

Salter, A., and Blodgett, B. (2012). Hypermasculinity and dickwolves: The contentious role of women in the new gaming public. *Journal of Broadcasting and Electronic Media, 56(3),* 401–16.

———. (2017). *Toxic geek masculinity in media: Sexism, trolling, and identity policing.* Cham, Switzerland: Palgrave Macmillan.

Sarkeesian, A. (2012). The mirror: Online harassment and cybermobs [video file]. *TedxWomen Talk*, December 4. Retrieved from: http://tedxwomen.org/.

Scharrer, E. (2004). Virtual violence: Gender and aggression in video game advertisements. *Mass Communication & Society, 7(4),* 393–412.

Schott, H. R., and Horrell, K. R. (2000). Girl gamers and their relationship with the gaming culture. *Convergence: The International Journal of Research into New Media Technologies, 6(4),* 36–53.

Schulte, B. (2014). "The Second Shift" at 25: Q&A with Arlie Hochschild. *Washington Post*, August 6. Retrieved from www.washingtonpost.com/.

Shanley, M. (2013). How *Candy Crush* makes so much money. *Business Insider*, October 8. Retrieved from www.businessinsider.com/.

Shapiro, M. A., Pena-Herborn, J., and Hancock, J. T. (2006). Realism, imagination, and narrative video games. In P. Vorderer and J. Bryant (eds.), *Playing video games: Motives, responses, and consequences* (pp. 275–89). Mahwah, NJ: Erlbaum.

Sharlet, J. (2014). Are you man enough for the men's rights movement? *GQ*, February 3. Retrieved from www.gq.com/.

Shaw, A. (2010). What is video game culture? Video games and cultural studies. *Games and Culture, 5(4),* 403–24.

———. (2012). Do you identify as a gamer? Gender, race, sexuality, and gamer identity. *New Media & Society, 14(1),* 28–44.

———. (2014a). From "snacks" to "binges": Player accounts of casual play. Paper presented at the Annual International Academic Conference on Meaningful Play, East Lansing, MI, October.

———. (2014b). *Gaming at the edge: Sexuality and gender at the margins of gamer culture.* Minneapolis: University of Minnesota Press.

Sheffield, B. (2014). What makes *Gone Home* a game? *Gamasutra*, March 20. Retrieved from www.gamasutra.com/.

Sherry, J. L., Lucas, K., Greenberg, B. S., and Lachlan, K. (2006). Video game uses and gratifications as predictors of use and game preference. In P. Vorderer and J. Bryant (eds.), *Playing video games: Motives, responses, and consequences* (pp. 213–24). Mahwah, NJ: Erlbaum.

Shontell, A. (2014). *Candy Crush* is doing more than $1 billion in sales. *Business Insider*, February 18. Retrieved from www.businessinsider.com/.

Simons, J. (2007). Narrative, games, and theory. *Game Studies, 7(1)*. Retrieved from http://gamestudies.org/.

Sinclair, B. (2013). *The Last of Us* dev says AAA can learn from indies. *GamesIndustry*, September 13. Retrieved from www.gamesindustry.biz/.

Smith, D. (2012). A personal journey: Jenova Chen's goals for games. *Gamasutra*, May 18. Retrieved from www.gamasutra.com/.

Smith, S. L., Lachlan, K. and Tamborini, R. (2003). Popular video games: Quantifying the presentation of violence and its context. *Journal of Broadcasting & Electronic Media, 47(1)*, 58–76.

Sommers, C. H. (2013). *The war against boys: How misguided policies are harming our young men*. New York: Simon & Schuster.

Spock, J. (2012). Endless space: When triple-A developers go indie. *Gamasutra*, November 29. Retrieved from www.gamasutra.com/.

Squire, K. (2006). From content to context: Videogames as designed experience. *Educational Researcher, 35(8)*, 19–29.

Stabile, C. (2014). "I will own you": Accountability in massively multiplayer online games. *Television & New Media, 15(1)*, 43–57.

Statt, N. (2013). Is *BioShock Infinite* the last gasp for the Triple-A "art game"? *ReadWrite*, April 4. Retrieved from http://readwrite.com/.

Stenros, J., and Sihvonen, T. (2015). Out of the dungeons: Representations of queer sexuality in RPG source books. *Analog Game Studies, 2(5)*. Retrieved from http://analoggamestudies.org/.

Stokes, M. (2017). Access to the page: Queer and disabled characters in *Dungeons & Dragons. Analog Game Studies, 4(3)*. Retrieved from http://analoggamestudies.org/.

Stuart, K. (2012). E3 2012: Aisha Tyler takes on the gamer haters with Facebook rant. *Guardian*, June 14. Retrieved from www.theguardian.com/.

Takahashi, D. (2016). With just 3 games, *Supercell* made $924M in profits on $2.3B in revenue in 2015. *Venture Beat*, March 6. Retrieved from https://venturebeat.com/.

Taylor, N., Jenson, J., and de Castell, S. (2009). Cheerleaders/booth babes/Halo hoes: Pro-gaming, gender, and jobs for the boys. *Digital Creativity, 20(4)*, 239–52.

Taylor, T. L. (2003). Multiple pleasures: Women and online gaming. *Convergence: The International Journal of Research into New Media Technologies, 9(1)*, 21–46.

———. (2008). Becoming a player: Networks, structure, and imagined futures. In Y. Kafai, C. Heeter, J. Denner, and J. Y. Sun (eds.), *Beyond Barbie and* Mortal Kombat (pp. 51–65). Cambridge, MA: MIT Press.

———. (2012). *Raising the stakes: E-Sports and the professionalization of computer gaming*. Cambridge, MA: MIT Press.

Torner, E., Trammell, A., and Waldron, E. L. (2014). Reinventing analog game studies. *Analog Game Studies, 1(1)*. Retrieved from http://analoggamestudies.org/.

Totilo, S. (2012). If you're female, online gaming is a festival of compliments and flattery, comic asserts [update]. *Kotaku*, April 4. Retrieved from http://kotaku.com/.

Trammell, A. (2014). Misogyny and the female body in *Dungeons & Dragons*. *Analog Game Studies, 1(3)*. Retrieved from http://analoggamestudies.org/.

———. (2016). How *Dungeons & Dragons* appropriated the Orient. *Analog Game Studies, 3(1)*. Retrieved from http://analoggamestudies.org/.

Tyler, A. (2012). Dear gamers [Web log post], June 13. Retrieved from www.facebook.com/notes/aisha-tyler/dear-gamers/10151040991508993/.

US Census Bureau. (2017). The digital divide: By Internet, computer, race, and Hispanic origin. Retrieved from www.census.gov/.

Vanderhoef, J. (2013). Casual threats: The feminization of casual video games. *Ada: A Journal of Gender, New Media, and Technology, 2.* doi: 10.7264/N3V40S4D.

Vickerman, K. A., and Margolin, G. (2009). Rape treatment outcome research: Empirical findings and state of the literature. *Clinical Psychology Review, 29*, 431–48.

Vorderer, P., Bryant, J., Pieper, K. M., and Weber, R. (2006). Video games as entertainment. In P. Vorderer and J. Bryant (eds.), *Playing video games: Motives, responses, and consequences* (pp. 1–8). Mahwah, NJ: Erlbaum.

Waddell, T. F., Ivory, J. D., Conde, R., Long, C., and McDonnell, R. (2014). White man's virtual world: A systematic content analysis of gender and race in massively multiplayer online games. *Journal of Virtual Worlds Research, 7(2)*. Retrieved from https://journals.tdl.org/jvwr/.

Walker, J. (2011). Only 18% of *Mass Effect* players play female. *Rock, Paper, Shotgun*, July 20. Retrieved from www.rockpapershotgun.com/.

Wenner, L. A. (1998). In search of the sports bar: Masculinity, alcohol, sports, and the mediation of public space. In G. Rail, (ed), *Sport and postmodern times* (pp. 301–32). Albany: State University of New York Press.

Westbrook, L. (2011). BioWare adding female Shepard to *Mass Effect 3* marketing. *Escapist Magazine*, June 16. Retrieved from www.escapistmagazine.com/.

White, J. (2011). What's the difference between the men's rights movement and feminism? *A Voice for Men*, September 16. Retrieved from www.avoiceformen.com/.

Williams, D. (2006). A brief social history of game play. In P. Vorderer and J. Bryant (eds.), *Playing video games: Motives, responses, and consequences* (pp. 197–212). Mahwah, NJ: Erlbaum.

Williams, D., Consalvo, M., Caplan, S., and Yee, N. (2009). Looking for gender: Gender roles and behaviors among online gamers. *Journal of Communication, 59(4)*, 700–725.

Williams, D., Ducheneaut, N., Xiong, L., Zhang, Y., Yee, N., and Nickell, E. (2006). From tree house to barracks. *Games and Culture, 1(4)*, 338–61.

Williams, L. (1984). "Something else besides a mother": *Stella Dallas* and the maternal melodrama. *Cinema Journal, 24(1)*, 2–27.

Willis, S. (1993). Hardcore: Subculture American style. *Critical Inquiry, 19(2)*, 365–83.

Wingfield, N. (2014). Feminist critics of video games facing threats in "GamerGate" campaign. *New York Times*, October 16. Retrieved from www.nytimes.com/.

Wohn, D. Y. (2011). Gender and race representation in casual games. *Sex Roles, 65(3–4)*, 198–207.

Yee, N. (2008). Maps of digital desires: Exploring the topography of gender and play in online games. In Y. Kafai, C. Heeter, J. Denner, and J. Y. Sun (eds.), *Beyond Barbie and Mortal Kombat* (pp. 83–96). Cambridge, MA: MIT Press.

———. (2014). *The Proteus paradox: How online games and virtual worlds change us—and how they don't*. New Haven, CT: Yale University Press.

———. (2017). Beyond 50/50: Breaking down the percentage of female gamers by genre. *Quantic Foundry*. Retrieved from https://quanticfoundry.com/.

INDEX

"geek girls," 17
geek masculinity, 6, 8, 20, 97, 203
Geguri, 163–64
#GirlGamer, 200
"girl gamer" stereotype, 100–107, 204, 210, 236n4
"girl games," 5, 89, 90, 127
girls' games movement, 5, 53, 81, 147
Girls Who Code, 10
Gone Home, 51, 53–54
Gramsci, Antonio, 9, 24, 32, 36, 54, 235n7
Grand Theft Auto (GTA), 68, 122, 135, 148
Gray, Ann, 12, 80
Gray, Kishonna, 78, 168, 173
Grayson, Nathan, 207
Green, Melanie, 124, 126
grinding, 134, 238n8
grounded theory, 219, 222, 226
Guba, Egon G., 219, 226–27
guilds/clans, 152, 164, 173–74
    in *World of Warcraft*, 78, 120, 163, 167
Guild Wars 2 (GW2), 174, 188–89

Hale, Jennifer, 93
Hall, Stuart, 14–15, 58, 86
Halo, 77, 123
Haraway, Donna, 137, 211
"hardcore" discourse, 45–46
    contrasted with "casual," 36, 39–40, 144, 207
    gendered, 25–26, 29–32, 95, 144
    See also core gaming
Harley, 3, 20, 72, 78, 139, 229
Harrison, George, 41
Harvest Moon, 154
hegemony, 10–11, 48, 110, 114, 145–46, 208, 212, 235n7
    challenges to, 36, 57, 94, 169, 181
    core/casual binary and, 20–21, 25, 36–37, 42, 94, 178–79
    definition, 9
    gender and, 25–26, 84–85, 94, 149, 156, 214–15

harassment and, 168, 174–75, 181, 202–3
hegemonic masculinity, 5–6, 24, 30, 32, 71, 124, 128, 141–42
hegemony of play, 24
    See also counterhegemony
hegemony of play, 24
Helix, 96, 118, 161–62, 229
    on characters, 61–63
    on game choice, 132–33
    response to harassment, 78, 163, 166–67
Her Story, 54
Hochschild, Arlie, 91
homophobia, 76–77, 97, 172, 175–76, 191, 235n5
homosociality, 8, 17, 19–20, 79, 191
Horn, 36, 236n7
Hulu, 52
Humble Bundles, 48
Humphreys, Sal, 212
hypersexualization
    of characters, 62, 66–69, 84, 125, 131, 134, 203
    players and, 57, 71, 74
hypodermic needle model, 147

identification, 42, 78, 137, 209, 213
    definition, 59
    gamer identity and, 15–17, 59–60, 66, 88, 110, 134, 140–45, 199–200, 220–25
    gendered, 13, 56–57, 69, 79, 99, 131
    representation and, 61–65, 84, 92, 113, 122–27, 209–12, 237n1, 237n5
identity tourism, 122
imagined communities, 138–39, 142, 145
Independent Games Festival, 43, 52
Indiegogo, 49
#INeedDiverseGames, 10–11, 210
inferential racism, 58, 86, 99
inferential sexism, 21, 85
    definition, 58–59, 86
    examples, 56, 86–107

ABOUT THE AUTHOR

Amanda C. Cote is Assistant Professor of Media Studies/Game Studies in the School of Journalism and Communication at the University of Oregon. Her work focuses on video game culture and industry, with an emphasis on questions of gender, identity, and power.